The Urbana Free Library

To renew materials call
217-367-4057

vespa

60

1946 _ 2006

Vespa®

The author and the publisher would like to express their sincere thanks to Antonio Corona, one of Italy's leading Vespa authorities. His contribution in terms of both his historical consultancy and his generosity in making available much of his immense iconographical archive has been fundamental to the success of the book. That we are able to enjoy the greater part of the historical illustrations that enrich these pages is down to him.

vespa

Giorgio Sarti

MOTORBOOKS

This edition published in 2006 by Motorbooks, an imprint of MBI Publishing Company, Galtier Plaza, Suite 200, 380 Jackson Street, St. Paul, MN 55101-3885 USA

MBI Publishing Company titles are also available at discounts in bulk quantity for industrial or sales-promotional use. For details write to Special Sales Manager at MBI Publishing Company, Galtier Plaza, Suite 200, 380 Jackson Street, St. Paul, MN 55101-3885 USA.

ISBN-13: 978-0-7603-2577-3
ISBN-10: 0-7603-2577-4

Printed in Italy

To my wife Roberta.
She climbed onto my Vespa 200 Rally for the first
time in 1978.
And she is still riding with me.

Acknowledgements
Special thanks to the publisher, Giorgio Nada, for his faith in this project.
Warmest thanks to Luciano Greggio for his fundamental editorial coordination. Without his professionalism, energy and cooperation this book would have celebrated the 70th rather than the 60th anniversary. Thanks also to Roberto Zerbi, Piaggio Group Chief Press Officer.
A thought for Ingegner Carlo Doveri, who passed away in 2005.

CONTENTS

FOREWORD

Piaggio celebrated the 60th anniversary of the birth of the Vespa on 27 April 2006. The ceremony was held at Pontedera in the Piaggio Museum, a place devoted to the conservation and promotion of the historical values of a vehicle that has represented – and above all continues to represent – extraordinary success in terms of design, research and technical innovation and creativity, labour and enterprise.

When Enrico Piaggio presented the first Vespa 98 to the public in 1946 and put the first 50 examples on sale, contemporary reports show that he received a very discouraging response from the experts. And yet, without hesitation, Piaggio the businessman decided to proceed with the production of a further 2,500 Vespas! It was a courageous move that paid spectacular dividends. Corradino D'Ascanio, the aeronautical engineer and inventor of the helicopter, was called upon to work swiftly and create a series of new models: the 98 was followed by the Vespa 125 introduced in 1949 and then by the Vespa U, the Vespa GS, the Vespone and numerous remarkable racing and trials prototypes. By 1952 the Pontedera-based company had already negotiated four foreign licences to satisfy growing demand for the vehicle, and by 1956 one million Vespas had been sold throughout the world. These were intense years in a country anxious to leave behind the drama of wartime destruction, a period in which a desire to construct and the challenge of the future were key elements in the success of not just Piaggio but other Italian businesses too.

The Vespa was born with the characteristic of originality and was proposed as a small, useful and attractive vehicle capable of responding to the economic and social changes that ranged from the period of construction through to the boom years of the Fifties and Sixties, from the uncertainties and difficulties of the Seventies to the triumph of the society of mass consumption. There are very few products that have managed to conserve their capacity for market penetration for so long: if it happens it is because those products express values capable of overcoming any barrier raised by changes in mentality, usage, taste or, more banally, obsolescence. Rather than merely enduring, the Vespa has proved capable of acting as a true protagonist of change, the interpreter of the dynamics of customs, aesthetics, language, fashion and the mentalities of men and women, adults and youngsters within the complex development of the economy and society.

While this is the story that has led to the construction of over 17 million Vespas, in one of the most recent economic and financial crises Piaggio risked going under and losing the patrimony of innovation and creativity embodied by the world's most popular scooter and shared by the other two-, three- and four-wheeled vehicles produced by the Piaggio Group.

That disaster was avoided. In fact, the changes in the structure of the company and the new management team have rapidly brought back into play those values rooted in the history and the abundance of ideas and skills represented by the men and women working at Pontedera; values they have successfully strengthened and renewed, giving a new impetus to the production process and, above all, to the thread of creativity, technological innovation, entrepreneurship and labour running through the creation of revolutionary new models that – today, just as 60 years ago – interpret when they do not anticipate the most modern demands for mobility and quality of life.

Giorgio Sarti's book, authoritatively published by Haynes in collaboration with Giorgio Nada Editore, and which it is my pleasure to commend, illustrates the various stages in the Vespa's history and documents the dynamics of a product that has become the stuff of legend and proved capable of retaining a leading position in its market sector. Above all, the book underlines the success of the Vespa, the evolution of an all-Italian project that has negotiated difficult times and today continues to represent the originality, the enterprise, the capacity for research and the achievements of Italian industry in the global economy.

For these reasons, the greatest tribute that we can pay to the first 60 glorious years of the Vespa – and to all its enthusiasts – is to plan for an equally extraordinary future.

Roberto Colaninno
President of the Piaggio Group

INTRODUCTION

In 1973 a very young Vespa enthusiast sent a proposal to the Piaggio management in Genoa for an advertising campaign based on the slogan: "Vespa, overtaking the times". The reply was a polite refusal: for this kind of thing there are advertising agencies, but thanks anyway. Satisfaction at having actually been contacted by the powers-that-be only partially made up for the disappointment at having been rejected. I know the story well, for I was that boy. My adolescent motorcycling development was, in fact, Vespa-based: a Vespa 50 Special at 14, a Vespa 125 Primavera at 16 and a Vespa 200 rally at 18 years old. My relationship with the Vespa then cooled a little as more demanding motorcycles in terms of size, price and performance arrived, but I never lost my affection for Pontedera's jewel, quite the contrary. In 1984 came the pleasant surprise of a first prize in a Mondadori competition for the best film script based on the Vespa and a fine 125 PK Automatica found a place in my garage. I began to feel the appeal of the models of the past ever more strongly in the 1990s, pride of place now going to a perfectly preserved 1963 GL 150. As you might imagine, like any good enthusiast I have always collected all the books imaginable that featured the Vespa. However, I always felt something was missing; either they were too technical and written for restorers or they were too illustrative and lacked information. I never managed to find a single volume that would satisfy both the lover of a single model and an enthusiast capable of falling for a model in the legendary calendar. And so I set about the task myself and this is the result. It is just a shame the publisher politely rejected my suggested title: "Vespa, overtaking the times".

The author

Part one

ORIGIN AND DEVELOPMENT

Birth and protagonists

Birth and protagonists

12 o'clock midday, 23 April 1946, the patent office, Florence. Piaggio deposits the following patent: "Motorcycle with a rational arrangement of organs and elements, with a frame with mudguards and covers concealing all mechanical parts."

Such was the official birth of the Vespa. Even though other scooters (vehicles with two small-diameter wheels) had already been built prior to the Second World War, there is no doubt that with the Vespa the genre took a significant step forward. Of significance in this respect is the wording of the official Piaggio press release. Firstly, the vehicle is deliberately described as a "motorcycle" because the scooters that had gone before had failed to leave a particularly positive impression. Above all, however, Piaggio was at pains to emphasise how the mechanical elements were fully enclosed by the side panels with the clear intent of drawing parallels between the new scooter and cars rather than traditional motorcycles.

It was no coincidence that the first prototype was presented on the Lancia stand at a motor show in November 1945. Enrico Piaggio was keen to associate the Vespa with a prestigious marque boasting a widespread and consolidated sales and distribution network. However, that attempt at an alliance with Lancia came to nothing, as was the case

Piaggio & C.

The original "Società Rinaldo Piaggio" was founded by Rinaldo Piaggio at just 20 years of age in 1884. The next step was the limited partnership Piaggio & C. established in 1897. The general partner was again Rinaldo Piaggio, with four partners: Oreste Odero (shipowner), Pietro Costa (sculptor) and Giacomo Pastorino (landowner). In the years 1892 and 1893 Rinaldo Piaggio bought out his partners and in 1920 relaunched the firm as Piaggio and Compagno, with the "compagno" being Attilio Odero. Odero was a leading player: he was formerly the director of the Odero factory of Sestri Ponente before becoming the chairman of the Terni steelworks and founder of San Giorgio. He was to be the chairman of Piaggio & C. and remained in the position through to 1943. The company capital was increased from 15 million lire to 30 million in 1930. The following years of crisis reflected the American financial collapse of 1929: the company capital dropped in 1932 from 30 to 10 million lire, but Rinaldo Piaggio wisely decided to invest in human resources and brought a number of the most talented aeronautical engineers of the era to the company. They included: Giovanni Gabrielli, Giovanni Casiraghi and Corradino D'Ascanio the man who was to play such a major role in the birth of the Vespa.

In 1934, the shareholders Rinaldo Piaggio and Attilio Odero were joined by Elena, the wife of Rinaldo. In 1936, a further six shareholders were added, the sons and son-in-laws of Rinaldo. On his death in 1938, the company capital was raised from 22.5 to 52.5 million lire. It was at this point that the two male heirs divided responsibilities for the company: the factories at Pisa and Pontedera in Tuscany being run by Enrico and those at Sestri and Finale Ligure in Liguria by Armando.

Birth and protagonists

*Enrico Piaggio
signed off the birth
of the Vespa in
green crayon.
(30 August 1945).*

*The first and last
page of the
document relating
to the purchase of
the land on which
the Piaggio factory
at Sestri Ponente
was built.
(3 October 1882).*

Birth and protagonists

with similar overtures made to Moto Guzzi, and Piaggio eventually decided to go it alone and organize the launch of the Vespa itself.

The official presentation of the production model, the 98, took place at the prestigious Golf Club di Roma in the March of 1946, while in April the general public was able to admire the first Vespa at the Milan Trade Fair: a legend was born.

Piaggio then founded a company devoted exclusively to the distribution of the new scooter, "S.A.R.P.I." or Società Agenzie Rappresentanze Prodotti Industriali, and official sales of the Vespa were to begin.

Piaggio, more than just Vespa

Many enthusiasts are so accustomed to associating the manufacturer's name with that of the Vespa scooter that they assume the two came into being at the same time. In actual fact, by the time the Vespa was introduced Piaggio had already been in business for exactly sixty years.

The company took its name from Rinaldo Piaggio who was born in Genoa on the 15th of July 1864. At just twenty years of age he started his own woodworking business at Sestri Ponente. As increasingly significant orders began to be taken thanks to the skill

Two views of the Sestri Ponente factory during the woodworking period.

Birth and protagonists

of the company's craftsmen, Rinaldo Piaggio began to specialise in naval furnishings, obtaining numerous foreign commissions. In 1901, the workshop was enlarged and along with the joinery, metalworking began to be undertaken and the firm started building railway carriages. A natural follow-on from this was the production of trams and cable cars. During the First World War, Piaggio built anti-submarine motorboats but also began to devote resources to the field of aviation, firstly repairing engines and subsequently constructing aircraft. At the end of the war the company built an extremely advanced fighter, the P2, while in 1928 it inaugurated a facility for research into aerodynamics (in a wind tunnel) and hydrodynamics (using tanks). This period saw the birth of the P7, a sophisticated hydrofoil-equipped seaplane with two propellers for propulsion in both water and air. During the 1930s, Piaggio engines conquered no less than 21 aviation world records, while the company continued to develop its railway carriages. The firm's founder, Rinaldo Piaggio, died in 1938 and was succeeded by his son Enrico. The Pontedera factory was bombed during the Second World War yet it was from the ruins that the scooter to be known as the Vespa emerged.

Among the Piaggio marine furnishings, of particular note was the salon created for the steamship Sicilia belonging to the Compagnia Navigazione Generale Italiana.

Birth and protagonists

Piaggio at sea

Dozens of ships and motorboats boasted furnishings and fittings by Piaggio, 63 different vessels to be precise. Among the most important were the elegant passenger vessels, Cristoforo Colombo, Marco Polo, Galileo Galilei (Navigazione Generale Italiana) and Venezuela (Società la Veloce), the fast cruiser Liguria, the powerful battleships Giulio Cesare and Andrea Doria, the transatlantic liner Lorelei and a military vessel for the Imperial German Navy of Emperor Frederick. Such was the quality of the firm's work that Piaggio was awarded prizes on the occasion of various international expositions: at Genoa in 1892, at Paris in 1900, at Milan 1906 and at Turin in 1911.

With respect to the sawmill founded by his father Enrico, Rinaldo Piaggio's company expanded enormously and developed into one of the finest woodworking firms of the period.

One of the anti-submarine motorboats delivered to the Italian Navy during the First World War and used in numerous missions in the Adriatic.

1. ORIGIN AND DEVELOPMENT

Birth and protagonists

**Piaggio
on rails**

Early in the twentieth century the Italian railway was experiencing rapid growth, with the network in continual expansion. Piaggio constructed all kinds of railway rolling stock, from sophisticated first class luxury coaches to the spartan third class carriages, from post trains to goods wagons. In 1924, the company created a train for the king, the queen, the queen mother and the young prince, a commission worth no less than 6 million lire. From 1937, Piaggio began constructing a seriess of sophisticated electric railcars and carriages in stainless steel under license from Budd of Philadelphia. The relative patents concerned above all the welding of the sheet metal and allowed a new generation of innovative and lightweight trains to be introduced.

The use of stainless steel guaranteed extended durability with no need for periodical maintenance or painting. An electric railcar, the MC2 (used by the Ferrovie Calabro-Lucane), is today exhibited at the entrance to the Piaggio Museum in Pontedera.

A tram built in great numbers by Piaggio (left) and a postal wagon with two axles that entered *service in the early years of the 20th century.*

Birth and protagonists

Piaggio and the automobile

After having ranged throughout the transport sectors, it was only natural that Piaggio also began to think about motorcars too (FIAT was formed in 1899). Piaggio made contact with Mario Tolomei, then the De Dion Bouton and Motori Jupiter representative in Florence through his Società Italiana Costruzioni Automobili company. The agreement involved the construction of chassis at Pontedera together with the production of Jupiter engines under license. In the end, however, the negotiations broke down and nothing more was heard about Piaggio cars until the launch of the Vespa 400 in 1957.

Piaggio in flight

While early in the twentieth century trains were still part of an innovative sector, aeroplanes represented a new frontier. Piaggio's aeronautical activities got underway in 1920 when Piaggio bought out Francesco Oneto's Pisa-based Officine Aeronautiche. The new company was constituted with capital of 10 million lire.

In 1923, Piaggio attempted to lure the great designer Giovanni Pegna away from the Pegna-Bonmartini aeronautical company. Faced with the straight refusal by Bonmartini who had no intention of losing an engineer of such prestige, Rinaldo Piaggio made him an offer he could hardly refuse: he would buy out Pegna-Bonmartini for the exorbitant

On the facing page, three examples of Piaggio railway rolling stock: a celebrated "Cento Porte" or "Hundred Doors" (top), the special carriage of the President of the Senate (centre) and the MC2 railcar of the Ferrovie Calabro-Lucane with a stainless steel body. Below, the first aircraft built under license by Piaggio in 1915, a Franco British Aviation seaplane.

Birth and protagonists

sum of 1,700,000 lire. The company further strengthened its position with the acquisition of Costruzioni Mecchaniche Nazionali and began producing radial engines. The most famous was the double row P XII RC with a total of no less than 18 cylinders and a maximum power output of 1,750 hp, the most powerful piston engine ever built in Italy.

1938 saw the introduction of a particularly advanced four-engined aircraft, the P 108. Among the innovations that made it so sophisticated was a remote control system for the machine guns.

The P 148, designed by D'Ascanio and Casiraghi, was a training and aerobatic aircraft introduced in 1951. The first 70 examples were supplied to the Italian Air Force. A 5-seater version known as the P 149 was introduced in 1953. An example of the P 148 is on show in the Piaggio Museum forecourt in Pontedera.

It has been suggested on a number of occasions that when looking for a way of using a batch of aircraft engine starter motors that were lying redundant in the stores, Enrico Piaggio asked the engineer Corradino D'Ascanio to design a vehicle that could be powered by them. However, this is nothing more than unfounded legend.

It is true, however, that the auxiliary engines used for generators and compressors used to start Piaggio S.M. series aircraft shared the 98

The Piaggio P.3 biplane, powered by SPA 6A engines (top left). The Piaggio P. 11 with a Lynk MK4 engine (top right). The Piaggio P.9 monoplane with a Circus MK2 engine (bottom left). In the mid-Thirties Piaggio abandoned wood and canvas construction in favour of all-metal frames (bottom right). On the facing page, a Dernier Wal built under license in 1926 (top); the Piaggio P. 23 R from 1935 (centre) and the four-engined P. 108 from 1938 (bottom).

Birth and protagonists

Birth and protagonists

engine's piston and connecting rod, but the crankcase of the motor/generator or motor/compressor assembly was a one-piece casting.

Piaggio and saucepans

In 1943, allied bombing flattened the Pontedera and Pisa factories. Only part of the 2,100 machine tools used for building aircraft were saved in time, but it was thanks to that machinery that in 1945 the company was ready to initiate a new production venture. A new factory was raised on the ruins of the old one and the ex-combatants returning from the war turned up at the gates ready to work. But what were they to produce? It was up to Enrico Piaggio to shoulder this enormous responsibility. Given the post-war economic situation, the firm had to focus on a cheap consumer good for which there was, above all, widespread demand. The first idea that came to mind was… saucepans! Had Piaggio gone ahead and launched a range of kitchenware the Vespa would never have come into being. Fortunately, Enrico Piaggio had a corporate image to protect and could hardly afford to compromise the factory's prestigious reputation for producing trains and planes by making pots and pans. Perhaps if they had thought of some kind of vehicle instead…

The birth of the Vespa

Italy in the period immediately following the Second World War was a shattered country. While there was a passionate desire for reconstruction, the problems to be overcome were immense and the workers were beginning to feel the effects of unemployment and inflation.

Within this context Piaggio was facing severe difficulties. The bombing had destroyed much of the production facilities in both Liguria and Tuscany. At Pontedera (7,000 employees and a covered area of 70,000 m²) the greatest damage had been incurred by the foundries, the stores and the shipping department. The mechanical workshops were all but razed to the ground. In contrast, damage to the company's offices and administrative buildings was much less severe. The air raids that caused the most damage were those of the 6th, 18th, 21st and 22nd of January and the 14th of February 1944. Since 1943, the number of skilled workers employed by the Piaggio group had been reduced from 12,000 to 2,000, while the number of office staff had fallen from 2,000 to 300. 30 office staff and 60 workers remained at Pontedera.

The key to survival was the conversion from wartime to civil production, a problem faced by all those companies that had been engaged in the production of munitions. In a country strewn with rubble and that had yet to see the revival of an efficient public transport system, economic private transport was of primary importance. The bicycle was no longer sufficient over long distances, the motorcar was an absolutely inaccessible dream and the motorcycle was too adventurous for many. What was needed was… the Vespa!

Birth and protagonists

The desolate scene of the Piaggio factory following the heavy bombing of January 1944 (above). The Pontedera factory (below) seen from the sky in the 1950s.

Birth and protagonists

Corradino D'Ascanio

Corradino D'Ascanio was born at Popoli in the Abruzzo region on the 1st of February 1891. A flying enthusiast from a very early age, he attached a sail to a bicycle in an attempt to achieve lift-off. During the First World War, D'Ascanio made a name for himself with experiments with two-way radio equipment installed in aircraft. In 1918, he was appointed as head of the experimental department at Pomilio Brothers, an Italo-American aircraft factory located in Indianapolis. He designed and constructed modern fighters and bombers, but after the war Pomilio Brothers was unable to convert its military aircraft for civil use and the factory closed. D'Ascanio returned to his homeland and after having worked on a number of projects, focussed on his true passion, flight. In 1926, he designed and built his first helicopter, the DAT2, while in the early Thirties, thanks to financial backing from Baron Trojani, a prototype was constructed that immediately proved its potential by setting three world records. In spite of this promising debut, the D'Ascanio-Trojani company closed as a result of the problems caused by internal jealousies within the Italian air ministry. Moreover, an agreement signed by the Fiat president, Senator Giovanni Agnelli, also fell through as a result of Trojani's economic demands that were judged to be excessive. At least partial recompense for these disappoints came in 1933, when D'Ascanio was given a position at Piaggio. Here, his irreplaceable experience finally found the appropriate setting that would permit him to complete a number of aviation projects, above all in the field of helicopters. It was there that, at the end of the Second World War, Corradino D'Ascanio was asked to create a scooter that would permit mass mobility with an economical vehicle.

Strange as it might seem, the enormous success of his Vespa was not a source of pride for Corradino D'Ascanio, but rather one of irritation: for a designer who

The experiments conducted by Piaggio with pioneer helicopters dated from the second half of the 1920s with the DAT2 (D'Ascanio-Trojani) prototype equipped with fixed blades. The DAT3 (photo on this page) successfully flew between the 8th and 13th of October, establishing the world straight-line flight endurance record (8 minutes 34") at a height of 8 metres from the ground. Ing. D'Ascanio is portrayed in the photo at the bottom (second right) while the pilot seen aboard the helicopter is Major Marinello Nelli.

Birth and protagonists

yearned for the sophisticated engineering of aviation projects, and above all helicopter design, having to take on a "simple", utilitarian two-wheeler must have represented a significant come-down.

Corradino D'Ascanio died at Pisa in 1981. Corradino D'Ascanio's fame is naturally associated with his helicopters and the Vespa, but the dynamic inventor also explored a vast range of areas including:

- Perforated card calculators: (an "electro-pneumatic machine for the cataloguing and rapid research of documents" from 1929)
- Bread makers (an "electric oven for the baking of bread and pastries" from 1919)
- Fireworks ("delayed ignition fireworks for aircraft" from 1926)
- Cigarette holders with a timer (for personal use...)

D'Ascanio's memoirs recall his meeting with Enrico Piaggio:
On the way up to Biella I asked myself what it was he could want from me. I knew he had been reduced to making saucepans and I had no illusions: there would have been no talk of aeroplanes or helicopters. He welcomed me enthusiastically and said to me, "I want a vehicle that will put Italy on two wheels, but I don' t want the usual motorcycle." He then led me to a scooter built by a technician from Biella. Baptised as the Paperino [the Italian equivalent of Donald Duck], it was derived from an unsuccessful light motorcycle born in 1940 in Turin.
Then again, there had been numerous scooters: Krupp built one in 1919, the French and the English in 1920. But they had not been successful. And were too expensive. They had not been designed for mass production. This Paperino too closely resembled a motorcycle and Piaggio rejected it. I knew nothing about motorcycles. That is to say, I knew motorcycles from the outside, but I had

never had anything to do with their engineering. Moreover, as vehicles they did not appeal to me at all and I had never ridden one. I tried to play for time, but Piaggio would not give me any. He had intuited that in order to escape from post-war stagnation, the average Italian would have to overcome, among many others, one enormous obstacle: that of traffic. Individual traffic. Piaggio wanted to solve the problem and realised that the future of his company depended on it".

On the facing page, two sketches drawn in the Piaggio offices of the PD3 helicopter prototype for which D'Ascanio devised an extremely elongated fuselage, at the end of which was located a second small propeller, while the principal, large diameter horizontal rotor was set towards the front (photo on this page). Bottom right, the PD4 prototype from 1952 with two twin-bladed contra-rotating rotors.

Birth and protagonists

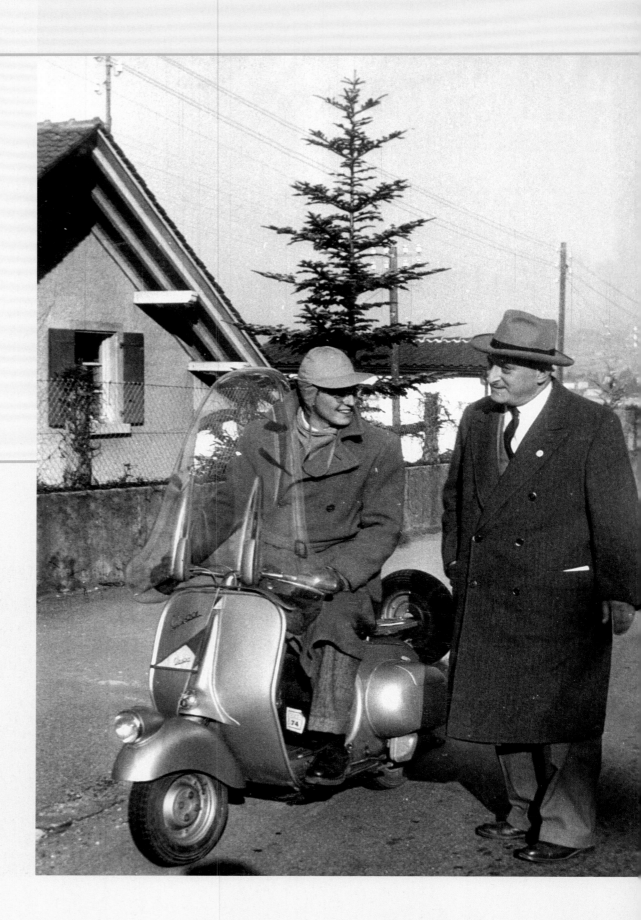

Corradino D'Ascanio

(From the Piaggio Magazine, year 1, number 1, January 1949):

Not knowing motorcycles, I was in the ideal position to create a vehicle without precedents. Piaggio was counting on this. "Only you can tackle the problem with a wholly new outlook" he told me. I followed intuitive criteria. I felt that the machine ought to serve those who, like me, had never ridden a motorcycle and hated the machine's lack of manoeuvrability. I thought it over for a while and one Sunday the basic idea came to me. The most important factor was being able to mount the vehicle comfortably, something that had already been resolved with the ladies' bicycle. So I started out with the concept that is fundamental in the ladies' bicycle. I felt that a seated position was more comfortable and more rational than having to straddle the frame. Then we had to make it as manoeuvrable as possible. We had to take into consideration its urban use. It had to be ridden without taking one's hands from the handlebars. How could this be done? Simple, I put the gearshift on the handlebar. Another thing: it should not dirty hands and trousers, one of the most conspicuous inconveniences with motorcycles. My motorcycle therefore had to have a covered engine isolated from the rider: a single assembly with the rear wheel. As a consequence, I created a transmission with no chain, the in-line gearbox being incorporated in the engine-wheel assembly. Another feature was dictated by my aeronautical experience: the mono-strut support for the front wheel rather than the bicycle-derived fork. Moreover, I introduced an innovatory monocoque body, eliminating the tubular system. In aeronautics there is a dogma among designers: lightness does not prejudice strength, as long as you do not go too far. Another requirement: the spare wheel. Remembering that on many occasions, travelling by car, I had seen motorcyclists at the side of the road struggling with a punctured inner tube removed from the wheel, I decided that all in all a mere puncture should not be a problem requiring a mechanic. I wanted my motorcyclist to have something in common with car drivers. In short, I was trying to build the machine as simply as possible. One of my favourite maxims has always been that of old Henry Ford: "if you don't fit it, it won't break".

The prototype Vespa came together in a flash. The engineering difficulties, and there were more than a few, in part because a brand-new approach was required, were overcome with a rapidity unthinkable today. The fact is that some of my assistants had worked with me for years and I had workers who had understood the importance of the vehicle and were determined to make it a success. There was a great desire to lift ourselves above the ruins of the war, to rise again, to serve a cause that was actually a common cause, not just that of the owner. We all knew our future was at stake. My innovations were noted and admired. The more innovations I presented, the more the enthusiasm of the workforce grew. A miracle took place in Biella. The proof is here: between the design and the construction of the first examples to be tested passed just three months. The Vespa, which initially had an engine of Sachs derivation, was tested in the September of 1945.

Facing page, D'Ascanio proudly poses alongside a first generation Vespa and (on this page), the father of the Vespa portrayed on the occasion of the production of the millionth example (April 28 1946).

Birth and protagonists

Carlo Carbonero

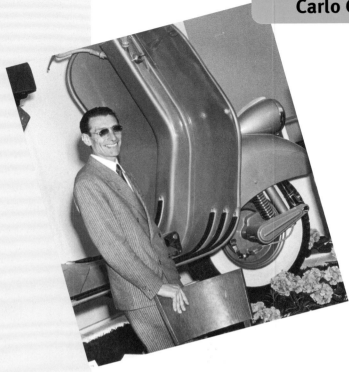

The engineer Carlo Carbonero, a talented aero-engine designer who worked closely with Corradino D'Ascanio, made a highly significant contribution to the development of the Vespa. The "father" of the Vespa frequently recalled how useful Carbonero's assistance was in the creation of the prototype. "Once the design had been defined, the prototype was constructed in record-breaking time thanks to the dynamism and the intelligent collaboration of Carlo Carbonero. I remember that one morning I presented the engineer with a drawing of a wheel and by that same evening the wheel was already made! And it was the engineer Carbonero himself who personally tested the prototype on the 4th of November 1945."

Francesco Lanzara

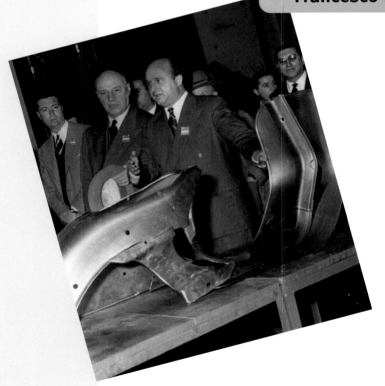

The engineer Francesco Lanzara, born in Naples in 1914, played a significant role in the Piaggio story. He graduated in civil engineering in Naples in 1936 and in aeronautical engineering in Rome in 1940. He met Rinaldo Piaggio in Africa and subsequently became director of the Pontedera factory for over 30 years from 1946 to 1979. When he joined the company he was given the unenviable task of organizing all production in the factory. The magnitude of this undertaking in the post-war years and the passage from industrial reconversion to subsequent expansion can only be imagined. However, Lanzara's affinity with the Piaggio board meant that he was able to express his great talent to best effect and it was at least in part thanks to his managerial contribution that Piaggio was able to operate rapidly and efficiently.

Birth and protagonists

**In search
of a market**

Now that the Vespa was born, Piaggio was faced with the by no means easy problem of how to distribute it. The first idea was that of associating it with established marques with which it could share the same "shop window". And which was the name of the moment in those years? The celebrated Moto Guzzi, of course, a company that could also boast an established distribution network.

In any case, the question was resolved almost before it had been posed: at Mandello, Count Parodi refused any form of commercial agreement. He had no faith in the so-called small-wheeled vehicles and the new scooter was seen as an inevitable commercial fiasco.

Despite this setback, Piaggio continued in his attempts to find a partner by aiming even higher through an association with the world of luxury cars. Contacts were made with the Lancia sales network and following a positive response the wonders of the new scooters were explained to the dealers one by one. Many were attracted by the idea, but again the initiative soon collapsed: sales were poor, well below expectations. At this point Piaggio decided to go it alone and thanks in part to successful advertising campaigns and the possibility of hire purchase the situation was overturned.

The first advertisements with which the Vespa 98 was launched also carried the names of the first distributors of Piaggio's new product.

Birth and protagonists

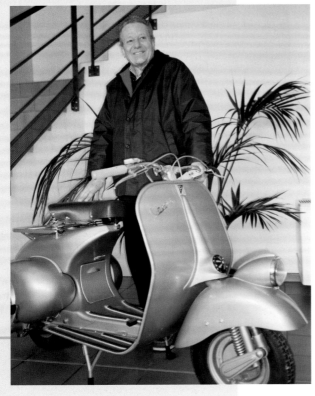

35 YEARS IN THE PIAGGIO TECHNICAL DEPARTMENT

Carlo Doveri was born at Viareggio in 1923. He graduated in engineering from the University of Pisa, a student of Corradino D'Ascanio. When this last moved to Piaggio he asked Doveri if he would like to follow him. Doveri accepted the offer and joined the Pontedera firm in 1950. He remained in the technical department through to 1984 and then worked a further two years as a consultant. In short, a 35-year career at the forefront of Vespa technical development.

Q. Engineer Doveri, what were your first tasks at Piaggio?

A. *I joined Piaggio in 1950 and immediately worked on an aeronautical problem: the in-flight measurement of stress on metal aircraft propeller blades. I remember that we had to fabricate manifolds with special bladed channels with mercury, not an easy problem but one we resolved satisfactorily.*

Q. And with regard to the Vespa?

A. *I was working on the Vespa too at the same time. I worked on the flexible cable gear change in place of the so-called "rod" system. A propos of this, I remember that Engineer D' Ascanio was so keen to see this feature finished that he chewed me out because I kept him waiting for an hour. And yet I'd got to the office by 7.30 in the morning! It was just that he'd got there by 6.30... I also worked on the carburettors that tended to ice up in the winter. We created an aluminium manifold that would channel warm air over them.*

The author with engineer Doveri during the interview held at his Pontedera office.

Q. You had direct contacts with Enrico Piaggio as well as Corradino D'Ascanio. What were their characters like?

A. *They both had very determined characters. D' Ascanio was always calm, but when he did get riled it was rough. Enrico Piaggio certainly knew his business. When Enrico Piaggio asked D' Ascanio if he could work on the Paperino, he refused because it had been created by another engineer. So Piaggio spluttered, "you're as stubborn as ever! Do what you want, but do something!"*

Q. What was the standard of training of your immediate colleagues?

A. *Extremely high. You could see that their aeronautical experience had instilled in all of them the need to work to the highest qualitative levels. In aeronautics it is simply a question of pure safety, but transferring these skills to a vehicle as spartan as this meant that the Vespa was born well, with no defects. The "mentality" was right for doing things well.*

Q. Who chose the colour for the first Vespa?

A. *Enrico Piaggio himself. At that time he though like Ford: any colour as long as it was green.*

Q. Before joining Piaggio had you ever tried riding a scooter?

A. *Actually, yes... A scooter I built myself. I called it "Cleofe" and it was powered by a British JAP 100 engine. I later also installed a Vespa engine.*

Q. And had you already had a chance to try a Vespa?

A. *Yes, I remember I'd ridden one belonging to a friend when I lived at Aosta. I liked the engine, the roadholding a little less.*

Q. How was the experimental department organized?

A. *In effect, there were two. One smaller one directed by Fausto Taranto where parts were worked on directly, without drawings. There were just a few workers here, but all highly skilled and used little machinery, a lathe, a milling machine.*
But they knew how to do everything. Then there was the experimental department proper directed by Averaldo Martini where projects were designed.

Q. One of the most important technical modifications was that of the passage from a 5% oil-fuel mixture to a 2% mix. Were there any problems?

A. *We called it "DR" for distribuzione rotante or rotary valve. Initially we couldn't work out why the con-rod roller bearing was always wearing out. Especially given that the same defect never occurred with the 400 light car. What was happening was that the air-petrol flow was not heated and reached the crankcase directly. When cold the residual oil lacked viscosity and the rollers consequently wore. We then found out that the only difference was that in the case of the 400, the rollers were caged while the others were not. All it took was to use caged bearings and the problem was solved.*

Q. Did you ever get to test any Vespas personally?

A. *Yes, even though we generally relied on testers. In fact, I could tell some stories...*

Q. Please do...

A. *The ones who crashed too often we'd send to other departments, that of the Ape or the Hydrojet for example. At that time we would stage events to demonstrate the potential of jet thrust, with no propellers, even setting up jumps from a ramp. One time the tester, Natale Biasci, took the ramp at high speed but sideways and completed a full spin before touching down perfectly on the water. Everybody applauded enthusiastically thinking it had all been*
planned and he raised his arms in triumph. But when we saw in him in flight we had our hands in our hair!

Q. Other episodes...

A. *One day the tester, Cau, had a terrible accident, crashing head-on with the Vespa into a car coming the other way. But he completed a somersault in mid-air and landed practically on his feet, unhurt. So then he goes up to the driver of the car, who in the meantime had stopped, white in the face, convinced he'd killed him. When Cau smiled at him, knocking on the window, the driver fainted from the shock. Well, when the ambulance arrived they picked up the guy who was driving the car, still unconscious...*

Q. The Vespa sidecar: where were the sidecars built?

A. *We didn't build them directly. They were made by an outside firm in Turin. In fact, here at Piaggio, we didn't even assemble them. We sent the Vespas to Turin and they saw to marketing them.*

Q. You spent a lot of time on the Vespa 400, didn't you?

A. *Yes. I worked at the Fourchambault factory for some time. I have to say they loved the Vespa even more than Pontedera did. They even built a monument to the Vespa.*
The Vespa 400 really was a good design; above all, it weighed a good two quintals (200 kg) less than the Fiat 500. But it was never supported by adequate marketing. There was talk of a joint venture with Peugeot, but Enrico Piaggio didn't want to be tied down. It was also sold in the United States, Great Britain and Germany. But of course, with a single model you couldn't do much more. In recompense, the 400 that participated in the Monte Carlo Rally did 140 kph!

Q. At ACMA in France, they also built the famous military Vespa.

A. *Yes, but it was a project developed by Giorgio D'Ascanio, son of the great Corradino.*

Q. At one time the Vespa was presented at shows with veritable special effects...

A. *Yes, and they were stunning. Once we had it moving on its own on a sheet of glass. But the true showstopper was when we had it moving, again on its own, on a wire! This was possible thanks to a gigantic gyroscope occupying the full width of the body. At the end of the wire the Vespa went behind a door, the gyroscope recharged and the Vespa came out again!*

Q. Who came up with these ideas?

A. *What a question, Corradino D'Ascanio of course!*

Q. The best of the Vespa models constructed!

A. *The PX, without doubt. A true distillation of all the experience gained previously. Apart from a minor aerodynamic problem, it was practically perfect straight out of the box.*

Q. What problem was that?

A. *There was a certain instability especially in the slipstream of other vehicles. We even went to the Fiat Research Centre in Turin to study the aerodynamics in the wind tunnel. We conducted an analysis with a gyroscopic platform and we realised that the problem stemmed from the handlebar set too far away. The rider was inadvertently moving the handlebar because his arms were over-extended. All we had to do was set the handlebar further back and the problem disappeared.*

Q. Let's talk about the Moscone, the outboard motor: was it a success or a fiasco?

A. *Neither one nor the other. What's certain, however, is that it was launched too early and then when we'd finished producing it there was a boom in recreational boating...*□

Birth and protagonists

Enrico Piaggio

Enrico Piaggio was born in Pegli in 1905. He graduated in Economics and Commerce from the University of Genoa in 1927 and received an honorary degree in engineering from the University of Pisa in 1951. He died in Pisa in 1965.

The following obituary was published in the Vespa Club d'Italia magazine No. 162 in 1965: *"Enrico Piaggio, the father of the Vespa, of the Vespa Club of Italy, is dead. Enrico Piaggio, generous supporter and constant benefactor, but also the figure spiritually closest to our endeavours and an understanding, enthusiastic participant in our associative passions despite being so averse to all forms of exhibitionism. Even from a distance, he always took an interest in the birth and development of our club and never failed to appreciate its efforts and to take pride in the successes that have marked the Vespa Club of Italy and of Europe's 16 years. We remember him present at the start of the first 1000 km race at Brescia, wishing the Vespisti, one sportsman to another, good luck for the race, and we remember him happy and smiling at the Viareggio conference celebrating the tenth anniversary of the Vespa Club of Italy; the long applause of all the delegates touched him and showed him both how sincere that wave of affection actually was and how he was recognised as the artificer and moving spirit behind the many celebratory events that had been held in Italy and elsewhere in Europe thanks to "his" Vespa and in the name of concord and fraternity between peoples of different nationalities and languages. Once again, at a now long past Conference of the Vespa Club of Europe at San Remo, on the occasion of the first Eurovespa, Enrico Piaggio joined the Vespisti present and felt vibrate in his great heart*

Enrico Piaggio and his wife Donna Laura - early Fifties – on the occasion of an event celebrating the extraordinary success of the Vespa. Behind them, with glasses, Renato Tassinari, the volcanic founder and chairman of the Vespa Club.

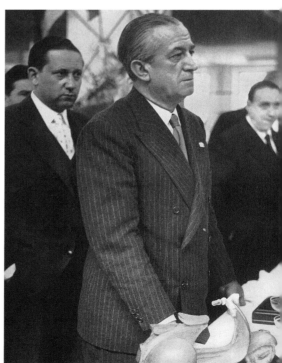

the affectionate enthusiasm and the fervid support of the representatives of all the Vespisti of Europe. He gracefully accepted the title of honorary member of the Vespa Club of Europe and belonged to the select group of founders of the Vespa Club of Italy. He had always believed in the rise of the Vespa Club and in its beneficial social role, above and beyond any propagandistic goal and he wanted the Vespa Club to unite young people and enthusiasts of the small engine in a harmonious and attractive touristic and sporting activity. The Vespisti of all the nations of Europe knew him, we felt him present and alive at our races and rallies and would always acknowledge him with an affectionate salute. Excited, we would always remember him when witnessing the endless parades of Vespisti in a festival of sun and flags, along the broad avenues of Madrid, or the boulevards of Paris through to the vastness of the Champs Elyseés, along the streets of Rome on the occasion of the Olympic Games. Along the avenues of Salzburg and Munich, along the roads winding through the Dolomites to Misurina and Cortina, along the roads of England and Switzerland, "Dottor Piaggio" would never be far from our thoughts, we always hoped that he would be present and that he would share with us the joy of those festive and triumphant sights that were, after all, the remarkable result of all his determined, intelligent work. We would lay on his table, on our return, photographs of numerous events, myriad landscapes and picturesque scene in which the Vespista appeared as a victorious protagonist. He would hide his deep satisfaction with a quick, "good, good", and as if looking at those photos was a frivolous distraction he would add "and now let's get down to work" and tackle the more pressing problems of the great industrialist. Enrico Piaggio lives on among all Vespisti with his unforgettable smile of intelligent integrity".

A number of shots of Enrico Piaggio during the years in which he led the company to the conquest of the domestic market with the Vespa, the revolutionary scooter that changed the lives of millions of people throughout the world. He was also an enlightened businessman in the social field, constructing the modern Piaggio village.

Birth and protagonists

Umberto Agnelli

Umberto Agnelli was born at Lausanne in Switzerland on the 1st of November 1934. He was the last of Edoardo Agnelli and Virginia Bourbon del Monte's seven children. Umberto was just a year old when his father died and was eleven when he lost his mother. His brother Gianni was his elder by 13 years and it was he who was the first to take up the company reins. Umberto graduated in law and at 22 years of age took on his first important position when he became president of the Juventus football club.

On the 15th of June 1959, in the chapel on the Piaggio estate at Veramista (near Pontedera) Umberto married Antonella Bechi Piaggio. In 1962 he became chairman of SAI (the insurance company) and in 1964 was appointed head of Fiat France. In 1965 he became chairman of Piaggio & C., the first successor to Enrico Piaggio. A year later the Era River broke its banks, the ensuing floods causing great damage to the Pontedera works. The restoration phase was to be one of the key episodes in Umberto Agnelli's chairmanship at Piaggio. He himself recalled the workforce's great commitment to the restarting of production in the shortest possible time. In particular, the shutting down of the furnaces (which might have exploded) is always cited as one of the events that made the greatest impression on him. In the early years of his chairmanship, the structure of the Piaggio firm remained virtually unchanged, both in terms of organization and production. Given their consummate technical skills, both Corradino D'Ascanio (Technical Department) and Francesco Lanzara (factory director) were naturally retained. In the late Sixties, Umberto Agnelli nonetheless began to appoint new members to the board of directors in order to form a broader group with greater attention to diversified activities. In 1970 he was appointed as managing director of

Fiat. In 1974 he separated from Antonella Piaggio and married Allegra Caracciolo. In 1980 Umberto was appointed vice president of Fiat. In the 1990s he had operational responsibility for IFI and IFIL (the family treasure chests). He was appointed president of Fiat in 2003, an hour after the death of his brother Gianni (on the 24th of January). However, a little over a year later, on the night of the 27th of May 2004, Umberto passed away at his Mandria estate near Turin. He was 69 years old.

ANTONELLA BECHI PIAGGIO

Antonella was the daughter of Colonel Alberto Bechi. During the war, Bechi was dismissed by Galeazzo Ciano for having covered his photo during a meeting and a few days after the armistice he was killed in a fire fight in Sardinia. His widow remarried Enrico Piaggio who "adopted" the little Antonella. At 20 years of age, Antonella married Umberto Agnelli. In an interview by Oriana Fallaci published by L'Europeo, Antonella Bechi Piaggio declared: *"They've said that it's a six-wheeled marriage, or that it's not a marriage but an industrial agreement. I don't even bother getting angry. It's such a stupid argument. I've loved Umberto since I was ten years old. I'd always thought we would get married and our families knew nothing: so why would they say it was them who organized everything?"*.

However, the marriage only lasted 14 years and in 1973 Umberto and Antonella separated in great secrecy. It was again in secret that in 1974 Umberto married Allegra Caracciolo di Castagneto (cousin of Marella Caracciolo, wife of Gianni Agnelli) at Villar Perosa, while Antonella married Umberto Visconti di Modrone.

Giovanni Alberto Agnelli

Giovanni Alberto Agnelli was president of Piaggio from 1988 through to his premature death in 1997 at just 36 years of age. From the outset he emphasised the "three missions": internationalization, innovation and ethics.

The first objective, that of expanding the markets, was explained with an anecdote: *"I'd like to quote a personal example. I have a watch that I wear frequently and that once belonged to my grandfather, Enrico Piaggio. It was presented to him in 1955, on the occasion of the 100,000th Vespa sale on the South African market. 38 years have passed and we no longer sell anything in South Africa".*

The second objective was that of making Piaggio a leading company in the search to find innovative solutions to the problems of personal urban transport, without losing contact with the environment.

The third objective was making sure that Piaggio was distinguished not only as an innovative company, but also as an ethical, transparent and collaborative company capable of generating a profound sense of shared objectives at all levels: *"In sign of a continuity with the traditions, values and culture that have enabled it to grow. In the interests of the company, of those who work for it and of the shareholders. But also, and above all, in the interest of our country."*

Giovanni Alberto Agnelli was keen to reinforce Piaggio's roots and to create a strong sense of belonging. "Attachment to the company is long–held value at Piaggio".

Nominated as president of the group in 1988, Giovanni Alberto Agnelli succeeded his father Umberto who handed over the reins to the company after 23 years. His presence contributed to a revolution within the company, with an emphasis on the strategic importance of the concept of globalization: *"This is no trend of the moment. In order to be a leading*

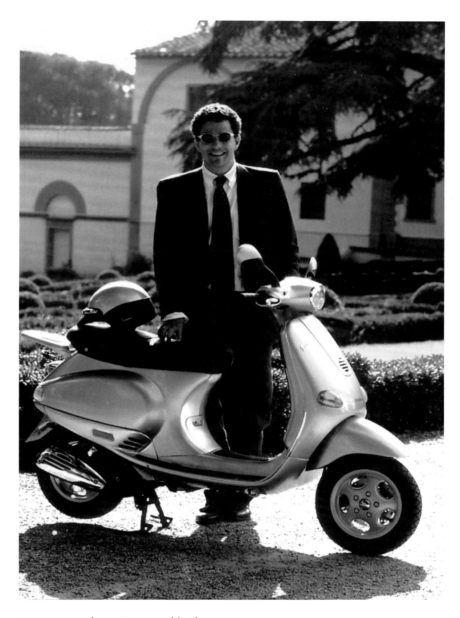

company we have to expand in the area accounting for over 80% of the market. Europe, our domestic market on which we are incontrovertibly the protagonists, represents just 12% of the global market. Restricting ourselves to Europe signifies being excluded from this market, a situation that within a few years would signify the absolute loss of competitiveness".

The Vespa beyond 2000

The Piaggio-Morgan Grenfell agreement

In the December of 1999, a remarkable piece of news spread among Vespa enthusiasts and the financial world: Piaggio was being "sold". The purchasers were the Morgan Grenfell Investment Funds, a subsidiary of Deutsche Bank, with 81.5% and the Texas Pacific Group (TPG) with 8.5% of the capital. The remaining 10% remained in the hands of Umberto Agnelli.

This was an important event in the history of the company, that through a strong shareholding could set ambitious objectives such as, for example, a return to the American market (abandoned in the 1980s) or flotation on the stock exchange. That the management structure remained Italian and production continued at Pontedera was evidence of the new investors' appreciation of the way the firm's business had been conducted through to the acquisition. The third millennium was to see Piaggio launch numerous new models and continue the development of new power units with increasingly innovative features oriented towards extremely low pollution levels. Another significant event was the revival of the Gilera marque, not only with scooters but also large motorcycles such as the 600 presented at the Milan Motorcycle Show in the September of 2001.

Joint statement by Piaggio and Deutsche Morgan Grenfell, the 16th of December 1999:

"The operation leading to the acquisition of a controlling share in Piaggio & C. S.p.A., the European leader on the two-wheeled vehicle market, was concluded today. Morgan Grenfell Private Equity (MGPE) shall control 81.5% of Piaggio, Dr. Umberto Agnelli shall retain 10%, while 8.5% of the capital shall be held by the Texas Pacific Group (TPG). MPGE shall involve a number of selected international financial investors and Mediocredito Lombardo. With managed capital of over 1.8 billion dollars, MGPE is one of the largest private equity funds in Europe. Since its constitution, MGPE has completed 478 investments for an overall value of 9 billion dollars. Mediocredito Lombardo (the merchant bank of the Gruppo Intesa), which will hold a 4.5% share of Piaggio, is responsible for the structuring of the entire operation and has organized credit lines made available by Banca Intesa to support Piaggio's development plans in view of its great opportunities for growth. Today, the assembly of Piaggio and CSPA shareholders nominated the new board of directors in the persons of A.Barberis, S.Roselli del Turco, D.Razzano, M.Garulli, E.Barachini, A.Giraudo and G.Scassellati; the new board of auditors is composed of M.Maffeis, L.Marchetti and M.Vanzetta. The board of directorss confirmed Ing. Alessandro Barberis as chairman of the company and Ing. Roselli del Turco as managing director and general director; on the same occasion Dott. Razzano was nominated vice - president."

Birth and protagonists

The Colaninno
Era

In the September of 2003, Vespa returned to Italian hands. An important financial operation was concluded that saw control of Piaggio pass from Deutsche Morgan Grenfell to IMMSI, a real estate company owned by the Mantuan financier Roberto Colaninno. The agreement involved the constitution of a new Dutch de jure company (local law permits shares to be differentiated on the basis of a right to vote), Piaggio Holding B.V. The company capital is constituted by four classes of shares (A,B,C, and D) with different company and administrative rights. IMMSI invested 100 million Euros in the operation and holds 100% of the Class A shares. This constitutes 31.25% of the company capital and provides a majority vote and a majority of board members.

The new chairman of Piaggio is Roberto Colaninno himself, while the managing director is Rocco Sabelli. The group's debt was reduced thanks to the 100 million Euro cash injection by Colaninno and the 150 million converted into shares by the creditor banks. The agreement between Piaggio and IMMSI was not easy to reach. The previous year an agreement had been signed whereby Piaggio was to have acquired the MV Agusta marque, but the operation was never concluded.

Dr. Roberto Colaninno (on the left in the photo), the new chairman of Piaggio, *celebrates the acquisition of the company with Dr. Rocco Sabelli, the new managing director.*

Birth and protagonists

Vespa Italian
once again

The acquisition of Piaggio by IMMSI: The official communication (Piaggiornale, No. 10, October 2003)

Milan, 23 October 2003

"Following the execution of the company procedures requested, today saw the closing of the contract signed on the 24th of September 2003 between IMMSI SpA, the "Dep IV" fund (managed by Morgan Grenfell Private Equity Ltd), Morgan Grenfell Development Capital Syndications Ltd (a company forming part of the Deutsche Bank Group), Piaggio Holding SpA and PB srl, a company constituted by the Piaggio Group's financing banks. Transfer of control over the management of Piaggio group affairs in Italy and abroad thus becomes operational.

The shareholders' assembly of Piaggio & C. SpA the company dealing with all the group's industrial and operational affairs, has nominated the new board of directors, on which IMMSI has a majority of seats. This board will remain in force for three years, through to the approval of the balance sheet on the 31st of December 2005, and is composed as follows: Roberto Colaninno (nominated as chairman by the assembly), Rocco Sabelli, Luciano La Noce, Giorgio Magnoni, Matteo Colaninno, Pietro Faraoni, Gaetano Miccichè, Graham Clemson and Vincenzo de Bustis Figarola. The board subsequently nominated Rocco Sabelli as managing director.

Within the new structure of the group, Piaggio is wholly controlled by the newly-formed Dutch de jure company Piaggio Holding Netherlands B.V., which has entirely subscribed an increase in Piaggio & C. SpA capital for a total of 235 million Euros following debt restructuring with the creditor banks. With a patrimony of 320 million Euros, Piaggio Holding Netherlands B.V. is itself controlled by IMMSI SpA (31.25%), a company constituted by the former Piaggio Holding SpA and by other shareholders. IMMSI has a majority of voting rights in the Piaggio Holding Netherlands B.V. assembly, as well as a majority among the members of the firm's Supervisory Board composed of Roberto Colaninno (President), Rocco Sabelli, Luciano La Noce, Michele Colaninno, Carlo d'Urso, Teresio Testa, Patrizio Menchetti, Graham Clemson and Diarmuid Cummins".

Birth and protagonists

**IMMSI becomes majority shareholder Official communication
(Piaggiornale No. 11/12 November/December 2004)**

Milan 28 December

*"IMMSI SpA, the holding company controlling the Piaggio
Group, announces that it has acquired for 45 million Euros,
within the ambit of the Aprilia operation, 28,334 class C
shares in Piaggio Netherlands BV held by Scooter Holding 3
BV, the company bringing together the former Piaggio shareholders. Following the operation, which will also involve a 50
million Euro capital injection in Piaggio & C. SpA, Piaggio
Netherlands B.V. will own 86.9% of Piaggio & C. SpA. Following this acquisition, IMMSI, which already holds a majority of
the voting rights in Piaggio Netherlands BV and in Piaggio
and C SpA, saw its capital holding in Piaggio Netherlands B.V.
grow from 31.25% to 40%, thus becoming the majority shareholder in the holding company controlling the Piaggio Group.
The growth of IMMSI's share of Piaggio capital is in line with
the Pontedera group's industrial development plans both in
Italy and abroad, and permits a significant valorisation of the
potential of the IMMSI investment, especially in view of the
future quotation of the Piaggio Group on the stock exchange."*

**A colossus
with five
two-wheeler
marques**

The Italian two-wheeler industrial pole was born in 2005: Piaggio
acquired 100% of the Aprilia Group (which in turn comprised the
Moto Guzzi and Laverda marques). The figures are significant: a
turnover of 1.5 billion Euros, a 24% share of the European market
and 35% in Italy. The group has a production capacity of over
600,000 vehicles a year and employs over 6,000 men and women.
It has eight factories around the world, six research centres and
is present in 50 countries. It is the world's fourth largest motorcycle group. The terms of the operation provide for the subscrip-
tion of the entire Aprilia capital increase of 50 million Euros, subject to the making good of all losses (amounting to 108 million
Euros) at 31 October 2004 and the zeroing of the company capital. Piaggio takes over credit extended by the banks to Aprilia
amounting to 98 million Euros and issues in favour of the same
banks to a maximum value of 64 million Euros. The bank credit
lines of the Aprilia Group were restructured for 78 million Euros,
of which 70 million with a duration extended to seven years and
at market rates and the remainder with a short-term credit line.

Part two
ORIGIN AND DEVELOPMENT
Technical and styling evolution

Technical and styling evolution

Over its first 60 years the Vespa has obviously evolved, yet has always managed to remain true to itself. The less that was changed the better, in fact. At a certain point, Piaggio actually decided it could do without the Vespa name (introducing the Cosa in the 1990s), but was eventually obliged to make an about turn. The Vespa is the Vespa, it would be like changing the taste of Coca Cola. The Vespa scooter is a very special industrial product that half a century after its introduction has the extremely rare privilege of being "updated" with a series of features that deliberately introduced stylistic elements from the past. In order to celebrate the 2006 anniversary, for example, the headlight was mounted on the front mudguard, a reference to the 98 model from 1946.

The scooter's technical evolution can be divided into two fundamental periods. The first lasted no less than 50 years and focussed on the single-cylinder two-stroke engine. This configuration signified particularly simple engineering, but also high atmospheric pollution values. From the 50th anniversary in 1996, the engine adopted was a more sober and sophisticated four-stroke unit and it is right to speak of a second life for the Vespa. In that first period, the two-stroke engine was developed continuously, but the evolution was a slow and gradual

The basic concept of the new scooter was established in the very first sketches by Ing.

D'Ascanio and the vehicle went into production in the spring of 1946 under the Vespa name.

Technical and styling evolution

process. One particularly important innovation was the passage from a 5% to a 2% oil-fuel mixture, with a significant reduction in exhaust smoke, dirt and coking. Another key episode in the development of the two-stroke was the introduction of the automatic premixer. The fuel system continued to feature a carburettor through to the introduction of the 250 and the adoption of sophisticated fuel injection. A manual gearbox was retained into the third millennium, but automatic transmission began to be offered from the 1980s onwards. It was initially regarded with a certain diffidence, but by the 1990s few were prepared to do without it. With regard to the frame, there were no true generational revolutions. The bodywork composed of the steel monocoque is a common denominator for all models, an element of distinction with the competition offering tubular frames with plastic body panels. The side-panels were originally removable and later fixed, but this was a detail that hardly overturned the original design. Over the years, the wheels were increased in diameter from 8" to 10", at which point they remained for a long period. Only in the third millennium have we seen the introduction of 11" and 12" wheels. The suspension also evolved, although without straying far from the configuration adopted in the 1940s with a trailing link at the front.

The experimental models

A three-wheeled Vespa

Among the many projects developed at Piaggio, those concerning the three-wheeled Vespa were without doubt the most original. The project was born in 1950 when Giorgio D'Ascanio tested a version of the Vespa fitted with a kind of hood as protection from the rain.
The testers noted a certain difficulty in holding the road in the case of turbulence such as when they were passed by a truck at a certain speed. In order to retain the advantages of protection without losing stability, in 1953 it was decided to construct a prototype Vespa with three wheels, two at the back, one at the front; of the two rear wheels, only one was driven.

However, as the vehicle was less stable than expected a second prototype was constructed in 1955 with two wheels at the front using arms and rockers. This design proved to be effective but a little too complex and was therefore abandoned. The Paris-Dakar rally held largely in Africa became famous in the early '80s. It was and continues to be a gruelling test for competitors and their machinery. Piaggio built a prototype featuring a supplementary tank to extended the vehicle's range and allow great distances to be covered between refuelling stops. Tyres with an aggressive tread pattern were fitted to cope with the rough terrain.
The prototype remained a one-off, however.

The '40s

Engine

The first engine fitted to the 98 had a modest power output of just 3.2 hp at 4,500 rpm. With the successive 125 the output rose to 4.5 hp at the same engine speed. The power unit was a horizontal, single-cylinder, two-stroke with three ports (intake, transfer and exhaust) and a deflector piston. Cooling was taken care of with a forced air system using a fan mounted on the flywheel magneto and a manifold on the cylinder head and barrel assembly. Cylinder head and piston were in light alloy, while the cylinder barrel was in cast-iron. The fuel system featured a Dell'Orto TA 17 carburettor and used a 5% oil-fuel mix. Ignition was via a flywheel magneto. The clutch was a multiplate oil bath unit. The gearbox had three speeds, with a handlebar grip-shift and rigid control rods. The transmission to the rear wheel was direct, with an intermediate flexible coupling.

The engine-transmission assembly was a simple, robust unit, exactly what was required in those years. Virtually everything was constructed in-house, with just two components being brought in from external suppliers: the carburettor (Dell'Orto) and the sparkplug (Marelli). The forced air cooling absorbed power and was an added complication, but proved to be necessary. The prototype, which relied on vents on the engine cover, was in fact subject to overheating.

Technical and styling evolution

Frame,
suspension,
brakes and
wheels

The steel frame constituted the Vespa's most characteristic element, so much so that its structure was to remain substantially unaltered throughout the scooter's production life. It was a true monocoque and Piaggio's own definition of the Vespa as a "two-wheeled small car" deliberately associated it with the world of the automobile. The load-bearing structure proved to be exceptionally robust and far stiffer than a tubular frame of the same weight. Below the monocoque was a tubular swinging arm supporting the engine-wheel assembly. A pair of rubber bump-stops provided a minimal springing effect. The side-panels were in sheet aluminium. The engine cover was attached via clasps and could be removed to access the power unit. The left-hand side-panel was fixed but had a hatch giving access to the interior and allowing it to be used to carry small objects. In terms of comfort, that provided by the Vespa's suspension was undeniably scarce. The 98 model was particularly spartan, lacking any form of rear suspension, while at the front there was a simple ribbon spring. It was not even fitted with a stand: when parked the 98 was laid on the running board (having first closed the fuel tap to prevent flooding). The successive 125 was slightly more comfortable. The front suspension was switched to the right-hand side and featured a more effective coil spring combined with an hydraulic damper. The new rear suspension was also

Technical and styling evolution

composed of a coil spring and hydraulic damper. The single arm struts with cantilevered wheels rather than forks were of clearly aeronautical origin. Contrary to popular belief, the Vespa's wheels were not actually offset to compensate for the engine located on the right-hand side. However, the front wheel was set with a camber angle of 1.5°.

Styling

The engine cover of the 98 had an aperture in line with the cooling fan. The handlebar was tubular, with the headlight mounted on the mudguard. The gearshift rods ran outside the central tunnel. The front mudguard of the first series was particularly deep and had removable walls. In the second series the mudguard was fixed (and less deep). The round rear light was to remain virtually unchanged throughout the 1940s.

The engine cover of the 125 retained the aperture in line with the cooling fan. The handlebar was tubular and the headlight was mounted on the mudguard. During its production run the 125 benefited from the introduction of a side-stand (instead of being leant on one side like the 98) and then a proper centre stand. The gearshift mechanism also evolved with the rods being run through the centre tunnel before a mixed system of rods and flexible cables was adopted.

PORTA BAGAGLI

SELLINO POSTERIORE

RUOTA DI RICAMBIO

CARRELLO DI RIMORCHIO

Ditta Giuseppe Lang · Genova

The '50s

Engine

The engine evolved, albeit without being subjected to any radical modifications. It remained a simple and extremely robust unit.

The 98 cc displacement was dropped with production concentrating on the classic 125 cc cylinder capacity. In the mid-Fifties, this unit was flanked by the 150 version. With respect to the first generation, the power output was increased slightly: the 125 now gave 5 hp and the 150 5.5 hp. The induction system was modified, with the old three-port and deflector piston configuration being replaced with a cross-flow system with two opposing ports and a flat piston. The gearshift system was significantly improved. The rigid control rods or "bacchette" fitted to the early models were subject to excessive play and required continuous adjustment. In the 1950s gears were selected via far more efficient flexible cables that permitted much greater precision. The GS version of the 150 had a maximum power output of 8 hp and provided significantly improved performance: its maximum speed of 100 kph began to rival that of many motorcycles of the period. One important innovation was the relocation of the carburettor directly above the cylinder. The gearbox was also new and for the first time offered four speeds. The highest specific power output was actually provided by the Sei Giorni version with 7 hp from 125 cc, but this extremely expensive machine was designed specifically for competition.

Technical and styling evolution

Frame,
suspension,
brakes and
wheels

The steel bodywork made the Vespa instantly distinguishable among the various rivals that were beginning to crowd the market. In various areas, however, the monocoque was nonetheless reinforced, above all in the central section. The original aluminium side-panels were replaced with cheaper steel panels with the 1955 version of the 125. The hinged hatch giving access to the carburettor housing remained in the curved centre section of the frame. The presence of hydraulic dampers on both the front and rear suspension helped to improve roadholding as performance levels rose. In order to improve comfort the handlebar was mounted on a cushioned support. The wheels were interchangeable and retained the 8" diameter and consequently the brake drums were also unchanged and began to be somewhat undersized and inefficient in critical situations. The GS version represented significant progress as along with the uprated engine it boasted an improved chassis specification. The suspension featured biconical variable rate springs and dual-acting hydraulic dampers. The diameter of the wheels was increased to 10". The brakes were also improved, with self-ventilating drums to prevent overheating.

SCHEMA INTERNO DELLA VESPA 125 cc.

Technical and styling evolution

Styling

In the early Fifties the Vespa was still being fitted with a tubular handlebar and a headlight mounted on the mudguard. From 1953, a full engine cover was fitted with no aperture in correspondence with the cooling fan and the styling thus became more uniform. The control cables were external. The only model that was significantly different was the U, the first Vespa with a high, handlebar-mounted headlight. In reality, there was very little special about this version, the U standing for Utilitaria and the fittings reduced to the bare bones to save costs: the bodywork even featured the open engine cover and a cutaway mudguard. The saddle lacked a front spring and the platform lacked rubber strips.

The styling was enhanced and the lines became sleeker in the second half of the Fifties. The left-hand side-panel featured a hatch giving access to the interior. The cables were routed inside the handlebar, providing cleaner lines. The leg-shield still lacked the metal edge trim. The platform was fitted with rubber strips only and the raised portion lacked the rubber mat. A long two-seater saddle was fitted as standard for the first time on the GS. The hatch on the inside part of the monocoque was eliminated in 1957.

Technical and styling evolution

The '60s

Engine

The '60s saw the introduction of the new 50 cc displacement expressly designed for fourteen-year-olds. Despite having the restricted performance imposed by the Italian Highway Code (a maximum power output of just 1.5 hp) it proved to be an enormous success. Its single cylinder was inclined at 45° rather than being horizontal. There were also innovations in terms of the other displacements. The classic 125 and 150 versions were flanked by the 90 and the 160. Towards the end of the decade the maximum cylinder capacity rose to 180 cc and the engine was subjected to constant development. Thanks to the new induction system the oil-fuel mixture was sprayed directly onto the con-rod assembly, lubricating the bearings. The intake port was located on the crankcase and regulated by the left-hand counterweight of the crankshaft. The first version to adopt this system was the 150 presented in 1958 (it was fitted to the 125 the following year). This important innovation provided numerous advantages in terms of the fuel and lubrication systems, with the possibility of passing from a 5% to a 2% oil-fuel mixture. The major benefit was that of drastically restricting the amount of smoke produced, with less coking and reduced fuel consumption. The electrical system was uprated to take into account the addition of the stoplight required by the new Italian Highway Code. The power output rose constantly and reached a maximum of 10 hp in the 180 Rally, which also boasted the new rotary valve engine.

The engine-gearbox assembly of the Vespa 90 (1963-1967), top left. Left, a cutaway of the Vespa 160 GS engine (1963-64). Below, a longitudinal sectional view of the model.

Technical and styling evolution

Frame, suspension, brakes and wheels

The new 50 presented an interesting new bodywork variation: it was, in fact, the first model to feature fixed rather than removable side-panels. This feature was also adopted on the Nuova 125 that retained the small frame in virtually unaltered form. Access to the engine was gained via a hatch opening transversally via a pair of hinges. The side-panels were instead removable on all the other larger models. The frame was nonetheless innovative in that it was assembled from two half-shells in sheet metal that were welded together with a central reinforcement. In the GS series, a hatch was let into the rear part giving access to a small locker. However, this was not a practical arrangement and the successive model instead featured the more convenient and capacious glovebox located behind the leg-shield. The last series to use the now obsolete 8" wheels was the 150 Super, all the other models now being fitted with 10" wheels.

Technical and styling evolution

Styling

An option was introduced for the first time that would be a constant feature of the Vespa range: the doubling up of the monocoque in small and large frame forms. The 125 displacement was unique in that it was found in both categories. In these years the small frame models boasted more up-to-date styling: the side-panels were fixed and well integrated with the principal structure. The 50 and 125 were light and responsive. The 90 was less successful, although the model's reputation was saved by the Super Sprint version that was the dream machine of many enthusiasts. It boasted particularly sleek styling, with a shapelier leg-shield and a lighter front mudguard. Even the handlebar was narrower. The spare wheel was positioned vertically in the centre of the platform with a glovebox mounted on top of it that resembled a motorcycle fuel tank and could be gripped between the knees when riding fast. It even had a chest pad for when you were really tucked in and looking for maximum speed. The 90 SS was also equipped with another component that was eagerly sought after by enthusiasts: that elongated silencer promising ultimate performance that was very different to the "tea kettle" fitted to the other versions with the same frame.

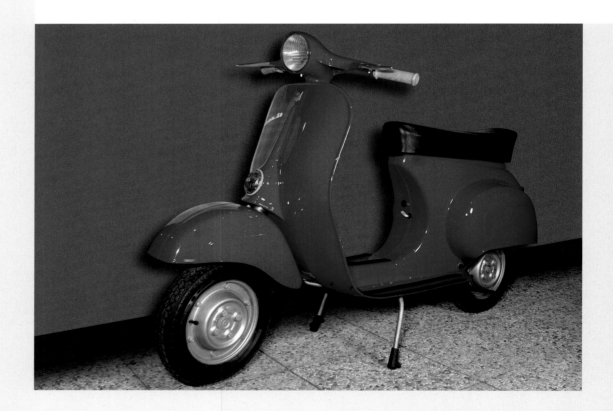

Technical and styling evolution

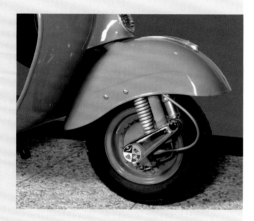

The large frame models were not ageing so well and suffered to some extent from the dated styling. They were frequently characterised by chromed trim on the side-panels and mudguard, but soon began to reflect the passing of the years. The chromed trim around the edge of the leg-shield was attractive. The headset of the early models was still the type composed of two half-shells, the one-piece unit being adopted later. The rounded tail became more square-cut from 1963 when a registration plate holder was incorporated. The most attractive model remained the Vespa GL, the first to boast the four-speed gearbox, the 2% oil-fuel mixture and the 10" wheels. These are all details still found on the PX of the third millennium, 40 years later... It was also the only model to boast wheels and brake drums in the same colour as the bodywork. One important detail was the capacious glovebox placed behind the leg-shield, a feature destined to last many years. The lively colours such as bright red helped make the 180 SS particularly attractive in the eyes of many enthusiasts.

The '70s

Engine

The decade saw the introduction of numerous modifications, from the smallest displacement up. The 50 was in fact offered in the Elestart version, which as the name suggests boasted the sophistication of electric starting. Even though in these years the feature was frowned upon (especially by the male clientele…), it was without doubt interesting and well ahead of its time. Apart from the higher cost, the disadvantages consisted of the greater weight and size of the batteries located behind the left-hand side-panel: the weight increased by 11 kg and the spare wheel had to be eliminated. An interesting device controlling lubrication was fitted to the 125 and 150 models. It was offered from the end of the previous decade, initially only on those models reserved for export to markets where there was a lack of facilities for the correct oil-fuel mixtures (as in the USA for example). This was the "Automatic Fuelmix", in effect an automatic premixer providing variable percentages and offered as an optional extra (L. 20,000). The sporty 125 ET3 from 1976 featured three-port induction. The maximum displacement rose to 200 cc in 1972; this represented the largest engine ever fitted to a Vespa and was to remain so for no less than 35 years. The 200 Rally was also the most powerful and fastest ever produced: the engine produced 12.5 hp and was good for a maximum speed of over 115 kph. The 200 also boasted another important innovation, as it was the first Vespa to be fitted with electronic ignition.

Technical and styling evolution

Frame,
suspension,
brakes and
wheels

The Vespa frame evolved very little in this decade with the design having becoming a classic and no need for significant changes being seen. The coachwork continued to feature a steel monocoque with fixed side-panels on the small frame series (50 and 125 Primavera) and removable covers on the large frame series (125 GTR and TS, 150 Sprint Veloce and 200 Rally). The suspension layouts were also standardized, the front always continuing to feature a trailing link, variable rate coil spring and a duel action hydraulic damper. The rear suspension retained the swinging engine-wheel assembly, again with a variable rate coil spring and a dual action hydraulic damper. The small frame series were fitted with 3.00x10" wheels, with the large frame instead being fitted with 3.50x10" rims. In this period performance was improved, particularly in the case of the 200 Rally series. The chassis began to reveal its limitations and a need was felt for radical modifications. Front end diving in the case of sudden braking became increasingly apparent and revealed itself to be a weakness of the design as a whole.

Technical and styling evolution

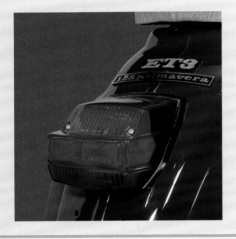

Styling

The small and large frame series were slightly diversified. The small frame series enjoyed great success, particularly among the younger generations. The fourteen-year-olds loved the 50 Special, the sixteen-year-olds were dazzled by the 125 Primavera. Both models had sleek lines that appealed to the youngsters. A lively range of colours was offered, including audacious tints such as bright green and orange. In order to modernize the appearance of the scooter, the diagonal scripts identical to those of the 98 from 1946 were soon set horizontally and more up-to-date graphics were adopted. There were also new graphics elsewhere on the bodywork, such as the longitudinal stripes applied to Primavera ET3 to emphasize its sporting aspect. The ET3 also featured a matte black elongated exhaust similar to that of the 90 SS from the '60s.

In terms of styling, the large frame series were a little more subdued. Despite the same displacement, the 125, initially offered as the GTR and then as the TS, was not received by the Piaggio's younger clientele with the same enthusiasm reserved for the Primavera, compared with which it lacked both appeal and per-

Technical and styling evolution

formance. The 200 rally was in a class of its own; it was the fastest Vespa and announced the fact with its longitudinal stripes and the "Electronic" script drawing attention to the ignition system. The 150 Sprint Veloce was in effect better balanced, but was located in what had become a largely ignored category.

With the same displacement, the 125 GTR and TS could not compete with the slim-line Primavera and both were given scant consideration by the teenage market.

The image of the large-frame models began to feel the weight of the passing years and was overly reliant on dated styling. The 200 Rally was a case apart and highly prized by the younger clientele for its uncompromised sporting look. Those longitudinal "racing" stripes may have put off the adults but they certainly appealed to the kids. The motif of contrasting longitudinal bands was not one that was to be revived over the following decades.

The '80s

Engine

In this decade the revolution was more concerned with styling than mechanical aspects, with the engines substantially retaining the characteristics of the corresponding displacements in the previous series. The new PX 125 and 200, for example, had maximum power outputs of 8 and 12.5 hp respectively, the same as those of the TS and the Rally they replaced. The performance figures also coincided.

Separate lubrication had now been extended throughout the range. The PX 125 T5 series broke the mould in that it featured a five-port engine producing a healthy 11 hp. While the situation was relatively stable in terms of the large frame series, there was much more going on among the small frame series. Here too, the power outputs and performance of the PK 50 and 125 remained close to those of the earlier 50 Special and 125 Primavera ET3, but there was one highly important innovation (a veritable revolution in fact) in the transmission department. For the first time, the traditional version with the gripshift gear change was flanked by a new series with an automatic gearbox. The system involved the use of expanding pulleys together with a belt drive to provide continuously variable ratios. The system was fairly sophisticated and was governed by the throttle opening and road speed (via an hydraulic servo mechanism). Although the design was effective it was over-complicated.

Technical and styling evolution

Frame, suspension, brakes and wheels

The bodywork of the new series, while being thoroughly revised in stylistic terms, retained the original steel monocoque in unaltered form. Another aspect that was left unchanged was the size of the wheels, now established at 3.50x10". The suspension department, one long in need of development, was instead thoroughly revised. The performance of the last models was capable of seriously embarrassing the front suspension, especially in the case of sudden braking. The front geometry was therefore completely revised, albeit without straying far from the general configuration previously adopted. The damper was anchored to the brake back-plate and attached to the trailing link in correspondence with the stub axle. In this way the notorious nose-diving effect under braking was considerably reduced and roadholding was significantly improved. Thanks to these improvements, the Vespa was once more an up-to-date vehicle and, above all, well balanced in relation to its new performance potential. From this point of view, the greatest benefit was felt by the 200 version, the most powerful scooter on the market.

Technical and styling evolution

Styling

There was a clearly differentiated public response to the small and large frame series. The PK series, was intended to replace the previous models (the 50 Special and the 125 Primavera) but failed dismally. Compared with the corresponding models from the '70s the styling was excessively square-cut and had nothing like the same appeal. An attempt was made to repair the damage with the launch of the PK XL series, but in styling terms it only made matters worse with its conspicuous saddle support that was ill at ease with the rest of the body. Among the technical details, mention should be made of the internal rather than overlapping bodywork welds. The Automatica was the first Vespa not to feature a foot brake (replaced by the left-hand headset lever).

The sports series was called the ETS and had longitudinal bands and an elongated exhaust like that of the ET3 from the '70s. The only feature that was truly appreciated in terms of the styling of the small frame series was the fact that the indicators were now incorporated within the leg-shield and at the rear end of the two side-panels. This provided much more modern lines compared with the previous series and represents a styling detail worthy of note.

Technical and styling evolution

The large frame was instead a remarkable success. From the very outset the PX proved to be a masterpiece, demonstrated by the fact that it is still virtually unchanged and selling strongly well into the third millennium. Its presentation represented an epochal moment for Piaggio. Compared with the '70s generation everything changed and there was the risk of alienating a large section of the public. Instead the PX retained all the qualities of the previous models, but was revised and improved in every respect. It was also updated; indicators perfectly integrated with the bodywork were offered as optional extras and proved to be so popular that examples without them are rare.

There was also a more sporting version, the T5. It was more powerful and faster but stylistically flawed, with an ugly rectangular headlight. It was also over-styled: there was even a spoiler below the platform! The front end of the pre-production examples of the PX tended to float, provoking excessive wallowing. In order to correct this problem, the scooter was taken to the Fiat wind tunnel for aerodynamic testing.

The '90s

Engine

In this decade too there were no major changes to the power unit, the revolution being largely aesthetic. The engine retained what were now the three classic displacements, 125, 150 and 200 cc. The maximum power outputs were also unchanged with respect to the PX series with the same displacements: 8, 9 and 12 hp respectively. The same was true of the various models' performance, with the figures close to those for the corresponding models from the '70s. Modifications were minimal: the ports were larger, the sparkplug was located more centrally and the cylinder head had a truncated cone configuration. Compared with the preceding models the choke and fuel tap controls were eliminated in favour of automatic devices. One enriched the oil/fuel mixture in relation to the ambient temperature (and closed automatically), the other closed the flow of fuel with the engine switched off and engaged the reserve supply, signalled via a tell-tale on the headset. The engine mounts consisted of larger flexible supports in order to further reduce the transmission of vibration. In the small frame series the only significant interventions concerned the automatic transmission that was simplified with respect to the first version, with the new Speedmatic system featuring a mechanical rather than hydraulic variator.

The Vespa Bimodale

The prototype Vespa 50 Bimodale was presented at the Cologne Show in 1990. It was equipped with a dual power unit: a classic internal combustion two-stroke engine and an electric motor. The batteries were located in the left-hand frame compartment and were charged by the internal combustion engine. The scooter had a maximum speed of 25 kph and a range of 15 km. This was an extremely interesting one-off experimental vehicle that never made it past the prototype stage.

The Bimodale was primarily an experimental vehicle designed to be ridden on all roads with the normal internal combustion engine while the electric motor could be used in urban areas without polluting the air with exhaust gases. The experiment was later repeated with the Sfera model.

1. ORIGIN AND DEVELOPMENT

Technical and styling evolution

Frame, suspension, brakes and wheels

The Cosa bodywork was all new and realized in Xenoil, a plastic material that once painted had an identical finish to the metal bodies. The frame, suspension and brakes package represent a clear advance in terms of safety. In particular, the designers focussed on the braking system in order to offer greater efficiency with respect to the previous generations. The Cosa was equipped with an integral braking system. This means that by depressing the pedal an hydraulic control is actuated that acts on both drums, automatically differentiating the braking force applied to the front and rear wheels. The handlebar lever instead actuated the front brake only, but when the pedal was already in action it did not increase braking force so as to avoid the risk of locking the front wheel. The hydraulic pump was located inside the central tunnel, close to the pedal and distributed braking force between the two units via a valve, giving priority to the rear wheel. ABS was available as an optional extra. With the Cosa, comfort was further improved thanks to more effective suspension, while wider tyres were fitted to increase stability. For the first time there was a space beneath the saddle to stow a helmet.

Technical and styling evolution

Styling

The small and large frame series were significantly diversified. The small frame was improved while the large frame suffered something of a disaster. With regard to the N and the FL2, Piaggio took steps to soften the excessively angular styling of the PK from the previous decade. While they were by no means masterpieces, they did begin to be accepted by the public.

The steering shroud was integrated more effectively with the front mudguard, the headset was better shaped in the area adjacent to the grips, the instrumentation was clearer and more comprehensive and the glovebox was more smoothly integrated with the back of the leg-shield. In the version with automatic transmission the lateral vents on the side-panels were eliminated. The plastic wheel covers were also more attractive (although rather impractical when the tyres had to be inflated).

The improvement with respect to the small frame models from the previous decade was significant. The larger instrumentation was particularly popular. For the first time the Vespa 50 was also fitted with a truly legible speedometer and well-positioned tell-tale lights; furthermore, there was also the luxury of a fuel gauge.

Technical and styling evolution

It was instead with the large frame that Piaggio made a major mistake in attempting to replace a "perfect" model, the PX. It was objectively difficult to improve on the styling of a masterpiece, but with the Cosa the firm managed quite the opposite. Then there was the fact that abandoning the Vespa name was a strategic decision that smacked of commercial masochism.

The styling of the Cosa paid great attention to the placing of the indicators within the bodywork; those at the front were angular and inset, while those at the rear formed a band that included the rear light in the centre. The result was harmonious and met with public approval.

The Cosa 2 was decidedly less successful and was penalised by the over-styled rear end. In this case, the registration plate was inserted between the two indicators with the rear light being squashed below the saddle creating a visual impact that upset and interfered with the lines of the tail. The Cosa seemed to do everything it could to make itself unpopular.

The 2000s

Engine

Major innovations for the small frame series: the birth of the 125 ET4 (an evolution of the LX) and the fitting of a four-stroke engine to the Vespa for the first time. This was not an absolute first for Piaggio: the technology had already been seen on the Sfera 125, but here modifications were made to the carburettor, the exhaust system and the ignition electronics. The engine also featured an overhead camshaft and an oil radiator cooled by the same flow of air cooling the cylinder barrel. The transmission was automatic, but of a simpler and more efficient design than that of the PK series. There was also exceptional changes to the smallest displacement model with the birth of the 50 ET2 powered by a two-stroke engine fitted with a sophisticated direct fuel injection system. Ten years on, the large frame system also evolved with the Granturismo model. This series featured liquid cooling with the radiator air intake concealed either side of the glovebox behind the leg-shield. The classic 125 and 200 displacements (the 150 was dropped) were later joined by the 250, the first time a Vespa displacement had ever exceeded 200 cc, 35 years after the introduction of the Rally. Power outputs and performance figures were improved, with no less than 22 hp propelling the scooter to a maximum speed of over 120 kph. The engine is extremely advanced: four-stroke, four valves, electronic fuel injection and ignition. The Vespa Granturismo was the first 250 in Europe homologated in accordance with the Euro 3 anti-smog norms.

Hybrid, an ecological Vespa

The world's first hybrid two-wheeler! In the spring of 2006 Piaggio presented the Municipality of Milan with the first example of the Vespa 50 LX bimodale, a development of the model introduced at the 1990 Cologne Show. This prototype, designated as the HyS (Hybrid Scooter), is effectively equipped with two power units, an internal combustion engine and an electric motor. The first is a classic catalyzed four-stroke, while the second instead turns the LX into a zero emissions vehicle able to circulate in city centres even when the level of atmospheric pollution leads to a ban on vehicles with internal combustion engines. A switch permits the selection of one of four operating modes: standard hybrid, high charge, low charge and electric only. In the first three, power is derived from both units (for example, the electric motor can give the internal combustion a boost when climbing) thanks to an integrated system, while in the last the internal combustion engine is disengaged. What is innovative is that when it is running the internal combustion engine is charging the electric motor's batteries. The differences with respect to the standard LX can be seen beneath the saddle with the compartment of the HyS occupied by the batteries: a top box has to be used to store a helmet.

Technical and styling evolution

Frame, suspension, brakes and wheels

The Granturismo large frame series revived the steel monocoque frame with welded reinforcements. The side-panels are fixed. The front suspension has a single-strut layout with a twin-chamber hydraulic damper and coaxial spring. The rear suspension has a pair of dual-action dampers with adjustable preloading. For the first time a Vespa was fitted with 12" diameter wheels. ABS was offered as an optional extra along with an integral braking system: the left-hand lever actuates both brakes, while the right-hand lever acts exclusively on the front disc. The braking system is servo-assisted. The discs have a diameter of no less than 220 mm. In the small frame series, the LX was fitted with 11" wheels of a new five-spoke design. In this period the question of active safety became increasingly important. While until then all models had been fitted with 10" diameter wheels, a significant increase in this dimension was introduced that provided greater stability on rough or loosely surfaced roads.

Technical and styling evolution

Styling

Moving into the new millennium with an all-new design, albeit one carrying the Vespa name, was always going to be a difficult task. With the benefit of the experience gained during the previous decades, Piaggio knew it was facing a terrible risk. In the 1970s everything had gone well for the firm, while in the '80s the large frame was extremely popular but the small frame failed to find favour. The '90s instead saw the resurgence of the small frame and the decline of the large frame. The world waited for Piaggio's 50th anniversary celebrations with bated breath: when the covers were removed a small frame scooter was revealed. This was the ET4 and toasts were made to both the anniversary and the beauty of the new model. It was so popular that in the middle of the following decade it was replaced by the LX series with only a few details having been revised. These included the headlight, with a round unit once again preferred to the oval version in a clear reference to the past. The small frame series proved to be a great success in terms of its perfectly balanced styling and details. The tapering side-panels were particularly popular and successfully rendered the idea of a dynamic vehicle. A small design masterpiece.

Technical and styling evolution

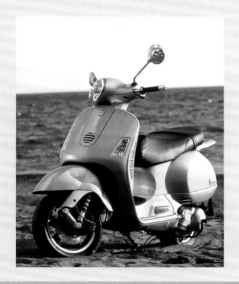

The public waited impatiently for the large frame – this was the first time that the two series were not produced in parallel. However, Piaggio wanted to be sure of offering a successful large Vespa and delayed for no less than 10 years. It was worth the wait, with the new Granturismo proving to be hugely popular.

The design is extremely up-to-date and skilfully manages to reference many stylistic elements that have contributed to the success of the Vespa over the years. For example, the script on the leg-shield is set diagonally and the Piaggio badge is the two-tone version, while the headlight is set off by a chromed bezel. For the first time, the liquid cooling posed the problem of where to locate air vents. The designers took advantage of the sides of the glovebox mounted behind the leg-shield to house modern features without disturbing the deliberately classical styling.

Another feature that has proved to be very popular is the incorporation of the passenger footrests within the body when they are folded. The luggage rack behind the saddle is useful, practical and sturdy. A body-coloured top box is also available for those looking for extra carrying capacity.

Part three

ORIGIN AND DEVELOPMENT

The forerunners

The prototypes

In the late '30s and early '40s four vehicles were built in Italy that represent the nation's first attempts at building a scooter, a vehicle with two small wheels: the Fiat, the Volugrafo, the Delta and the Simat. None of them actually made it into production, in part due to the rather basic, albeit fully finished, configuration of the projects. Other scooters had already gone into production abroad, but none had achieved commercial success. The most interesting models appeared in the Twenties in France (Monet Goyon), Germany (Lomos), Great Britain (Unibus) and the United States (Autoped). A number of models from the USA achieved moderate success in the Thirties (Cushman, Motoscoot, Salsbury).

Fiat, 1938

This was effectively the first Italian scooter. Built as a one-off, it was registered as being owned by Giancarlo Camerana, then Vice President of Fiat. At the time Camerana was a close friend of Enrico Piaggio.

The scooter was powered by a Type 32 Sachs two-stroke engine displacing 98 cc. It produced a power output of 2 hp and ran on a 6% fuel/oil mixture. The two-speed gearbox was controlled by hand via a lever. The front suspension was composed of a semi-elliptic spring linked to a system of struts. The rear suspension was rigid. Lateral drum brakes were fitted along with 8" wheels. The scooter weighed 55 kg.

The forerunners

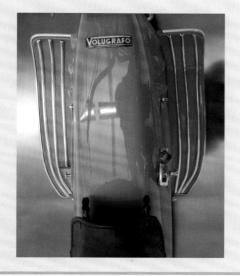

Volugrafo, 1939   Designed by the engineer Vittorio Belmondo, this basic scooter was built by Volugrafo of Turin.

It was also powered by a Type 32 Sachs two-stroke engine displacing 98 cc. It produced a power output of 2 hp and ran on a 6% fuel/oil mixture. The two-speed gearbox was controlled via a central lever. Both front and rear suspension was rigid. Drum brakes were fitted with 8" wheels. The scooter weighed 58 kg. There was also a version with a displacement of 124 cc.

The Volugrafo was a particularly interesting model and boasted a number of engineering features that were to have a future in the commercial development of the scooter such as small diameter wheels – this provided excellent manoeuvrability, but a spare wheel was not offered. The opening hatch in the side accessing the engine was to be copied faithfully on the prototype MP5 Paperino built by Piaggio in 1944.

The Volugrafo was conceptually spartan; it was neither comfortable to ride nor practical given the inconvenient positioning of the gear lever. There was no stand which meant that when parked it had to be leant with one running board on the ground. The colour scheme was very eye-catching with all components painted in bright red.

The forerunners

Simat, 1940

This scooter was virtually identical to the Volugrafo. It too was designed by Vittorio Belmondo who intended to market it himself and was again powered by a 98 cc Sachs two-stroke engine. The steel bodywork was pressed in a single piece. The running boards served as footrests but also as something to lean the vehicle on when parked given that it lacked a stand. The running boards were in aluminium. As with the Volugrafo, comfort was at a premium given that the Simat had no suspension other than the pair of springs set below the saddle. The fuel filler cap was placed behind the saddle. The wheels were fitted with spinners for rapid removal, an understandable feature given the frequency with which in those years tyres had to be repaired due to punctures; despite their small diameter, a spare wheel was not provided.

Compared with the Volugrafo from the previous year, the bodyshell was distinguished by a conspicuous hump beneath the saddle. The front mudguard also extended further forward than that of the Volugrafo.

The forerunners

Velta, 1941

The Velta was yet another design by Vittorio Belmondo. It was actually an improved version of the Simat, now equipped with front suspension and powered by the customary a 98 cc Sachs two-stroke engine. The Velta represents the final evolutionary stage of the scooter conceived by Belmondo. The bodyshell was identical to that of the earlier Simat, from which it also inherited the inconvenient gear lever location virtually in the centre of the body.

The presence of front suspension capable of providing a modicum of ride comfort instead represented significant progress. The layout featured a pair of coil springs located either side of the steering head, a configuration similar to that adopted in the same period on the far larger Harley Davidsons built in the United States.

In contrast with earlier prototype models by the same designer, the Velta features extensive use of the VBT initials standing for Vittorio Belmondo Torino. The initials are found all over the scooter, almost obsessively, from the front suspension struts to the handlebar levers.

The forerunners

MP5
Moto Piaggio
Paperino, 1944

In order to escape the bombing of Pontedera, Piaggio moved to Biella. Here the engineers Renzo Spolti and Vittorio Casini had the opportunity to admire the collection of motorcycles found in the castle of a great enthusiast, Count Felice Trossi. Among the various models, one in particular attracted their attention, Vittorio Belmondo's Volugrafo. With inspiration being drawn from this model, the first example of what was to be the forerunner of the Vespa was built by Piaggio: the MP 5, or Moto Piaggio 5, also known as the Paperino (Donald Duck) following on from the Fiat Topolino (Mickey Mouse). The entire project was realised within the experimental department. Only the engine (Sachs 98) and the tyres (Superga) were outsourced.

The Paperino had a number of interesting features: the voluminous bodywork, the handlebar controls, forced-air cooling and small-diameter wheels. However, the central tunnel had to be straddled to mount the scooter, something that did not please Enrico Piaggio. It was sufficient for production of the Paperino to be restricted to just a few dozen examples.

Following the Paperino episode, Enrico Piaggio decided to entrust the project to the engineer Corradino D'Ascanio who was responsible for the prototype of what was to become the first Vespa model, the 98.

The forerunners

**MP6
Moto Piaggio,
1945**

Following the Paperino episode, Enrico Piaggio decided to entrust the scooter project to the engineer Corradino D'Ascanio who was responsible for the prototype of what went on to become the first Vespa model, the 98.

This prototype was so successful that the Vespa that went into production was virtually identical. The only difference lay in the type of cooling: natural ventilation in the prototype and forced air in the production model. The prototype was, in fact, distinguished by large grilles at the front and rear of the engine cover.

A number of features that were to characterize the Vespa from then on were present at the outset. The bodywork was particularly extensive and the mudguards were deep to offer thorough protection and avoid soiling riders' clothes. The rear mounted engine allowed the scooter to be mounted easily without having to straddle a central tunnel and kept the engine-transmission assembly compact. The small-diameter wheels guaranteed great manoeuvrability and allowed a spare wheel to be carried. The handlebar controls made the Vespa easy to use for everyone. Minimal modifications were required for mass production: the asymmetric side-panels of the prototype became symmetrical

The forerunners

and the horn was shifted from under the saddle to the leg-shield. A number of prototypes were constructed, but they may be divided into two series. One version had the brake pedal on the right, angular side-panels (with a lower fold), no badging on the leg-shield, the gear-shift behind the shield part rigid and part flexible and a kick-start pedal with an articulated arm. A second version had the brake pedal on the left, rounded side-panels (with no lower fold), a Piaggio logo in the centre of the leg-shield (or a Vespa script on the left), rigid gearshift controls and a non-jointed kick-start pedal.

The prototypes were tested on the Biella-Oropa road by Vittorio Casini, who was to say, in his thick Tuscan accent: "Questo hoso qui ti va anche sui muri" ("This thing'll even climb walls").

Part two

THE ROAD TO SUCCESS

The '40s

The '40s

CINEMA
Citizen Kane (Orson Welles) - *Obsession* (Luciano Visconti) - *Casablanca* (Michael Curtiz) - *Gilda* (Charles Vidor) - *Sciuscià* (Vittorio De Sica)

MUSIC
Tulipan (Trio Lescano) - *White Christmas* (Bing Crosby) - *Nella Vecchia Fattoria* (Quartetto Cetra)

RADIO
Radio Londra - Canta Rabagliati - Oggi a Montecitorio - Arcobaleno - La Bisarca - Voci dal mondo - I notturni dell'usignolo - Radio plays

BOOKS
The Tartar Steppe (Buzzati) - *And Suddenly It's Evening* (Quasimodo) - *Don Camillo* (Guareschi) - *1984* (Orwell)

CARS
Renault 4 CV - Cisitalia - Alfa Romeo 6C - Citroën 2 CV - Fiat 500 - Land Rover

MOTORCYCLES
Solex - Ducati Cucciolo - Gilera 500 Saturno - Moto Guzzi 500 Astore - Matchless 500 G80 - Morini 125

FASHION
Nylon stocking production suspended in 1943 and reintroduced in 1947 - Wedge soles - bikinis - US military T-shirts

INNOVATIONS
Polaroid - Nikon 1 - Penicilin - Sonar - Teflon - Electronic calculator - Vitamin A - Transistor

ENTERTAINMENT
Pinball - Vinyl 33/78 records - Car radio - First TV ads in the USA - NTSC standard TV transmissions

SPORT
London Olympics (1948) - Post-war Mille Miglia and Le Mans 24 Hours - Gino Bartali wins Tour de France (1948) - Fausto Coppi wins Giro d'Italia

EVENTS
Second World War - Atomic bombs in Hiroshima and Nagasaki - Birth of Italian Republic (1946) - Marshall Plan aids Europe

The '40s

The diffidence shown towards a vehicle that was so different with respect to those the public was accustomed to was considerable, with the small wheels arousing concern over roadholding. However, those who tried the Vespa were enthusiastic and thanks to word-of-mouth it began to establish a following. Piaggio advertising did the rest and from the 2,500 examples produced in 1946, output rose to 61,000 in 1950. There were just two models in those years, the 98 and the 125. The gear change mechanism used the rod system and required a certain degree of maintenance.

The 98 had a power output of 3.3 hp at 4,500 rpm and a maximum speed of 60 kph. The gearbox had three speeds. In the 125 the power output rose to 4 hp at 4,500 rpm for a maximum speed of 70 kph. The most significant improvement introduced with the 125 was coil spring suspension on both wheels.

Piaggio moved to Biella in 1944. The offices were located in the warehouses of the Poma cotton mill and the Squindo foundry, while the production lines were set up in the textile factories belonging to Faudella at Pavignano, Barberis at Candelo and Pettinature di Vigliano at Gaglianico and Lessona. The two-tone logo was designed in the immediate post-war period when Enrico Piag-

In the early years of its career the Vespa presence was felt everywhere, from the great international expositions to local town fairs, ensuring that the message reached the widest possible public.

The '40s

gio decided to restart production. It is comprises a heraldic-style shield with a pointed tip, divided diagonally. Set in the upper part was a white "P" on a blue ground, while below was a blue Piaggio script on a light blue ground. The Boldoni font used was very traditional for that period.

Vespa, the story of a name

Legend has it that Enrico Piaggio's first words when he saw the prototype Vespa were, "It looks like a wasp!". In reality, it is by no means certain that he was actually the first to associate the new scooter with the insect. What is certain is that the name was a success from the outset. There are actually two strands to the scooter-insect correlation. There are those who see in the pinched shape the separation between the head-handlebar and the thorax-body, while others pointed to the similarity of the insect's buzz and that of the scooter.

Fortunately, the virtues of the new scooter were soon recognised by all those who were not motorcyclists but nonetheless wished for a means of individual transport that was simple, economical and – above all – non-sporting.

The advertising campaign involved well-known international personalities. This photo shows one of the first Vespas being personally presented to a young Prince Rainier of Monaco.

MOTO CICLISMO

ANNO XXXII - N.° 7
10 APRILE 1946

Questa copia
Lire Trenta
Sped. in A. Post. Gr. 2

RASSEGNA DELLA PRODUZIONE MOTOCICLISTICA ITALIANA

Caratteristiche della motoleggera "VESPA": motore a 2 tempi - cilindrata 98 cmc. - velocità massima 60 km. ora - consumo 1 litro per 50 km. - cambio a 3 marce - massima pendenza superabile 20% - sospensione elastica, anteriore e posteriore. Rappresentante per la vendita: S. A· R. P. I. - Genova - Via Galata 33 - Telefono 54770.

Anche la motocicletta appare oggi in una fase nettamente evolutiva e fra le costruzioni italiane del dopoguerra la nuovissima "VESPA" della PIAGGIO & C. di Genova che qui presentiamo costituisce una brillante incarnazione di tendenze profondamente innovatrici ma basate su principi razionali tradotti in concreto con attenta meditazione. I primi esemplari della "VESPA" hanno fornito in pratica eccellenti risultati. La serietà della ditta costruttrice garantisce d'altronde di per se stessa la bontà di questa macchina, la prima che, nella produzione su vasta scala, batta vie decisamente nuove.

The '40s

From the owner's handbook:

- *Gears may also be changed without disengaging the clutch. Exhaustive testing with this system has demonstrated that the transmission components do not suffer.*
- *The Vespa light motorcycle does not have a stand, it may be leant with the running boards directly on the ground or preferably on a kerb. When the motorcycle is leant on the running board the fuel tap should be closed to avoid flooding the carburettor. It is advisable to lean the motorcycle on the left-hand running board.*
- *Clean the exhaust silencer every 4,000 km by introducing water and caustic soda (25%) and then rinsing thoroughly with running water.*
- *If the carburettor is flooded when starting the engine, close the fuel tap and drain the fuel from the engine by unscrewing the plug in the lower section of the crankcase. Turn the engine over by hand until the fuel is completely drained, screw in the plug and actuate the starting lever with the fuel tap still closed, reopening the tap as soon as the engine fires.*

The voice of the press

From *Motociclismo*, 10th April 1946:

"In the last few days Piaggio & C. of Genoa has presented to the public the "Vespa" utilitarian light motorcycle mass-produced in its Pontedera factory. This machine represents one of the most important aspects of Piaggio's peacetime production programme which must provide work for its major industrial facilities, until recently devoted to the production of munitions, specifically aircraft, aero–engines and variable pitch propellers. Aviators and aviation specialists and technicians have always been enthusiasts of and frequently knowledgeable experts with regard to motorcycles. It should come as no surprise that these engineers, open–minded innovators by necessity and tradition, when invited to design a utilitarian light motorcycle, should have left to one side the classical school and attempted to resolve the problem on the basis of criteria that were their own, if not wholly new or revolutionary.

The practical result has proved more than satisfactory: both manoeuvrability and roadholding are very good, even on fairly rough roads and muddy terrain. The suspension offers excellent ride comfort. The front leg-shield, which to date has no provisions to this end, could be equipped with hooks and rings to carry bags and other objects you never know where to stow on a motorcycle. Overall, you get the impression that the "Vespa" should be favourably received and enjoy considerable success, especially taking into consideration the sale price that, even though it is still fairly high in relation to the reduced purchasing power of the general public, is excellent in comparison with the current prices on our market and reasonably in line with the prices on some foreign markets".

The '40s

Highly sought–after today by all collectors, when it appeared on the market the 98 was by no means as successful as had been hoped. According to a Piaggio report of the period, "the first months of distribution were not encouraging. It was a struggle to sell the first 50 examples produced. It is a year of losses for the group and it does not appear that the investment in the Vespa will bring the forecast results."

The reason is to be found in traditional motorcyclists' distrust of the "small wheels" and their consequent snubbing of this alternative vehicle. But then, the Vespa was not designed for them. Fortunately, the virtues of the new scooter were rapidly recognised by all those who were not motorcyclists but nonetheless wished for a means of individual transport that was simple, economical and, above all, non-sporting. Thanks in part to the extensive advertising campaign staged at the behest of Enrico Piaggio and the fact that from the outset the firm aimed to conquer a female clientele, the Vespa gradually began to acquire a reputation. However, true success only arrived with the successive 125.

The voice of the dealers

Testimony: the first dealer: the Fiat-Ghizzoni concessionaire in Milan, Tancredi di Giambattista, owner of the dealership, tells his story:

"*Ghizzoni had been a Fiat concessionaire since before the war. When Enrico Piaggio asked Osvaldo Ghizzoni whether we were interested in trying a new light motorcycle design, we went straight down to Pontedera. We were the first to be called among all the dealers in Italy, Lombardy was a highly attractive market. It was winter and at Viareggio they had already organized the first carnival. Half the factory was in ruins. There were no windows in the offices, we found Enrico Piaggio with an army blanket over his shoulders.*
The Vespa immediately made a... terrible impression on us. They showed it to us in a workshop. It was a prototype. We didn't like it because we were still tied to the image of the motorcycle. It looked like an abortion to us. An engineer, his name was Carbonero, invited me

to have a go in the workshop. And suddenly I changed my mind. The floor was rough, but right away I realized that the Vespa could be a brilliant solution to the problem of personal transport. I realized that it was a very clever vehicle with that handlebar gear changer, the monocoque body, the covered engine, the spare wheel and the opportunity to keep one's legs together.
Via Sarpi in Milan, there was a queue to try the Vespa. The test rides took place in the courtyard. A tester on a ramp in the workshop then demonstrated that the Vespa could also tackle steep slopes. It was a great success. To make sure Fiat wasn't overshadowed, Osvaldo Ghizzoni created an independent, parallel company, "Sarpi", again in Via Sarpi in premises close to our own. The Vespa constituted the first true Italian miracle. Capital was in short supply; at times Pontedera would call us because they urgently needed an advance, they lived from day to day...".

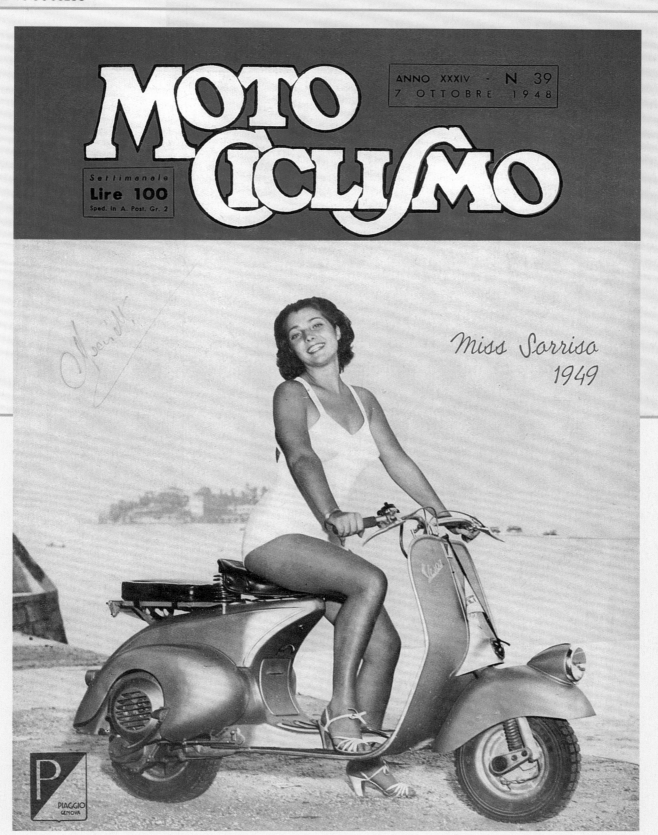

Part two

THE ROAD
TO SUCCESS

The '50s

The '50s

CINEMA
Totò - *On the Waterfront* (Elia Kazan) - *Poveri ma belli* (Dino Risi) - *I soliti ignoti* (Mario Monicelli) - *Ben Hur* (William Wyler) - *Sabrina* (Billy Wilder)

MUSIC
Rock Around the Clock (Bill Haley) - *Love Me Tender* (Elvis Presley) - *Only You* (The Platters) - *Volare* (Domenico Modugno)

RADIO
First transmissions in Germany and Italy - Lascia o raddoppia - Carosello - Musichiere - Perry Mason - Canzonissima - Rin Tin Tin - Festival di Sanremo

BOOKS
Piccolo mondo (Giovanni Guareschi) - *The Old Man and the Sea* (Ernest Hemingway) - *Il Gattopardo* (Giuseppe Tomasi di Lampedusa)

CARS
Porsche 356 - Lancia Aurelia - Alfa Romeo Giulietta - Ford Thunderbird - Fiat 500/600/1100 - Citroën DS 19

MOTORCYCLES
Ariel 500 Twin - Benelli 125 Leoncino - BSA 500 Gold Star - Gilera 500 Saturno - MV Agusta 125

FASHION
Leather bomber jacket - Pointed bras - Skirts and petticoats - Baby-doll - Stiletto heels - Jeans - Brilliantine - Christian Dior's "New Look"

INNOVATIONS
Television - Jukeboxes - Electric razors - Washing machines - Cinemascope - Transistors - Olivetti Lettera 22 typewriter - Sputnik

ENTERTAINMENT
Hula-hop - Polistil miniature models- Lego - Portable record-player - Fumetti Tex Willer - Drive-In

SPORT
Coppi wins Giro d'Italia/Tour de France (1952) - Ascari World Champion with Ferrari (1952 and 1953) - Helsinki and Melbourne Olympics

EVENTS
Berlin Wall (1952) - Edmund Hillary climbs Everest (1953) - Revolution in Cuba - Six European countries give rise to the EEC

The '50s

By the Fifties the Vespa was already an enormously successful product. The first calendars appeared, the scooter was seen on the covers of magazines and on film posters. The Vespa became recreational transport not solely a means of reaching work. The success was such as to generate the models built under license in various countries: Great Britain, France, Germany, Spain, Belgium. As the Vespa became more widespread, the first clubs were formed and owners had the opportunity to participate in numerous rallies.

There were two displacements, 125 (base and U) and 150 cc (base and GS). The transmission now used flexible cables rather than the rigid rods. Two particularly sporty models were also introduced, the Sport and the Sei Giorni, both produced in limited numbers. The general public was, however, won over by the GS 150 that boasted a number of innovations: it was the first Vespa fitted with 10" wheels and a four-speed gearbox.

In 1956, Piaggio was the world's largest motorcycle manufacturer with an output of 221 thousand units. That same year, Pontedera celebrated the production of the millionth Vespa.

While marketing had yet to be become a buzzword in Italy, Piaggio had come up with a perfect sales formula. In those years, the company had put together a winning combination of hire purchase, a one-year guarantee,

The Piaggio workforce crowd around the 500,000th Vespa built to celebrate the event (29 October 1953).

The '50s

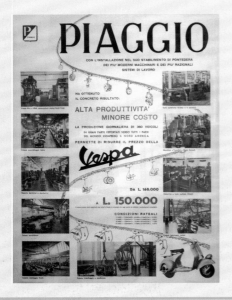

free maintenance coupons and a free theft and third-party insurance policy: how could one resist? Then, in 1954, came a masterstroke when the price of the 125 was dropped from 150,000 to 128,000 lire.

Post-war reconstruction had now been completed and Italy was enjoying a period of growth that was to be defined as the "boom" and the "economic miracle". Italian homes began to be equipped with domestic appliances as the first refrigerators and washing machines appeared. Television was born and these were the years of the famous quiz show Lascia o raddoppia (similar to The $ 64,000 Question), with the bars crammed with people determined not to miss a single episode. Even the cinemas were forced to cancel screenings on the evenings when the quiz show was broadcast. Within this context the Vespa became increasingly popular and could be seen in any urban location shots in the films of the period – when it was not actually playing a starring role as in Roman Holiday. Midway through the decade, a cyclone blew through the world of personal transport: Fiat presented its 600, the first utility car accessible to the masses. It was above all the two-wheeled sector that felt the effects with a vertical fall in sales as many clients, perhaps making recourse to delayed payments, finally moved up to four wheels. However, the Vespa had a different clientele and it was actually in this period that it consolidated its success.

The '50s

The Millionth Vespa

There were great festivities on the 28th of April 1956, with Piaggio celebrating not only the first 10 years of the Vespa, but also the millionth example to leave the Pontedera production lines. In order to mark the event Piaggio invited Italian and foreign authorities, hundreds of journalists from throughout the world and dozens of agents from Italy and abroad. When the millionth Vespa rolled off the line it was actually blessed by the Archbishop of Florence. Piaggio printed a celebratory envelope seal and the Italian Post Office granted a special frank for all correspondence leaving the internal Pontedera factory office.

The event was truly remarkable if you think that the production of the 500,000th Vespa had been celebrated on the 29th of October 1953. It had taken seven years to reach the first half million and just two and a half for the second. This gives some idea of the success and the boom in sales recorded by the Vespa in the early Fifties when it accounted for 34% of the entire motorcycle and scooter market.

The '50s

Vespa press

From "*Motociclismo*", 9th of March 1950:

"*Four years have now passed since the Vespa made its first, almost timid public appearance early in the spring of 1946. The Vespa immediately appealed to everyone without hesitation, in spite of its appearance that most felt to be decidedly revolutionary. This machine with its new and attractive line, with its completely enclosed engine, with its open frame allowing the rider to sit on the saddle without having to straddle the rear wheel, with no pretensions to speed, quiet and designed to protect the clothes of the rider, immediately won over all those who felt the need for a means of personal transport but would never have had the courage to use a true motorcycle. And it is by no means a common occurrence that Piaggio, despite being totally new to the construction of motor vehicles, managed to identify to perfection the tastes and requirements of the practically virgin clientele to which it turned and to* create for it a vehicle that from the very first example has proved to be so well thought out as to require subsequently no substantial modifications. The only changes of note were the increase the engine's displacement from 98 to 125 cc and the adoption of a more efficient sprung suspension system, both being introduced at the request of the clientele, who having taken to the new scooter, wanted to use it for even the most demanding of duties and therefore required far greater performance than originally planned for*".

This interesting testimony underlines how the arrival of the Vespa constituted a "revolutionary" episode in the two-wheeled world, bringing the new scooter to a clientele "that would never have had the courage" to tackle a conventional motorcycle for the first time.

The rapid spread of the Vespa in the 1950s was in part due to the extraordinary promotional activities of the numerous Vespa Clubs in Italy and abroad.

The '50s

— **Buon giorno, nonno!**
— **Bonjour grand'père!**
— **Hi there Grand pop!**
(Motocycles - Paris)

* * *

* * *

Dittatura stradale.
Prepotence routiere.
Road hog.
(Candido - Milano)

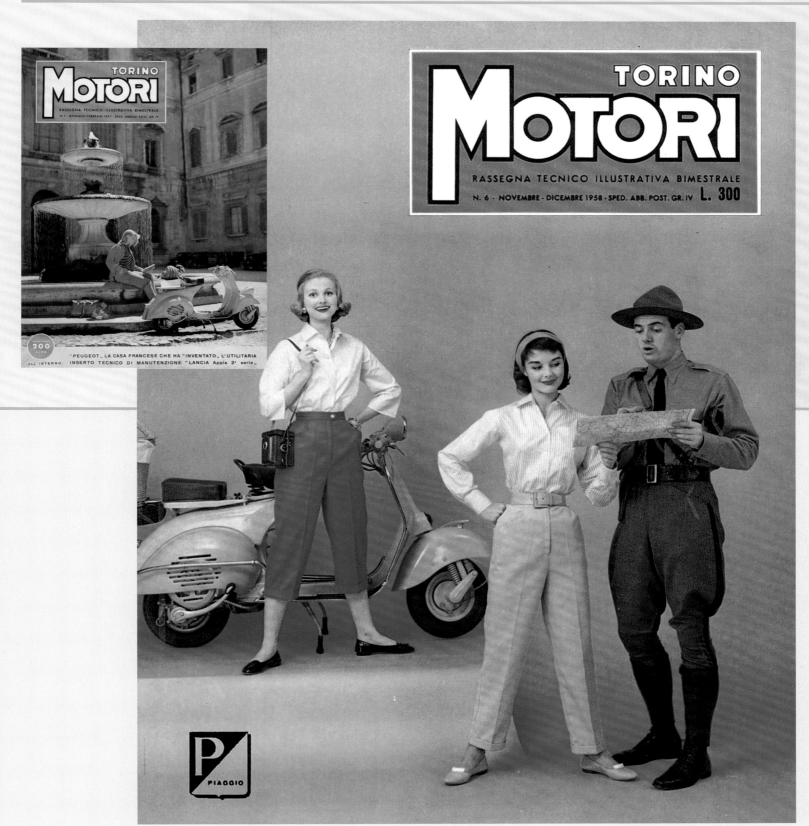

Part two

THE ROAD TO SUCCESS

The '60s

The '60s

CINEMA
007 James Bond (Robert Young) - *La Dolce Vita* (Federico Fellini) - *Il Sorpasso* (Dino Risi) - *The Magnificent Seven* (John Sturges) - *The Graduate* (Mike Nichols)

MUSIC
Love Me Do (Beatles) - *Blowing in the Wind* (Bob Dylan) - *Satisfaction* (Rolling Stones) - *Ventiquattromila baci* (Adriano Celentano)

TV
Civilisation - Arcobaleno - Dr Who - Z Cars - Star Trek - The Odyssey - The Citadel

BOOKS
Tropic of Cancer (Henry Miller) - *Farewell to Arms* (Ernest Hemingway) - *One Hundred Years of Solitude* (Gabriel Garcia Marquez)

CARS
Mini - Ferrari 250 GTO - Alfa Romeo Giulia - Lancia Fulvia - Jaguar E-Type - Porsche 911

MOTORCYCLES
Aermacchi 250 Chimera - Ducati 200 Elite - Laverda 200 - Moto Guzzi 125 Stornello - BSA 650 A 65

FASHION
First collections by: Valentino (1960) - Kenzo (1961) - Cacharel (1962) - Benetton brothers go into business (1965) - Hippies

INNOVATIONS
Credit cards - Jet airliners - Photocopiers - Laser - Birth control pill - First heart transplant

ENTERTAINMENT
The Twist - Barbie - Super 8 - Peanuts - American Pop Art - Radio transmission "Chiamate Roma 3131" - Panini stickers

SPORT
Olympics: Rome - Tokyo and Mexico City - Eddy Merckx wins Giro d'Italia (1968) - Ferrari win Constructors' Championship (1961 and 1964)

EVENTS
Assassination of John F. Kennedy (1963) - Vajont landslide (1963) - Florence flooding (1966) - Neil Armstrong first man on the moon (1969)

GARCÍA
MÁRQUEZ

CENT'ANNI
DI SOLITUDINE

PUNTₑMES
APERITIVO
un punto di amaro e mezzo di dolce

109

The '60s

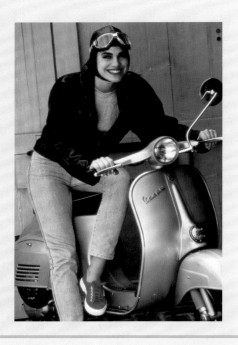

Towards the mid–sixties, there was a sudden decline in sales in Italy. Everyone now wanted a car, even the most basic model, and the scooter market suffered. In 1965 Piaggio recorded an operating loss of over 300 million lire, a figure that rose to a billion in 1966. Damage to the company was limited by the success enjoyed by a new model, the Vespa 50. Born in 1963, the model enjoyed immediate success thanks to the fact that it was exempt from the obligatory registration number and driving licence required by the 1962 edition of the Italian Highway code for vehicles of above 50 cc. The advertising campaign was therefore aimed at young people (the 50 could be ridden at 14), a new target group that from then on was to be an increasingly important component of the Vespa clientele. Student numbers were increasing and the Vespa 50 was the ideal vehicle to take them to school. Thanks to its compact dimensions and reduced weight, the Vespa 50 appealed to women as well as satisfying youthful desires for emancipation, freedom and independence. Piaggio also introduced the Elestart version with standard electric starting. In order to attract even more fourteen-year-olds, the company presented a moped at the Genoa Fair of the Sea on the 11th of October 1967 that was to symbolize an era. Numerous models were introduced during the

la Piaggio presenta il nuovo modello

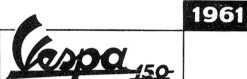

1961

Vespa 150

- motore migliorato – maggiore elasticità e ripresa
- carburatore con dispositivo per avviamento immediato
- impianto elettrico con elevate caratteristiche fotometriche

cambio a 4 velocità

PREZZO **L. 148.000**

VENDITE RATEALI A 6-12-16-20-24 MESI

lo scooter più venduto nel mondo

The '60s

1960s as alongside the 50 were the 90 models (base and SS), the small-frame 125 (Nuova), large-frame 125 (base, Super and GT), the 150 (base, GL, Super and Sprint), 160 (GS) and 180 (SS and Rally). In the early Sixties, all riders of two-wheeled vehicles were faced with an unaccustomed bureaucratic obstacle: the obligatory driving licence. Would Piaggio abandon its Vespisti in their hour of need? No, of course not. The firm organized courses at Vespa Club d'Italia premises to help its clients pass the test.

A great flood devastated the Pontedera district on the 4th of November 1966 when the River Era broke its banks and inundated the Pontedera factory. Thanks to the efforts of the workforce, the furnaces were shut down before the rising waters could cause an explosion.

During this decade there were further significant Vespa sales milestones. The two millionth example was celebrated in the July of 1960 and the three millionth in the March of 1965, while the four millionth came off the production line in the May of 1969. Progress was therefore constant, a million units being sold every five years despite the difficulties of the market. 1964 saw the completion of the Autostrada del Sole from Milan to Naples.

The '60s

The hexagonal Piaggio logo

Piaggio changed its logo on the 1st of October 1967. The new version was a blue hexagon with an arrow symbol. This symbol may also be seen as a mirror image double "P". With this change the company wanted to underline the major corporate revision undertaken in that period. The aeronautical and railway business was separated from the motor vehicle division, the company was reconfigured and the managerial structure was modified. The new chairman was Umberto Agnelli, the son-in-law of Enrico Piaggio.
The introduction of the new logo was announced to the press, the Italian dealers and the foreign importers and an entire issue of the Piaggio Magazine was devoted to of the changes: "This introduction will be, where possible, immediate and total, involving both vehicles and advertising; in other sectors, where this is not possible, it will be more gradual." The period in which the old and new logos co-existed, brief as it was, has to be considered as a sensitive moment with regard to the image of the brand with respect to the consumers. The extreme

importance of this delicate operation and the need for the complete cooperation did not escape the Italian dealers and the foreign importers. Naturally, such a significant change was reflected throughout the organization, from the office signing and that of the dealerships, from advertising to letterheads. It is interesting to note how this logo remained unchanged for 35 years of Vespa production. Following the error committed in the 1990s when the very name Vespa was rejected in favour of Cosa, in the new millennium the firm recognised that it was a key element in the valorization of the product.
From this point of view, everything possible was done to revive historical references, introducing diverse elements that were recognisable from previous models. This has led to the reappearance of the original shield, the one with the diagonal division and light and dark blue colouring. A smart decision, and one well received by many enthusiasts who, while being tied to the image of the hexagon, could hardly remain indifferent to a symbol so laden with history.

Stabilimenti Piaggio di Pontedera: una linea di montaggio Vespa.

5.300 punti di assistenza contraddistinti da insegne col marchio Piaggio Servizio sono distribuiti su tutto il territorio nazionale. Le parti di ricambio utilizzate sono le stesse che vengono prodotte negli impianti di Pontedera e montate sui veicoli nuovi di fabbrica.

PIAGGIO

con
Vespa
si
può

...per mettere in moto la Vespa 50 è sufficiente un colpo di pedivella...

15

...il suo uso non richiede abbigliamenti speciali, nè tute, stivali, giacconi od altro...

29

115

Part two

THE ROAD
TO SUCCESS

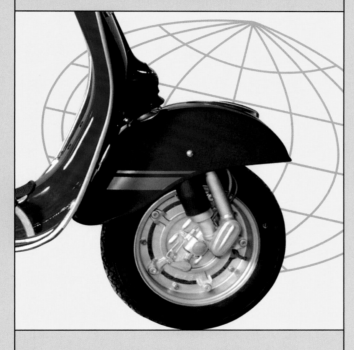

The '70s

The '70s

CINEMA

Love Story (George Hiller) - *Saturday Night Fever* (John Badham) - *Il Padrino* (Frank Coppola) - *Star Wars* (George Lucas) - *Amarcord* (Federico Fellini)

MUSIC

Let it be (Beatles) - *Wild World* (Cat Stevens) - *The Dark Side of the Moon* (Pink Floyd) - *Daniel* (Elton John) - *Staying Alive* (Bee Gees)

TV

First colour transmissions in Italy (1975) - HBO via cable - Charlie's Angels - Rischiatutto - Happy Days

BOOKS

The Invisible Cities (Italo Calvino) - *La Storia* (Elsa Morante) - *The Interior Life* (Alberto Moravia) - *A Man* (Oriana Fallaci)

CARS

Fiat 126/127 - Ford Fiesta - BMW 3 and 5 series - Range Rover - Ferrari Daytona/BB - Lamborghini Countach - Lancia Stratos

MOTORCYCLES

Honda 750 - Kawasaki 500 - Suzuki 750 - Moto Guzzi V7 750 - Laverda SF 750 - Ducati Supersport 750 - Bimota KB1 - Mondial Touring 125

FASHION

Miniskirt - Hot pants - Tanga - Jeans - Bell-bottoms - Big collars - Wigs and toupees - Ray Ban sunglasses - Man's handbag

INNOVATIONS

Boeing 747 Jumbo - Fibre optics - Pocket calculator - First Apple personal computer - Colour television - VHS video recorders

ENTERTAINMENT

Videogames - Bic lighters - Kinder eggs - Post-Its - Pulsar watch - Discos - Clik Claks - Action Man

SPORT

Olympics: Munich and Montreal - Thöni wins three skiing World Cups - Munari World Rally Champion - Ferrari win Constructors' Championship

EVENTS

Divorce and abortion legalised - World oil crisis - End of the Vietnam war - Watergate - Beatles break up - Birth of rap music

The '70s

This was a decade of light and shadow. Following the crisis of the 1960s, attempts were made at Pontedera to invest significant resources in the youth market. In this period the dreams of countless fourteen-year-olds were focussed on mopeds and Piaggio managed to satisfy this demand with a remarkably varied range of products. There was of course the Vespa 50, but it was not alone. In the years of the moped boom, the new Ciao enjoyed an exceptional degree of success and capillary distribution that was reinforced in 1973 with the introduction of the Bravo. Piaggio's acquisition of Gilera then allowed the firm to experiment with a scooter with innovative styling, the Eco, which flanked rather than replaced the Vespa. These were difficult years, with the decade witnessing no less than two energy crises. The first, in 1973, saw the price of petrol rapidly triple with the entire automotive sector thrown into disarray. Having a range of successful mopeds ensured Piaggio's survival. Nonetheless, the firm was looking to the future and continued to diversify its production activities. These were the years in which the firm acquired the Argom company (rubber goods) and Bendix (brake servos) and Borg Warner (limited-slip differentials) production licenses. Piaggio also produced a small agricultural tractor pow-

Piaggio and Gilera

On the 26th of November 1969, at the Circolo della Stampa in Milan, Piaggio's managing director, Nello Vallecchi, publicly announced the acquisition of Gilera of Arcore.
From the Piaggio magazine of April 1970:
"*Today, with the support of the Piaggio marque, Gilera represents one of the strongest Italian companies in its sector, with a range of models capable of satisfying the demands of enthusiasts of all forms of motorcycling: from gentle touring to extreme off-road and trials*".
From the very outset, Gilera's output had been characterised by interesting technical innovations that soon earned the firm a reputation around the world. The marque enjoyed significant sporting success, especially with its four-cylinder engines in the '30s and '40s. The Arcore-based company survived and was successfully revived thanks to the Piaggio buy-out.

The '70s

ered by the engine from the Ape MP. The second energy crisis in 1979 was tackled with a renewed policy of expansion. In the 1970s, the scooter was an extremely successful vehicle, flanking the motorcycle market and achieving significant results. The Vespa enjoyed a reputation for being a product that kept pace with the times although in this period it did lose some of the appeal it had enjoyed in previous decades: it no longer represented a novelty while the new superbikes, the dream of countless young men, began to make their appearance. While through to 1970 the motorcycle was largely a vehicle for those who could not afford a car, when the Honda 750 was presented large displacement bikes began to be objects of desire and were actually purchased as status symbols. Nonetheless, the Vespa success story continued apace: five years to reach the 5,000,000th example (September 1974) then just three years to reach the 6,000,000th (August 1977) and a further four to reach 7,000,000 (March 1981).

This represented an important achievement in a decade marked by the fuel crises of 1973 and 1979 that had serious consequences for the mobility and economies of all western countries. In Italy, the first car-free Sundays were introduced and the price of petrol rocketed.

The '70s

Per te che conosci la gioia della guida veloce. Per te che sai che un sorpasso è sicuro solo quando è sempre pronta una grande riserva di potenza. Per te che nello spunto da fermo, o nelle punte di velocità massima non vuoi essere secondo a nessuno. Per te abbiamo creato la Vespa Sprint Veloce.

The '70s

Part two

THE ROAD TO SUCCESS

The '80s

The '80s

CINEMA

Apocalypse Now (Francis F. Coppola) - *The Last Emperor* (Bernardo Bertolucci) - *E.T. and Indiana Jones* (Steven Spielberg) - *Blade Runner* (Ridley Scott)

MUSIC

Thriller (Michael Jackson) - *Every breath you take* (Police) - *Born in the USA* (Bruce Springsteen) - *Material Girl* (Madonna) - *Solo noi* (Toto Cotugno)

TV

Birth of CNN (June 1980) - Canale 5 - Rete 4 and Italia 1. Mixer - Dallas - Quelli della Notte - Fame - Miami Vice

BOOKS

The Name of the Rose and *Foucoult's Pendulum* (Umberto Eco) - *Satanic Verses* (Salman Rushdie) - *Palomar* (Italo Calvino) - *The Alchemist* (Paulo Cohelo)

CARS

Renault Espace - Audi Quattro - Fiat Panda and Uno - Lancia Delta - Ferrari Testarossa - Mercedes Benz SEC

MOTORCYCLES

BMW R 80/GS - Ducati Paso 750 - Kawasaki GPZ 900 - Honda VFR 750 - Suzuki GSXR 750

FASHION

Milan capital of Italian fashion - Explosion of Prêt-à-porter - Swatch watches - Timberland boat shoes - Moncler ski jackets - Nike and Reebok trainers

INNOVATIONS

Birth of the TGV high-speed train (1981) - ATMs - Portable video cameras - First Philips Compact Disc - Fax - First artificial heart - Apple Macintosh

ENTERTAINMENT

Cordless phones - Swatch watches - Rubik's Cube - the Lambada - Teletext - Aerobics - Hot Wheels cars - Atari consoles

SPORT

Italy wins World Cup in Spain (1982) - Olympics: Moscow - Los Angeles and Seoul - Ferrari wins World Constructors' Championship (1982 and 1983)

EVENTS

Itavia DC9 crash at Ustica - Perestroika - Fall of the Berlin wall - Chernobyl disaster - Space Shuttle disintegrates on take-off

Games of the XXIIIrd Olympiad Los Angeles 19

The '80s

Piaggio continued to pursue its policy of expansion and began producing automotive components in the Atessa factory. In 1981, Piaggio acquired the historic Bianchi firm, a producer of celebrated bicycles. In that same year, the company achieved its production record with an output of no less than 512,630 units, with a turnover of 626 billion lire in the process. The workforce also reached its highest ever total of 13,470 employees. However, the rest of the decade represented something of a decline. By 1989, for example, the total number of employees had dropped to 6,000 reflecting a fall in demand for two-wheeled vehicles during the 1980s. The decline in sales was exacerbated by the introduction of new laws that obliged riders to wear helmets from 1986. Compared with 10 years earlier, the second half of the decade saw a veritable collapse with sales falling by 50%. The scooter market was suffering something of an image crisis and was hardest hit. Young people no longer saw this type of vehicle as a symbol of freedom and independence and scooter registrations in Italy precipitated. From the over 100,000 units of the early '80s the figure dropped to just 10,890 in 1990, with the market essentially being identified with the Vespa given that it had virtually no rivals.

The PK "seed"

From the PK brochure:

"Every Vespa is composed of 1,200 pieces that during the course of 35 years of technical and stylistic evolution have been subjected to around 19,000 modifications. Today, thanks to this continuous evolution, only a single detail remains identical to the specification of the original design. A component the size of a seed around which everything has changed, but which to signifies the very seed of a success that is being renewed. This component, which we will never replace, is at the heart of our Vespa." For the record, the "seed" in question is the flywheel magneto spline".

The Vespa changes, but always remains the same. Such is the destiny of a unique industrial product. When the PK series was presented it was by no means difficult to recognise the mechanical and stylistic elements that identified it as a classic Vespa: the small diameter wheels, the steel monocoque, the two-stroke engine, the air cooling and the gripshift gear change. And yet... and yet the PK was an all-new Vespa, as it would only logical to expect given that no less than 35 years had passed since the birth of the first model. This demonstrates that over the years, while the basic design remained unaltered, there has been a continuous process of evolution. Certainly, from the outside, at least for the non-Vespisti, it is sometimes hard to see the differences, with many models appearing virtually identical. From this point of view, the designers have always faced a major challenge: that of allowing the Vespa to evolve continuously through focussed interventions and small steps, without ever making perilous leaps forward. Piaggio cleverly emphasised with the "seed" campaign just how far the development of the Vespa has actually progressed. Practically nothing has remained interchangeable with the models of the past, all the components have gradually been improved and perfected. However, it would be nice to think that it was a gesture of affectionate recognition; it is nice to know that at least one piece, as small as it may be, has remained unchanged. And knowing how the Vespa story proceeded, it might be said that the "seed" has borne excellent fruit.

The '80s

The Vespa Nuova Linea was presented as follows in the PK catalogue: "*Born as the present, born as the future. The present is born as a technical synthesis of the cardinal points of the Vespa. The present is born as the mature evolution of an ever-current technological concept. The future is born as the projection of a new aesthetic creed. The future is born to conjugate in time true values of safety and reliability. The Vespa Nuova Linea: a new dawn for the Vespa. The birth of the Piaggio programme for the '80s, a present–future programme*".

These were difficult years. The general public was turning its back on motorcycles throwing the sector into crisis and even the scooter firms were also sailing through troubled waters. However, the period also saw the rise of many forms of alternative entertainment that involved young people in other sectors such as those of computers, charter flights, various forms of personal stereo and CDs. New trends appeared, the first Swatch watches went on sale, the first McDonald's opened in Italy and the first Italian private TV networks were developed. In this period Piaggio did all it could to remain competitive by renewing the two Vespa series, but the operation was only partially successful: the new large frame Vespa PX was as popular as the small frame PK was ignored.

Panasonic

Portable VHS Video System

NV-100 Video Cassette Recorder
WVP-50 Colour Video Camera

VHS
PAL

nuovo giorno Piaggio nasce "Vespa domani".

« Vespa domani »:

NASCE PRESENTE come sintesi tecnica dei punti fermi Vespa: carrozzeria portante, trasmissione diretta, ruote intercambiabili. Nasce presente come evoluzione matura di un concetto tecnologico sempre attuale.

NASCE FUTURA per coniugare nel tempo ampie doti di sicurezza ed affidabilità grazie ad una nuova sospensione più funzionale e al migliore assorbimento delle vibrazioni. Nasce futura come esperta soluzione di un perfetto assetto di guida grazie ad un sapiente equilibrio delle masse, al manubrio di nuovo disegno che assicura maggior comfort e ad una maggiore sensibilità dei comandi.

« VESPA DOMANI » NASCE IN DUE MODELLI:
Vespa P 125 X - motore monocilindrico a due tempi con distribuzione rotante. Cilindrata 123,4 cc. Cambio a 4 velocità. Velocità max. 95 Km/h. Consumo: oltre 46 Km. con 1 litro di miscela al 2% (norme CUNA). Si guida a 16 anni.

Vespa P 200 E - motore monocilindrico a due tempi con distribuzione rotante. Cilindrata 197,97 cc. Accensione elettronica. Cambio a 4 velocità. Velocità max. 110 Km/h. Consumo: oltre 33 Km. con 1 litro di miscela al 2% (norme CUNA).

« Vespa domani » nuovo giorno Vespa: nasce dal programma Piaggio anni '80, programma « presente-futuro ».

PIAGGIO cambia il mondo in 2ruote

131

Part two

THE ROAD TO SUCCESS

The '90s

The '90s

CINEMA

Life is Beautiful (Roberto Benigni) - *Pretty Woman* (Garry Marshall) - *Thelma & Louise* (Ridley Scott), *Braveheart* (Mel Gibson) - *Titanic* (James Cameron)

MUSIC

Graffiti (Prince) - *Dangerous* (Michael Jackson) - *Faithful* (Cranberries) - *Barbie Girl* (Aqua) - *Last Night* (U2) - *Portami a ballare* (Luca Barbarossa)

TV

Birth of TG5 - Fantastico - La Ruota della Fortuna - Mille lire al mese - Il fatto - Carramba che sorpresa - Non è la RAI - La Piovra - ER

BOOKS

Sostiene Pereira (Antonio Tabucchi) - *The Celestine Prophecy* (James Redfield) - *The Pelican Brief* (John Grisham) - *Ocean Sea* (Alessandro Baricco)

CARS

Smart - Renault Twingo - Nissan Micra - Ford KA - Porsche Boxster - Dodge Viper - Daimler-Benz-Chrysler agreement - BMW buys Rolls Royce

MOTORCYCLES

Ducati 916 - Ducati Monster - Honda 900 Fireblade - Triumph Speed Triple 900 - Suzuki 1300 Hayabusa

FASHION

'60s and '70s revival (miniskirts, flared trousers, hippy dresses, wedges and punk clothes) - "Eco-ethnic-grunge" fashion

INNOVATIONS

Internet - Cell phones - Video cameras and palmtop computers - Apple iMac - Dolly the sheep: first cloning of a mammal - Viagra, the "blue pill"

ENTERTAINMENT

Rollerblades - Snowboard - Jacuzzis - GameBoy - Play Station - Introduction of GPS satellite navigation

SPORT

New Zealand wins the America's Cup - Tomba wins the skiing world cup - Ferrari wins F1 World Constructors title (1999)

EVENTS

Unification of Germany (1990) - "Tangentopoli" (1992) - Channel Tunnel (1994) - Birth of the European Union (1993)

I Narratori ✦ Feltrinelli

ANTONIO TABUCCHI
SOSTIENE
PEREIRA

FROM THE DIRECTOR OF 'ALIENS,' 'T2' AND 'TRUE LIES'

LEONARDO DiCAPRIO   KATE WINSLET

TITANIC

NOTHING ON EARTH COULD COME BETWEEN THEM.

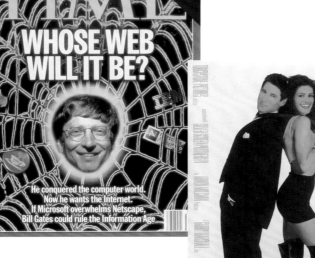

SLAMMING
SADDAM

TIME

WHOSE WEB
WILL IT BE?

He conquered the computer world.
Now he wants the Internet.
If Microsoft overwhelms Netscape,
Bill Gates could rule the Information Age

RICHARD GERE
JULIA ROBERTS

PRETTY WOMAN

She walked off the street,
into his life
and stole his heart.

Susanna Tamaro

Va' dove ti porta
il cuore

Baldini&Castoldi

oasis Definitely Maybe

The '90s

Piaggio continued with its strategy of expansion and diversification with further acquisitions. In line with what was happening elsewhere in this period, attempts were made to diversify production as much as possible and Pontedera moved away from its historical roots and into the financial markets. The decade also saw a new chairman installed at Piaggio. In 1988, after 23 years in the job, Umberto Agnelli handed over the company reins to Gustavo Denegri. The organisational structure became more functional and a holding company was formed to head the group. From the 1st of January 1989 the general management moved from the historical offices in Genoa to Pontedera. Attempts were also made to profoundly renew the product lines in this decade. New scooter models were introduced for the first time as Piaggio tried to expand the market in the face of more incisive competition. The first of these new models was the Sfera featuring automatic transmission and plastic bodywork. It was followed by the Quartz, Zip and Skipper models that all enjoyed considerable sales success.

Cosa, what's in a name (extract from: *"Cosa scooter project, the new generation"*, Piaggio brochure, November 1987):
Piaggio is presenting a new scooter: the "Cosa". This is an avant-garde product in terms of aesthetic and technical contents, the

PX Classic: the last true Vespa?

The Classic version of the PX, launched in 1996, celebrated the 50th anniversary of the Vespa. Like all the models that had preceded it, the Classic featured a steel body with removable side-panels, a two-stroke engine, a gripshift gear change and drum brakes. If we also take into account the 10" wheels, the four-speed gearbox and the 2% oil/fuel mixture, we can see that the basic configuration was unchanged with respect to the GL introduced no less than 35 years earlier. However, moving into the new millennium everything changed: to the new ET series characterised, among other innovations, by a four-stroke engine and an automatic gearbox. And the PX? It still retained the monocoque with removable side-panels, the two-stroke engine and the gripshift. A front disc brake was adopted however, in place of the original drum. The PX thus enjoyed a new lease of life in Classic form as what many Vespisti have defined as the last "true" Vespa.

The '90s

levels of quality and reliability it offers and its comfort, roadholding and performance. Rather than an evolution of other products, the "Cosa" represents an innovative approach to design and technological applications and solutions to the problems of the scooter. The new scooter has a sleek, aggressive appearance. The styling, developed in the wind tunnel, is soft and aerodynamic. The ergonomic problems have been tackled and resolved with particular care in order to offer elevated comfort: the riding position, instrumentation and controls guarantee convenience and safety. Piaggio has invested 35 billion lire in the research and development project and the renewal of tooling.

It is never easy to find a name for a product with an international background and destination. Above all when this product is born in a sector, such as that of the scooter, in which for years Piaggio has enjoyed leadership with a vehicle called "Vespa" that has become the stuff of two-wheeled legend. A name was needed that was simple and communicative, valid in every language and perfectly at home in the world of youth. A new name. Not one bound up with an albeit glorious past, a name that opened to the future and represented a change of direction, a

All collectors naturally gravitate towards the most significant historic models, those that are well known for having introduced particular technical or styling features. In general these models are eagerly sought-after by enthusiasts and attract high prices. It might be of interest to take a look at the relatively recent models that could be of interest to collectors in the future. From this point of view the Classic is in pole position and from the outset promised to be an "instant collectible", much in the same way as the last air-cooled Porsche 911. The fortunate owners of the PX Classic have plenty to celebrate: their Vespa is the most highly evolved and developed of the drum-brake PX series and is already sought-after by collectors. Clearly a Vespa worth taking care of!

The '90s

technical and industrial revolution expressed through a totally innovative scooter. Here, therefore, on the basis of careful studies and analyses, is the "Cosa". A courageous choice, but one that finds support in significant predecessors in the automotive and design fields. This is the case with the Fiat Uno and the Tizio, the world's most famous lamp. "Cosa", therefore, as the name/symbol of a new product. "Cosa" is easy, immediate, creative. A name suitable for a scooter that exalts Piaggio's technical experience and offers new horizons and opportunities for those that will use it. Quality and technology for lovers of two-wheeled transport. In the avant-garde with Piaggio.

These were difficult years for the Vespa: the large frame series was a commercial fiasco, not so much because it was unattractive but above all because it was called the Cosa, the small frame series did slightly better than in the previous decade, but was hardly a runaway success. Fortunately, the 50th anniversary of the Vespa in 1996 was exploited to launch in advance what was to be the Vespa of the third millennium. By the end of the decade things were looking far rosier and Piaggio was able to look confidently to the future.

The '90s

The Vespa at the Guggenheim

In 1998, a particularly important exhibition devoted to the motorcycle was inaugurated in New York. It was housed in the celebrated Guggenheim Museum, in the spiral building designed by Frank Lloyd Wright and located on the city's glamorous Fifth Avenue.

The title of the exhibition was "The Art of the Motorcycle" and there were not a few people who were surprised to see the world's most famous paintings replaced by motorcycles. However, the show was so successful that the organisers were obliged to extend its stay. It went on to become the most popular exhibition in the Guggenheim's history. Enthusiasts were able to admire the 100 most significant motorcycles of the 20th century including many examples of extraordinary historical value. Could the Vespa be left out? No, of course not. A fine GS was in fact on display. It was just a shame about the colour: that yellow was never offered!

Part two

THE ROAD
TO SUCCESS

The 2000s

The 2000s

CINEMA

The Lord of the Rings (Peter Jackson) - *Matrix* (The Wachowski Brothers) - *Mission Impossible* (Brian De Palma) - *Kill Bill* (Quentin Tarantino)

MUSIC

Come Away (Norah Jones) - *X & Y* (Coldplay) - *Tracks* (Vasco Rossi) - *Home* (Simply Red) - *Messaggio d'amore* (Matia Bazar) - *Per dire di no* (Alexia)

TV

Big Brother- Mai dire gol - C.S.I. - Alias - Sex and the City - Desperate Housewives - Il Commissario Cordier - O.C.

BOOKS

Harry Potter (J.K. Rowling) - *The Da Vinci Code* (Dan Brown) - *La pazienza del ragno* (Andrea Camilleri) - *Timeline* (Stephen King)

CARS

Enzo Ferrari - Toyota Prius - Alfa Romeo 159 - Renault Avantime - Lancia Thesis - BMW 1 - Hummer 3

MOTORCYCLES

MV Agusta F4 - Benelli Tornado - Aprilia RSV - Ducati 999 - Yamaha R1 - BMW R 1200 S - Suzuki GSR-600

FASHION

Return of: the boob tube, Dungarees, Women's braces, The schoolgirl look, Hot pants, Pointed shoes - Low waists - Guru t-shirts

INNOVATIONS

First photos of Titan by the European Huygens probe - Cloning of stem cells - First face transplant

ENTERTAINMENT

MP3 files - Apple iPod - Digital cameras - Videophones - Plasma TV screens

SPORT

Sydney, Athens and Peking Olympics, Turin Winter Olympics (2006) - Ferrari win World Constructors' Championship (2000, 2001, 2002, 2003, 2004)

EVENTS

New York 2001 Twin Towers terrorist attack - War in Iraq - EU expanded to 25 countries - Adoption of the Euro (2002)

The 2000s

The Vespa approached the third millennium in fine form. The ever more chaotic urban traffic situation encouraged many motorists to forgo their cars in favour of a vehicle better suited to wriggling through the jams and easier to park. This was a clientele that was not necessarily attracted to motorcycles and was actually looking for something that would offer greater protection and be closer to a car. In this period, the range of scooters available expanded greatly and many manufacturers offered interesting models. However, the Vespa remained unique, which accounted for much of its appeal. Technically, it was extremely up-to-date: it had a four-stroke engine and automatic transmission, but these were features common to all scooters. What the Vespa had that was unique was its history, it was the only scooter to have been in production since 1946. It was the only one with such a pedigree. Thanks in part to Roberto Colaninno's IMMSI group, the Vespa even found the resources to explore new markets such as that of the United States. Here the Vespa enjoyed great success, its presence expanding year by year to the point where it represented a true phenomenon. The range of models offered is wide and well defined. The small frame LX series is particularly suitable for

The 2000s

urban use thanks to its compact dimensions and great manoeuvrability. The large frame Granturismo series allows even highway and motorway trips to be undertaken in complete safety and even long distance touring is possible. For the die-hard Vespisti there is still the glorious PX with its rear brake pedal on the platform and a gripshift, just like back in 1946.

Piaggio heads for the Stock Exchange. The board of directors had hinted as much in the December of 2005 and it was confirmed on the 10th of March 2006. On that date, the Piaggio Group applied for inclusion on the Italian Stock Exchange's Telematic Share Market. This was the first step taken by the group led by Roberto Colaninno towards the placing of a part of the company capital. The coordinators of the offer are: Banca Caboto, Deutsche Bank, Citigroup, Mediobanca and Lehman Brothers. Following quotation, IMMSI intends to increase its share in the group from 40 to 54%, thus bring increasing stability and reinforcing the majority group.

The Vespa at the Fondazione Mazzotta

A major exhibition at the Fondazione Mazzotta's Milan headquarters was inaugurated in 2005. It featured the most important Italian motorcycles from a century of production history. They ranged from the Gilera of 1907 to the Grand Prix Ducati from 2004, with a large section being devoted to the Vespa. Pride of place was taken by the first model produced, the 98, naturally displayed lying on one side as at that time it had yet to be fitted with a stand. A rare racing Vespa and the streamlined record-breaker from 1951 could also be admired.

The 2000s

The Vespa-Ferrari, displayed in the Ferrari Store at Maranello, one of four examples of *the ET4 150 created as a tribute to the Prancing Horse's Formula 1 triumph in 2000.*

Part three

THE VESPA FAMILY

The Vespa abroad

Beyond the borders

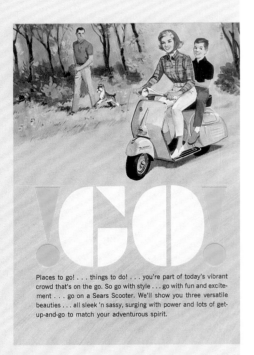

Places to go! . . . things to do! . . . you're part of today's vibrant crowd that's on the go. So go with style . . . go with fun and excitement . . . go on a Sears Scooter. We'll show you three versatile beauties . . . all sleek 'n sassy, surging with power and lots of get-up-and-go to match your adventurous spirit.

The Vespa's success was not confined to Italy. The scooter also became an extremely popular vehicle elsewhere, with a huge following, especially in Europe. Many manufacturers attempted to compete with Pontedera on their local markets with models of all shapes and sizes, but without success. Whether those manufacturers were called BSA or Triumph (in England), Peugeot or Motobecane (in France), NSU or Zundapp (in Germany), not one managed to produce a scooter to rival the Italian model. In many countries, the Vespa itself thus began to be produced under license. ACMA was born in France, with its production lines in the Fourchambault turning out not only standard models but also a version for military use carrying a large cannon. A more traditional Vespa was built in Germany, first by Hoffman and then by Messerschmitt, and in England, by Douglas. Compared with the original models, the variations generally concerned just a few components, including the front headlight, which was changed to meet local regulations. The major exception was the Russian Viatka, a straight copy… and built without a license.

The Vespa abroad

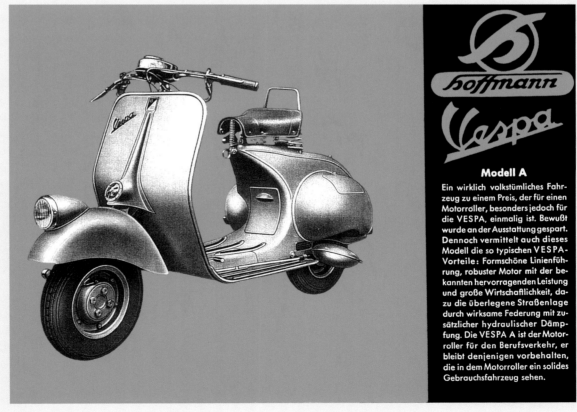

Modell A

Ein wirklich volkstümliches Fahrzeug zu einem Preis, der für einen Motorroller, besonders jedoch für die VESPA, einmalig ist. Bewußt wurde an der Ausstattung gespart. Dennoch vermittelt auch dieses Modell die so typischen VESPA-Vorteile: Formschöne Linienführung, robuster Motor mit der bekannten hervorragenden Leistung und große Wirtschaftlichkeit, dazu die überlegene Straßenlage durch wirksame Federung mit zusätzlicher hydraulischer Dämpfung. Die VESPA A ist der Motorroller für den Berufsverkehr, er bleibt denjenigen vorbehalten, die in dem Motorroller ein solides Gebrauchsfahrzeug sehen.

France

A.C.M.A.

The Vespa was built under license by A.C.M.A. in its factory at Fourchambault. Two models were offered, the 125 and the 125 GL. In contrast with Pontedera's 150, the A.C.M.A. version was fitted with an engine derived from that of the 125 and had different bore and stroke dimensions.

However, the most interesting A.C.M.A. model was the military Vespa. The project was initiated in 1953 when the French army decided to replace its now obsolete American Cushman scooters that dated from the Second World War. A competition was organised with the Valmobile 100, the Bernardet 250 and the Vespa 150 being entered. The eventual winner was the Vespa and production got underway in 1956. Designated as the TAP 56 and revised in 1959 as the TAP 59 (TAP standing for Troupes Aéro Portées), the military Vespa was finished in a typical dark olive green only and was produced exclusively in France. It boasted a number of special features, including a reinforced frame as it was designed to be able to be parachuted. What is most striking, however, is the presence of a 3" cannon protruding from the leg-shield, while on either side the side-panels were fitted with ammunition racks. 500 examples of the military Vespa were constructed and the vehicle saw active service in Algeria and Indochina.

The Vespa abroad

Belgium

M.I.S.A.

The Vespa models marketed in Belgium came out of the M.I.S.A. factory at Jette, near Brussels. Production ran from 1954 to 1962 with 125 and 150 cc versions of the GS series being offered. The Belgian Vespa was initially distributed by Bevelux, with an organisation extending into Holland and Luxemburg. There were over 150 sales outlets, but Vespas could also be purchased at a number of major stores in Brussels including: Bon Marché, Galeries Anspach, Innovation, Grands magasins de la Bourse and Cado-Radio.

When the marketing side was handled directly by M.I.S.A. the network was extended with over 400 dealerships being established in Belgium. The 125 was sold at 16,200 Belgian francs, with the 150 offered at 17,500 BF. The more expensive 150 GS was instead available for 19,900 BF.

Even the Ape series was offered: the first model to be distributed was Tipo C, on sale from 1957. In order to encourage sales, the Ape was offered with a 36-month instalment plan.

There was great interest in the Vespa on the local market and the production lines were kept running at full capacity: no less than 55 examples of the Vespa and the Ape left the factory each day in 1958.

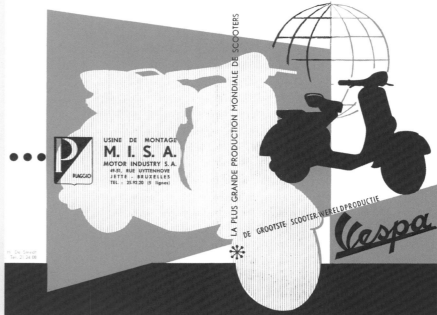

Germany

HOFFMANN/
MESSERSCHMITT

From 1950, the Vespa was built under license in Germany by Hoffmann of Lindorf, near Dusseldorf. After 1955, production was instead organised at the Messerschmitt works at Augsburg in Bavaria. Two models were offered, the 150 Touren and the 150 GS. It is interesting to note that Messerschmitt had a good reputation in the aeronautical industry, just like Piaggio. The Vespa was exported to Germany after 1956.

In Germany the Vespa failed to attract the same degree of success it enjoyed in other countries such as Great Britain and France. Among the various motives were those associated with the local Highway Code: the same driving licence and level of insurance was required whether a vehicle had a displacement of 100 cc or 250 cc. For this reason, there was no demand for the classic 125 cc displacement with the market preferring large displacement scooters with imposing dimensions. Of the 124,000 scooters sold in 1955, 32,000 were built by Zundapp (Bella), 27,000 by NSU (Prima), 16,000 by Heinkel (Tourist) with just 900 being Vespas. Messerschmitt therefore abandoned distribution in 1964 with Piaggio operating directly on the German market from the following year.

Die *Vespa* mit dem *Vespa*-Seitenwagen

ist eine harmonische, vollendet aufeinander abgestimmte Konstruktion. Hier haben Sie das richtige Gefährt für eine Fahrt zu zweien! Man sitzt in dem geräumigen Seitenwagen äußerst bequem, angenehm gefedert und vor Fahrtwind geschützt.

Technische Daten:

Fahrgestell geschweißte Rohrkonstruktion, Anschluß durch Rohrtraverse. Weiche Federung, Windschutzscheibe. Getriebeübersetzungen der Beiwagenmaschine: 12,2:1, 8,2:1, 5,83:1. Eigengewicht des Gespannes 130 kg; zulässiges Gesamtgewicht des Gespannes 285 kg. Lackierung: Fischsilbergrau, Vespa-grün.

Hoffmann-Werke LINTORF BEZ. DÜSSELDOR

KÖNIGIN DER MOTORROLLER

Vespa MODELL 1954

Motor: 123 ccm gebläsegekühlter VESPA-Motor mit direkter Kraftübertragung.
Leistung: 5 PS bei 3000 U/min.
Höchstgeschwindigkeit: ca. 75 km pro Stunde.
Kraftstoffverbrauch: etwa 2,3 ltr.
Dreiganggetriebe mit Handschaltung, Licht- und Zündanlage, Schwungradmagnet und Batterie.
Chassis: Selbsttragend aus geprägtem Stahlblech.
Federung: Vorder- und Hinterrad-Federung mit zusätzlicher hydraulischer Dämpfung.
Bremsen: Sturzsichernde vordere und hintere Trommelbremse.
Bereifung: 3,30-8.
Ausstattung: großer Scheinwerfer im Lenker, Nebellampe auf den vorderen Kotflügel, Rücklicht mit eingebautem Stoplicht, Luxusausführung mit reichlicher Chromierung.

Hoffmann-Werke LINTORF BEZ. DÜSSELDORF

hoffmann *Vespa*

Modell 1954

Noch eleganter, noch stärker in der Motorenleistung, das sind die hervorragenden Merkmale des neuen VESPA-Modells. Für den auserlesenen und wählerischen Geschmack anspruchsvoller Motorrollerfreunde wurde hier ein Fahrzeug entwickelt, das unter Beibehaltung einer hunderttausendfach bewährten Konstruktion der Vollkommenheit nahe ist. Neue Erkenntnisse auf dem Gebiet der Schalldämpfung machen diese Maschine zur geräuscharmsten aller Motorroller. Es vereinen sich in der VESPA, Modell 1954, zu seltener Harmonie: Architektonische Schönheit mit technischem Einfallsreichtum.

Great Britain

Douglas

Licensed production of the Vespa in Great Britain began in 1951 at the Douglas works in Kingswood, near Bristol. Two engine displacements were again offered, 125 and 150 cc with the last also available in GS form. Production ceased in 1957, with a total of 126,000 examples having been sold. While it was not as economical a machine as it was in Italy, the British Vespa enjoyed a degree of success and was widely used by the police forces. It also became an essential part of the Mod lifestyle, as seen in the cult film *Quadrophenia*. The sales strategy adopted in Britain saw the Vespa positioned as a high quality vehicle, with highly elegant and bowler-hatted aristocratic figures being photographed with their scooters (and even with their chauffeurs!).

In this period the Vespa became an extremely fashionable vehicle and numerous clubs were soon founded. In 1953 there were no less than 60 Vespa clubs with over 3,000 members. In the July of that year a national rally was organised at Brighton with over 500 Vespisti taking part. Many important British trendsetters were also photographed on their Vespas: from the Duke of Edinburgh to the Formula 1 driver Stirling Moss.

Spain

Moto Vespa

From 1956, the Vespa was built under license in Spain by Moto Vespa at Ciudad Lineal, near Madrid. Output comprised the 50, 125 Super and 150 Sprint models.

The Moto Vespa factory occupied 21,000 m² where the complete production cycle took place. The launch of the various models was accompanied by an advertising campaign highlighting the vast range of potential clients: from the student to the hunter, from the priest to the doctor. There was also a comparison with the world of the automobile, the scooter as usual being presented as a "small two-wheeled car". In order to create images of great impact, events were organised in the arenas where toreadors would perform aboard Vespas. In Spain too the Vespisti congregated in clubs that grew year by year. The first president of the Vespa Club of Spain was Don Luis Serrano de Pablo who, together with his wife Dona Matilde, travelled to the Vatican to donate a chalice to Pope Pius XII.

In contrast with other European countries, production in Spain continued through the following decades.

The 125 Primavera of the 1970s was sold for 16,900 pesetas, the 125 PX from the 1980s for 280,000 pesetas and the Cosa from the 1990s for 360,000 pesetas.

USSR

Viatka

From 1957, the Viatka 150 was built at Kirov in central Russia, then part of the Soviet Union of course. It was to all intents and purposes a Vespa 150, but rather than being built under license, it was a straight copy. The Viatka was named after the river that flowed near the factory, a typical custom in the Soviet Union in that period. The differences with respect to the original Vespa were minor but numerous. In terms of the engine they ranged from the displacement (from 145 to 148 cc) to the compression ratio (from 6.3:1 to 6.7), from the carburettor (from 18 to 200 mm) to the clutch (from 3 to 4 plates). With regard to the rest of the vehicle, the most distinctive feature was the wheels fitted with wider tyres (4.00 rather than 3.50"). As the monocoque was built from thicker steel, the Viatka was around 10 kilos heavier. Given the impossibility of asserting its rights to industrial protection regarding the product, Piaggio made recourse to irony. In a publication from 1959 a title proclaimed "They Make Satellites but Copy Scooters". The first man-made satellite was, in fact, launched by the Soviet Union, with the Sputnik being sent into orbit in 1957.

India

Bajaj

The Vespa was built under license in India by Bajaj from 1961, in the Poona factory near Bombay. It is still in production. The full name of the company is Bajaj Auto and it is in fact a large group whose main focus is on the production of cars; the scooter represents something of a sideline. The founder is proud to point out in his catalogues that he was a disciple of Mahatma Gandhi.

The Vespa was imported to India from as early as 1948. Bajaj then signed an agreement with Piaggio to build the various models locally before becoming independent in 1972. The first model to be manufactured at Poona was the Chetak, introduced in 1974. Production has continued into the third millennium with no significant technical or stylistic variations: the styling reflects that of the models built at Pontedera in the 1970s. The Indian models are all recognisable by the size of glovebox behind the leg-shield, much larger than those of the original models. The market is enormous and the Vespa-Bajaj is hugely popular in India. Over 4 million examples have been produced and in 2000 the vehicles circulating with the Bajaj marque numbered over 13,000,000. Remarkably, the Vespa-Bajaj has also been imported to Italy.

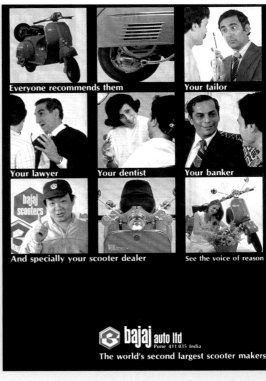

159

United States

Vespa of America

The 1970s saw the establishment in the USA of the Vespa of America Corporation. In this case scooters were not produced locally, but a number of models were imported: the 90 Sport, 125 Primavera, 150 Super and 200 Rally. In order meet US regulations a number of components were modified: indicators were added to the handlebars and side-panels, the rear light was detached from the body, the fuel tap was enlarged and reflectors were added to the side of the front mudguard. Sales ceased in 1981 but were revived in 2002. "Quick. What's the Vespa?" This was an advertising slogan used by the Vespa of America Corporation in the late '70s. In the United States there were still relatively few people with any awareness of the world's best-selling scooter. The American market is not easy and after just ten years Piaggio pulled the plug on its US operation. It was a hard decision to make, but understandable. In the USA, the public is accustomed to large vehicles such their V8 cars and Harley Davidson motorcycles; it is by no means easy to make inroads with a tiny scooter. Moreover, local laws are far stricter with regard to two-stroke engines that pollute more than four-stroke units.

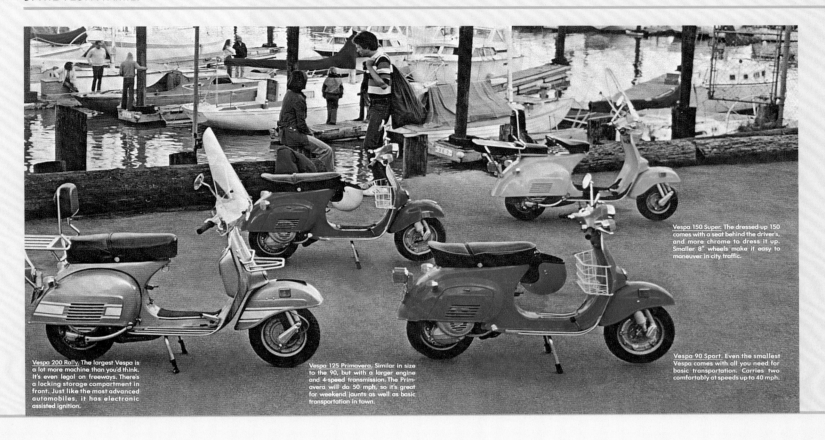

Vespa 200 Rally. The largest Vespa is a lot more machine than you'd think. It's even legal on freeways. There's a locking storage compartment in front. Just like the most advanced automobiles, it has electronic assisted ignition.

Vespa 125 Primavera. Similar in size to the 90, but with a larger engine and 4-speed transmission. The Primavera will do 50 mph, so it's great for weekend jaunts as well as basic transportation in town.

Vespa 150 Super. The dressed-up 150 comes with a seat behind the driver's, and more chrome to dress it up. Smaller 8" wheels make it easy to maneuver in city traffic.

Vespa 90 Sport. Even the smallest Vespa comes with all you need for basic transportation. Carries two comfortably at speeds up to 40 mph.

La dolce Vespa.

The Vespa P200E.

Anyone who appreciates "the sweet life" will likewise appreciate La dolce Vespa, "the sweet Vespa Scooter."

Vespa Scooters have welded, unitized bodies for safety and comfort. The unique design lets you ride inside with your feet on the floor. And direct drive to the rear wheel means there's no chain to stretch or break.

You'll find a Vespa Scooter is clean, quiet, incredibly powerful and easy to handle. And you can expect between 70 and 140 mpg. So you'll save plenty of gas and money.

Today's Vespa Scooter is the result of 30 years of engineering refinement. Our top models offer sophistications like electronic ignition, automatic oil injection and exclusive dampened hydraulic front suspension. With a hidden spare wheel included as

standard equipment. And the Vespa P200E, largest of three models, will take you anywhere. Even on the freeway.

Vespa products are made in Italy by Piaggio. Over the years, they've sold over 6,000,000 Scooters and 2,000,000 Mopeds. Which adds up to billions of dependable miles around the world. That's why both Vespa Scooters and Mopeds come with a 12-month warranty, with no limit on mileage.

Why not add La dolce Vespa to your life. You'll find your nearest Vespa dealer in the Yellow Pages. Or write to the address below.

Mileage is based on CUNA Standards. Yours may vary. Check Vespa limited warranty with your dealer. Wear helmet and eye protection. Check local laws.　Vespa of America Corporation, Piaggio Group, 355 Valley Drive, Brisbane, CA 94005.

give your life a little **vespa**℠

WOW. WHAT WAS THAT?

Something very special is taking to the roads of America. A totally unique variety of two-wheel transportation. The Vespa scooter.

There have been more than 6 million Vespa scooters and 2 million Vespa mopeds sold around the world, with good reason.

The Vespa scooter's superior convenience and comfort has made it a valuable supplement to the automobile. You ride inside—clean and quiet—with your feet securely on the floor.

The low center of gravity increases control and maneuverability.

The engine, fuel tank and direct drive system are all below and behind you, in a welded, unitized body.

The top models offer freeway speed power plus electronic ignition, automatic oil injection, hydraulic front and rear suspension and a hidden spare tire.

Rather than being all engine and tires, the Vespa scooter is all beauty. Its exquisite Italian design is a remarkable

pairing of panache and practicality. Over 30 years of engineering excellence and experience guarantees it. It's all in a machine that wiggles in and out of traffic while delivering between 70 and 140 mpg. Plus a 12-month, unlimited mileage warranty.

For a test ride, see your Vespa dealer now. Look in the Yellow Pages or write us for nearest location. And next time your friends wonder what went by—it'll be you.

Mileage is based on CUNA Standards. Yours may vary. Check with your Vespa dealer. Wear helmet and eye protection. Check local laws. Vespa of America, 355 Valley Drive, Brisbane, CA 94005.

vespa THE UNCOMMON CARRIER

QUICK. WHAT'S A VESPA?

Would you believe it's one of the world's most popular motor vehicles?

That's because it's also one of the world's most sensible, sophisticated street machines. The Vespa scooter. Not a motorcycle, not a motorbike, it's more like a two-wheeled car. You ride inside—cleanly and quietly —with your feet securely on the floor, protected by a welded, unitized body.

Its low center of gravity gives you a welcome sense of comfort, control and maneuverability.

Inside the top models lies an engine powerful enough for freeway driving and an automatic oil injection. There's electronic ignition and hydraulic front and rear suspension—even a hidden spare tire. Vespa scooters deliver between 70 and 140 mpg. Their stylish, sculptured body is delivered to you by super Italian designers.

We're talking about something Americans have seldom seen, yet are becoming increasingly interested in as supplemental, sophisticated transportation. The Vespa scooter. It's the result

of over 30 years of engineering excellence and experience. More than 6 million Vespa scooters and 2 million Vespa mopeds have been produced and sold so far. No wonder it's backed by a 12-month, unlimited mileage warranty.

We invite you to experience it now at your local Vespa dealer's. Look in the Yellow Pages or write us for nearest location.

Mileage is based on CUNA Standards. Yours may vary. Check with your Vespa dealer. Wear helmet and eye protection. Check local laws. Vespa of America, 355 Valley Drive, Brisbane, CA 94005.

PIAGGIO GROUP

vespa THE UNCOMMON CARRIER

Part three

THE VESPA FAMILY

A three-wheeled Vespa: the Ape

A three-wheeled Vespa: the Ape

While from the early years of its production the Vespa was seen as a means of personal transport, the Ape (pronounced "Ah-pey" and translated as "Bee") was born and developed exclusively as a commercial vehicle. From 1948 onwards, a number of versions were produced, all characterized by the same basic elements that contributed to the success of the original: great functionality and versatility, small displacement and low fuel consumption, easy to drive, excellent carrying capacity, modest purchase price.

The Ape appeared soon after the Vespa; that is to say, in the immediate post-war period when there was an increasing need for an economical means of transporting goods. Its history runs parallel with that of the Vespa and while not enjoying the same "legendary" status as the scooter nor benefiting from similar advertising resources, for decades it has represented a fundamental vehicle in the field of commercial transport. In certain regions of Italy the Ape was known as the "Lapa", while abroad it had very different names. On English-speaking markets, for obvious reasons Ape was dropped in favour of "Vespa Commercial". In France it was called the "Trivespa", in Portugal the "Vespacar" and in Germany the "Vespa Lastenroller". Naturally, the company tried to exploit the well-known Vespa brand as much as possible.

The birth of the Ape

"The Birth of the Ape", by Corradino D'Ascanio, from the Piaggio Magazine, February 1949:

"We had to fill a gap in the means of post-war utilitarian locomotion, bringing to the market a small displacement delivery vehicle with low fuel consumption, a modest purchase price and low maintenance that would be easy to drive, manoeuvrable in the heaviest city traffic and, above all, suitable, ready and available for home delivery of goods purchased in the shops. These characteristic three-wheeled vehicles are multiplying day by day in Italian cities as not only do they perform their duty of transporting goods from the shops to the homes of the clients, but also act as a highly visible and effective form of publicity for the companies that have adopted them. We are returning, albeit slowly and gradually, to a comfortable lifestyle and clients no longer want to have to leave shops laden with packages but rather today they prefer to give the shopkeeper their address and have their purchases despatched rapidly from the shop itself. Moreover, a home delivery service presupposes a certain frequency of trips from the central zones to the suburbs of the city and the shopkeeper can hardly demand constant physical labour from his deliverymen. Moreover, time is becoming ever more precious and what is saved in fuel and maintenance for an Ape delivery vehicle is lost in the hours taken by a delivery boy making home deliveries by bicycle or on foot. Means of public transport are detested for their incurably poor service and the now chronic overcrowding that puts the goods to be transported at risk".

A three-wheeled Vespa: the Ape

DOPO IL GRANDIOSO SUCCESSO DELLA MOTOLEGGERA "VESPA., LA S. p. Az. **PIAGGIO & C.** PRESENTA IL VEICOLO

MOTOFURGONE UTILITARIO

PORTATA : 2 Quintali

VELOCITA': 40 Km. all'ora

PENDENZA : massima superabile 18 %

CONSUMO : 35 ÷ 40 Km. per litro

La circolazione del Motofurgone "Ape,, è regolata dalle stesse norme valevoli per la Motoleggera "Vespa,,

S. A. R. P. I. CONCESSIONARIA ESCLUSIVA PER LA VENDITA

GENOVA - Via Galata, 33

A three-wheeled Vespa: the Ape

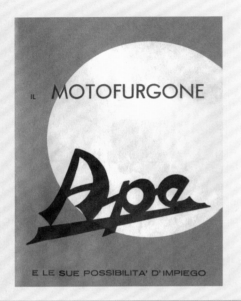

The Ape was clearly born out of the Vespa: the engine was the same 125 cc unit and the wheels, handlebar and controls were the same. The rear section instead presented an infinite series of variants: from a pickup to a van, from a canvas cover to a tipping body, while there was also a "people-moving" version initially known as the Giardinetta and then as the Calessino.

While in just a few years, the Vespa became a perfect vehicle for recreational activities, the Ape remained within the sphere of working transport. Advertising was therefore less creative and more concerned with the concrete advantages of the vehicle.

The Ape was used for carrying goods by numerous companies, from one-man outfits to the most successful corporations. All of them would have their name sign-painted on the rear body creating a lively series of mobile advertising hoardings. Among the most famous names were: Sant'Ambroeus (pastries, Milan), Upim (department stores), Motta (cakes and pastries), Negroni (ham and salami).

It was not just with Vespas that enthusiasts undertook adventurous trips around the world. In 1998, the Italians Brovelli and Martino travelled from Lisbon to Beijing with an Ape TM 703: 25 thousand kilometres on roads and desert tracks in the Eurasia Expedition.

The '40s

Ape A

The Ape was introduced in 1948, the A version having a displacement of 125 cc and a loading capacity of 200 kg. Two versions were produced, a pickup and a van. In 1949, these were joined by the Giardinetta series capable of carrying up to two people.

In the early years the emphasis was placed on the Ape's versatility: "The product delivered to the home accelerates the sales process", "the client is no longer the porter for his own purchase", "rapid home delivery revives the pleasure in purchasing", "a client satisfied in just a few minutes will remain faithful for a lifetime."

Images were drawn and were influenced by the style of the Corriere della Domenica front pages.

The brakes featured a pedal with hydraulic actuation for the rear wheels and a handlebar lever for the front wheel. There was also a car-like handbrake acting on the differential. The transmission was composed of a differential and two chains. The manual starting lever was located on the driver's right-hand side. The front suspension featured steel springs, while at the rear shock absorbers were combined with torsion bars. The wheels were in pressed steel. The Giardinetta version introduced in 1949 could be used to carry people or bulky goods.

IL PRONTO TRASPORTO A DOMICILIO ACCELERA IL RITMO DELLE VENDITE ● IL CLIENTE NON SIA IL FATTORINO DEL PROPRIO ACQUISTO ● LA RAPIDA CONSEGNA A DOMICILIO RINNOVA IL PIACERE DELLA COMPERA

A three-wheeled Vespa: the Ape

CARATTERISTICHE
T E C N I C H E

Motore : a 2 tempi - cilindrata cmc. 125 potenza massima HP. 4 a 4500 giri.

Cambio di marcia : a 4 velocità.

Messa in moto : con leva a mano azionabile dal posto di guida a sinistra.

Raffreddamento : è assicurato a qualsiasi velocità da un ventilatore centrifugo.

Telaio : di lamiera acciaio stampata e saldata elettricamente.

Trasmissione : con differenziale e due catene.

Sospensione : con molle acciaio a spirale per la ruota anteriore ; con barre di torsione ed ammortizzatori per le ruote posteriori.

Ruote : di lamiera, acciaio stampata, con freno a tamburo, intercambiabili tra loro.

Pressione gomme :
per la ruota anteriore   1,2 ÷ 1,5 Kg./cm.₂
per le ruote posteriori   1,5 ÷ 1,8 Kg./cm.₂

Freni : a pedale, idraulico, sulle ruote posteriori, a mano sulla ruota anteriore e a leva a mano sul differenziale.

Illuminazione : un faro anteriore a due luci e lampadina di posizione, due fanalini laterali ed un fanalino posteriore, l'alimentazione è fatta a mezzo del generatore collegato ad una batteria.

Cassone : di legno con nervature di rinforzo, sponda posteriore ribaltabile.

Lunghezza massima		m. 2,430
Larghezza »		» 1,280
Altezza »		» 0,860
Altezza della sella da terra		» 0,700
Altezza pedana da terra		» 0,150
Raggio minimo sterzata		» 1,885
Carreggiata		» 1,028
Altezza fondo cassone da terra		» 0,500
Dimensioni cassone		m. 1,110 x 1,110
Altezza sponde cassone		m. 0,200
Peso totale a vuoto		Kg. 125

Velocità massima a pieno carico 40 Km. all'ora.

Carico trasportabile   Kg. 200

Pendenza massima superabile a pieno carico 18 %.

Consumo a pieno carico : 1 litro di miscela ogni 35 Km.

The '50s

Ape B
Ape C
Ape D

The B version of the Ape appeared in 1953 and boasted an increased displacement of 150 cc and a 300 kg loading capacity.

The C version was introduced in 1956 and featured a 150 cc engine and pressed-steel bodywork. There was also a proper seat (rather than a saddle) for the driver, a reverse gear and electric starting.

The loading capacity rose to 350 kg. Pickup, van and calesse or rickshaw versions were available. The D series was introduced in 1958 with the same range of versions.

A vast range of models and versions was offered. Emphasis was placed on the Ape's potential as a capacious and efficient means of transportation in every situation and climatic condition. Piaggio also tried to encourage sales by offering hire purchase schemes.

The early Ape models enjoyed great commercial success: in the first 10 years no less than 200,000 examples were delivered. In 1960, on the occasion of the Olympic Games in Rome, it was used as an official vehicle within the Olympic Village. The Ape became an increasingly common sight in the large cities and many small businesses enjoyed excellent service from Piaggio's small three-wheeler.

A three-wheeled Vespa: the Ape

1

pianale normale

Il motocarro che diverrà il collaboratore indispensabile nell'industria nel commercio e nell'agricoltura.
Il mezzo che accelera il ritmo del vostro lavoro.

2

pianale metallico

3

ribaltabile

Il motocarro leggero che risolve il problema del trasporto rapido ed economico.

4

furgoncino

The '60s

Pentarò
Ape MP

With the Pentarò 250 of 1961 the Ape doubled up: a separate rear trailer with two wheels was added to the three-wheeled motorized unit. This led to a two-fold increase in loading capacity to 700 kg. 1966 saw a significant technical innovation with the introduction of the MP ("motore posteriore" or rear engine) 190: direct transmission to the rear half shafts provided significantly improved traction. The cabin was radically modified and more comfortable. Pickup, van, calesse or rickshaw and tipping versions were available. The loading capacity rose to 550 kg. The MPV version appeared in 1968 and featured a steering wheel rather than handlebars.

The success achieved with well-known companies encouraged Piaggio to publicize images of the Apes used by its clients. The slogan claimed: "The vehicle for you is the Ape, because the Ape produces, because the Ape helps you earn."

The Pentarò was a small articulated vehicle with a front three-wheeled tractor unit and a rear trailer on a pair of stabilising wheels. The tractor had the same form as the Ape while the semi-trailer could be unhooked as with large trucks. With the Pentarò, Piaggio ventured into a new area of the light transport sector with a practical, relatively economical and highly original vehicle.

A three-wheeled Vespa: the Ape

THE VESPA FAMILY

A four-wheeled Vespa: the 400

A four-wheeled Vespa: the 400

The Vespa 400 was designed and developed by Piaggio entirely in-house. However, Fiat, which supplied the sheet metal to Pontedera (and above all had a 96% share of all cars on the road in Italy), did not view this new utility car favourably. This was partly due to the fact that it was presented in 1957, just four months from the launch of the Fiat 500. Nonetheless it made its debut at the Paris Motor Show, with an exceptional product endorser: Juan Manuel Fangio. Production was started by the French company ACMA in its factory at Fourchambault. The car faced competition in France from the Citroën 2CV and the Renault 4CV, although they cost between 10 and 15% more. They did, however, have the advantage of carrying four people while the Vespa 400 had only room for two. Among the advantages of the 400 were good roadholding and the spaciousness of the cabin.

The Vespa 400 was reasonably successful: 30,000 examples were produced between 1957 and 1961, only around a hundred of which arrived in Italy.

The engine was an air-cooled two-stroke twin with a displacement of exactly 393 cc. The power unit was rear mounted and drove the rear wheels. Independent suspension was fitted all round along with four-wheel hydraulic brakes. With a total length of 2.83 metres the Vespa 400 weighed just 360 kg. Fuel consumption: 5 litres of oil/fuel blend/100 km.

Among the utility car designs developed by Piaggio that never saw the light of day was this front-engined, rear-drive model conceived by Carlo Doveri in 1954.

A four-wheeled Vespa: the 400

The Vespa 400 and expeditions

As with the Vespa, there were clients eager to demonstrate the reliability of the 400 over long distances. In the August of 1958, Raymond Miomandre and Renè Pari completed a return trip from Paris to Moscow: 7,000 kilometres in 140 hours, without any mechanical repairs being required. Four Vespa 400s entered and completed the gruelling Monte Carlo Rally, confirming the four-wheeled Vespa's great reliability.

A cutaway view of the Vespa 400 published in advance by the French press early in 1957.

Note the engine-transmission assembly, the fully independent suspension and the spare wheel behind the seat.

A four-wheeled Vespa: the 400

la plus pratique... la moins chère!

MANIABILITÉ : Le rayon de braquage de la VESPA 400, de 3 m 80, et l'encombrement réduit de la voiture permettent de se garer dans l'emplacement minimum.

BEAUTÉ DES LIGNES

La VESPA 400 est la voiture de l'actualité. Consommation, garage, assurances, entretien la rendent imbattable sur le plan économique.

Mais si elle est une voiture économique, la VESPA 400, ne le sacrifie en rien à la beauté des lignes et à l'élégance.

Alliant l'habitabilité et le confort à une recherche d'esthétique très poussée, la VESPA 400 est une "2 CV racée" aussi agréable pour le travail et les voyages, que pour les courses en ville d'une femme élégante.

A four-wheeled Vespa: the 400

La **Vespa 400** fait l'unanimité

La nouvelle VESPA 400 modèle 1960 présente toute une gamme de perfectionnements fort appréciables.

Un soin tout spécial a été apporté à son aménagement intérieur : sièges confortables, poches de portières, glaces de côté coulissantes, moteur beaucoup plus silencieux.

Les nouveaux coloris de sa carrosserie sont jeunes et variés.

Son moteur est garanti 50.000 km ou 2 ans, quelle assurance pour vous et quelle économie !

En ville vous ne pourrez plus vous en passer, à la campagne elle vous rendra de grands services.

Elle vous plaira par son élégance, son confort, sa rapidité et son extrême robustesse.

Vous, *Madame*, **vous serez séduite** par ses lignes, son élégance complétera la vôtre, elle augmentera la personnalité de votre charme.

Vous, *Monsieur*, **vous apprécierez** sa nervosité, sa tenue de route, sa maniabilité, son économie, et son faible encombrement.

... elle est **techniquement** parfaite

Moteur deux cylindres. Deux temps. 393 cm³. Alésage et course 63/63. Taux de compression 6,4, refroidissement par air forcé, puissance 2 CV (12 CV SAE) 4,7 au cent.

Mélangeur semi-automatique, une manivelle à tourner et l'huile est mélangée automatiquement à l'essence.

Boîte à 3 vitesses et une marche arrière (2ᵉ et 3ᵉ synchronisées), embrayage monodisque à sec.

Direction à crémaillère à récupération automatique du jeu.

Suspension indépendante sur les 4 roues, 4 amortisseurs hydrauliques à double effet et à ressorts coaxiaux.

Monocoque tout acier.

Planche de bord du modèle luxe. Commande des clignotants et commande phare code au volant. Compteur kilométrique panoramique. Large boîte à gants.

vive • élégante • sobre • pratique • agréable •

Capote s'ouvrant facilement. Vitres de côté coulissantes. Déflecteurs.
Voie avant 1,100 m, voie arrière 1,100 m, empattement 1,800 m, largeur hors tout 1,37 m, longueur hors tout 2,85 m, hauteur totale à vide 1,35 m, poids à vide 385 kg.

... son **habitabilité** est exceptionnelle

Deux sièges réglables, largeur aux coudes 122 cm, longueur du dossier aux pédales 110 cm, espace du coussin au plafond 88 cm.
La roue de secours posée dans un logement sous le siège droit est très facilement accessible.

Part three

THE VESPA FAMILY

An outboard Vespa: the Moscone

An outboard Vespa: the Moscone

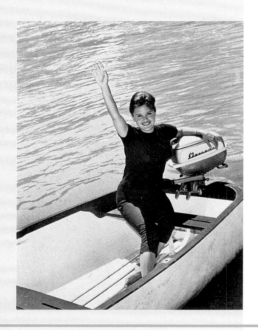

The Moscone (or Fly in English) completed the insect trio initiated with the Vespa and the Ape. It was, in fact, an outboard engine introduced by Piaggio in 1949 with the intention of making motor boating accessible to all. In Piaggio advertising, the Moscone was always photographed against highly attractive marine backdrops with the possibility of reaching these locations in a particularly economical manner. In the case of the Moscone too, albeit to a much lesser degree than with the Vespa, recourse was made to the world of actresses, in this case with Rossana Podestà.

"Moscone, the Long-Awaited Outboard ", from the Piaggio Magazine, by Vincenzo Balsamo, pioneer of Italian motor boating, navy officer and Vice President of the F.I.M.:

"The development and spread of the outboard engine in practical use; that is to say in the application of the marine power unit for recreational or utilitarian purposes has not followed that rising path it was logical to expect as a consequence of the sparkling results achieved in sporting competition. Within the complex technical and economical phenomenon of the spread of the means of locomotion on water; a need was felt to tend

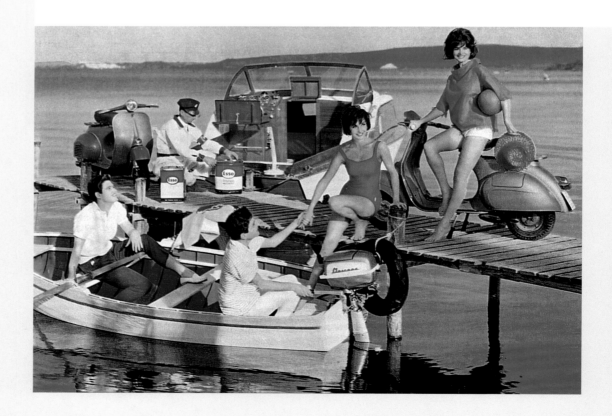

An outboard Vespa: the Moscone

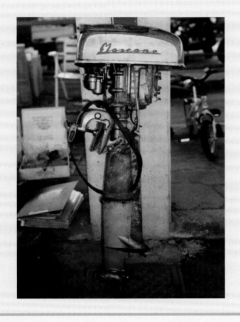

towards an engine with a very small displacement only from which could derive the required conditions for the popularity of the outboard engine. In other words, a large sector of the public needed to be put in the position of being able to own a motorboat that was easy and safe to use, of modest speed and with running costs accessible to the all.

A decisive step with wide repercussions for the outboard sector was taken in 1949 with the appearance of a concrete proposal from the Italian industry. This was not a one-off still at the experimental stage, but rather an engine with a displacement of just 100 cc that had already passed all the most severe tests and that entered the vast panorama of national and international motor boating as a factor of undoubted value for its expansion. The "Moscone" that has recently emerged from the Piaggio workshops embraces those prerequisites of an engine that wishes to be defined as utilitarian: materials carefully selected for their physical and mechanical properties, ingenious and practical controls, ease of starting, protection of the immersed components and the vital organs from the action of the water, lightness and robustness of the assembly,

An outboard Vespa: the Moscone

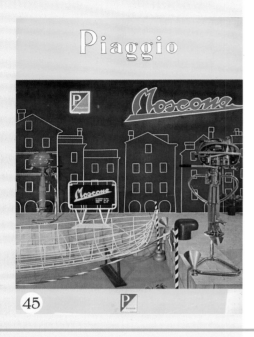

simplicity of application to any boat. The engine is a twin-cylinder two-stroke unit and develops 3.3 brake horsepower at 4000 rpm. Ignition is via a flywheel-magneto with special magnets, with coils, condenser and contact breaker for the alternate firing of the two cylinders; the cables and sparkplugs are suitably waterproofed. The unit is started with an automatic recoil cord and is water-cooled with a self-priming and self-adjusting pump.

The propeller is made of a special non-corroding aluminium-magnesium alloy, reverse is immediate through the rotation of the motor and the underwater exhaust ensures the unit runs quietly. The overall weight of the motor is just 17 kg. With this compact mechanical jewel, enclosed in a compact volume, with harmonically tapering lines in an elegant fairing, attached to an ordinary boat one may attain speeds varying from 2.5 to 12 kph and a range of 3.3 hours at cruising speed or 2 hours at maximum speed. It therefore provides the opportunity to undertake the kind of nautical cruising to which many aspire but have until now found the economic factor to be the greatest obstacle and limitation".

The Piaggio boatyard also presented an elegant clinker-built wooden boat on the occasion of the launch of the Moscone outboard motor.

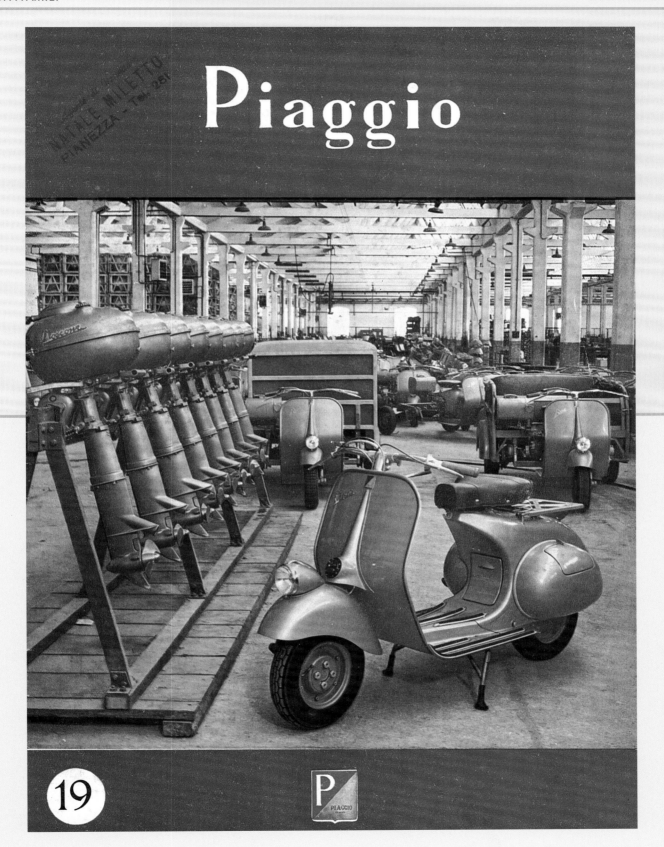

Part four

COMMUNICATION

Publicizing the Vespa

The '40s

In the early years of production, Piaggio concentrated on the novelty value of the Vespa.

The first full-page advertisement simply read: "Piaggio & C. S.p.A. presents the Vespa light motorcycle."

Subsequently there was a deliberate attempt to characterize the Vespa as a product far removed from the traditional image of the two-wheeled vehicles of the time. Parallels were instead drawn with the comfort of the car: "Not a motorcycle, but rather a small two-wheeled car." The copy emphasized the greater protection offered by the Vespa with respect to motorcycles: "You may continue to use it through the winters as you are protected from mud and you may travel swiftly, safely and comfortably without soiling your clothes with engine oil or dust from the road." All this in great safety "guaranteed on wet and slippery roads thanks to exceptional stability."

The financial resources of the potential clients were relatively modest in this period and Piaggio encouraged sales by offering the enticement of instalment plans. The advertising therefore avoided the superfluous and focussed on very concrete features. In this phase the Vespa represented not so much a recreational vehicle as a means of getting to work.

The '50s

alla loro felicità manca solo la
Vespa

At this point the Vespa's success was assured, but Piaggio's advertising continued to claim that it was the "smallest two-wheeled car" and that "better a Vespa today than a car tomorrow", so as not to confuse it with motorcycles. The qualities of the Vespa were emphasized as a means of competing with the rivals that began to appear in the wake of the Piaggio scooter's success: "the most widely-used scooter", "a product of quality", "the most comprehensive after-sale service". In order to attract a female clientele, the Vespa was frequently portrayed with girls alongside. Rather than a utiliatrian means of transport, it became a consumer good. Hence the exhortation "Vespizzatevi!" or "Vesparize yourselves!"

In this period, the general public began to enjoy greater economic resources; the "economic miracle" was in full swing and a clientele that could look upon the Vespa as a recreational vehicle had to be captured. People were perhaps now inclined to permit themselves a meal in a restaurant out of town, something unthinkable just a few years earlier. The marketing idiom changed accordingly as Piaggio turned to a broader clientele eager to shrug off the deprivations of the post-war years. However, the firm also had to defend itself against its first competitors: the Lambretta was not the only threat as by now all the motorcycle manufacturers had a scooter in their range.

*Quando
sarò grande
andrò in
VESPA*

Tra trent'anni

In Vespa

ci si ama meglio

The '6os

By now the Vespa was extremely popular and advertising began to emphasize its international success "throughout the world". The problem of traffic began to make itself felt, but with the Vespa this was "not a problem", "with the Vespa you're always on time". However, towards the end of the 60s, there was an increasingly powerful current of change stemming from the world's youth movements. These were the years of protest, long hair and miniskirts, the music of the Beatles and rebellious behaviour.

While previously, Piaggio's advertising campaigns had been fairly traditional, the late Sixties saw a sharp break with the past as the company decided to ride the revolutionary wave sweeping through the period. The Vespa was by now an established product and the advertising idiom could therefore become more creative, with highly innovative images and slogans. The historic slogan "Chi Vespa mangia le mele" (usually translated as "Who Vespas eats the apples") came out of this period. The years in which the Vespa served essentially as an economical means of travelling to work were long past. Other demands now had to be met and Piaggio tackled the period with advertising campaigns of great impact: a bold use of colour, attractive images and even daring poses with beautiful girls.

The '70s

In this period Piaggio exploited the success of the earlier campaigns with the slogan "Mela compro la Vespa", a play on words with Mela meaning both "apple" and "I'll... it", the slogan translating literally as "I'll buy it, the Vespa" and more idiomatically as "I'm getting a Vespa". However, the period also saw the rise of an ecologist movement, with pollution, above all in relation to cars, being discussed for the first time. A new campaign was created and here again there was a play on words: The invented term "sardomobili" associated cars stuck in traffic with sardines crammed into tins. "Sardomobili steal the air", "Sardomobili don't love others". Naturally, the Vespa instead offered freedom and happiness: "Enjoy Vespa!", "Who Vespas shines". In America a slogan suggested that "Perhaps your next car shouldn't be a car".

Publicizing the Vespa

Chi Vespa
mangia le mele

How did this successful slogan come about? The powers that be at Pontedera courageously decided to back a new advertising campaign that would reflect the period of great changes. The language was completely new and the style reflected the Pop Art of those years. There was considerable resistance to the campaign at first but it eventually appeared in the press, on posters and in the sales outlets with unprecedented coverage. "Who Vespas eats the apples" was taken up by the media and transcended the two-wheeled world to enter the collective consciousness. Umberto Eco and Oliviero Toscani talked about it in "L'Espresso" and Luca di Montezemolo did likewise in "Storia Illustrata".

Filippetti of the Leader agency of Florence explains how the campaign was born:
"That day I was on my way back to the agency after lunch, impregnated and soaked by the rain of stimuli coming from all directions. I was looking out of the bus, thinking about the new Vespa campaign on which I was working. As the driver suddenly braked, someone said, "here we go, the usual hassle with rowdy students on the march!" The whistles of the first smoke bombs and the sirens of the arriving Jeeps were in the air. Sitting down and protected from the smoke, I saw him from the window. Calm, impassive, taking no notice of the chaos around him, an apple gripped between his teeth he painted in white letters on the wall: "Trust no one over thirty." Stunning. A new, unheard of commandment. Words used as weapons that gunned down half the people on the bus and left me with the sensation that with an idea like that, with those words, an era of passion was about to begin.
Back at the agency I looked at the blank sheet of paper in front on me, reflecting on those words, on that idea. I felt a great urge to recount that new reality for Vespa, with the language that it was itself constructing. "Who Vespas yes, who doesn't Vespa no". The pen was writing by itself: Variant A: "Who Vespas touches the sun, who doesn't Vespa no". Variant B: "Who Vespas eats the apples, who doesn't Vespa no". That's it! Found it! Yes, that kid would have painted a phrase like this, that's all, cool. I called Pico Tamburini, head of the Leader agency, and he said, "Fine Gib! Fresh as rainwater! It'll be hell to sell though." I could already hear them, the "those that don't" coming to blows with the "those that do" during the presentation, bickering amongst themselves: "But why an apple?", "transgression and freshness, sir." "But we sell Vespas!", "Good eaters, Mr President." "But what about this strange slogan...? "We're selling to eighteen-year-olds, boss." And the worst of them: "But who's paying? The agricultural board?" Come on, Zancani, call Fillippetti at Leader, get him to correct the grammar at least. Put a nice verb after the noun, sweeten the phrase, it'll be less traumatic!"
The great Dr. Zancani, then the director of the publicity department at Genoa. He caught on to that campaign right away, and like a true Sessantottino [a participant in the 1968 protest movement] managed to impose it on the powers that be. "A very dangerous idea" said the tests, but he decided that there had to be a Piaggio contribution to the revolution of joy, a corporate way of sharing with the kids the power of imagination.
All sorts were said, but it was also immediately spoken of as a landmark campaign. "Who Vespas" became part of the collective consciousness.
From time to time I ask myself what and where he is now, that kid painting words as weapons on the walls. By now, he too will be one of "those that don't". I see him still riding fast on a Vespa, not telling anyone that the secret of his eternal youth is that "who Vespas yes".

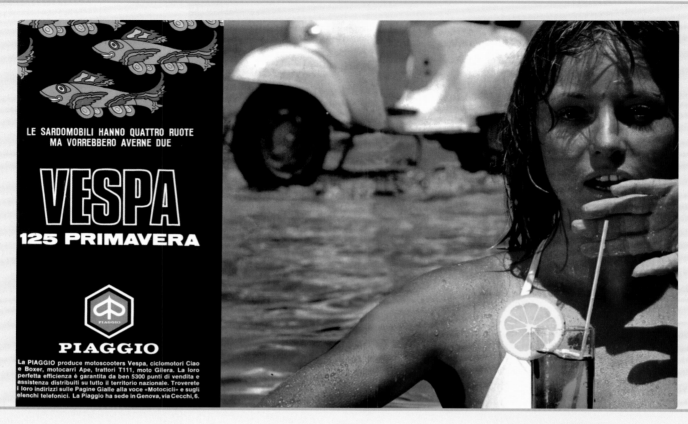

LE SARDOMOBILI HANNO QUATTRO RUOTE
MA VORREBBERO AVERNE DUE

VESPA
125 PRIMAVERA

PIAGGIO

PIAGGIO

La PIAGGIO produce motoscooters Vespa, ciclomotori Ciao
e Boxer, motocarri Ape, trattori T111, moto Gilera. La loro
perfetta efficienza è garantita da ben 5300 punti di vendita e
assistenza distribuiti su tutto il territorio nazionale. Troverete
i loro indirizzi sulle Pagine Gialle alla voce «Motocicli» e sugli
elenchi telefonici. La Piaggio ha sede in Genova, via Cecchi, 6.

**le sardomobili
non godono il sole..**

le sardomobili hanno 4 ruote ma vorrebbero averne 2;
hanno i fari sbarrati, urlano a clacson
e non trovano spazio;
respirano grigio e non vivono i cieli aperti;
soffrono di solitudine e vanno sempre in gruppo

..splende chi Vespa

PIAGGIO

**le sardomobili hanno quattro ruote
ma vorrebbero averne due
come la**

Vespa Rally
200

Vespa Rally 200:
due ruote potenti, scattanti
due ruote con i riflessi pronti
due ruote "rally" spinte dal nuovo motore:
accensione elettronica
cilindrata 200 cc
12 cavalli che crescono
fino a 5700 giri;
due ruote poderose
che sfrecciano
in piena sicurezza
sul filo dei 110 all'ora

Vespa Rally 200:
motore a 2 tempi
cambio a 4 rapporti
pendenza massima superabile, 40%
consumo: 2 litri
di miscela al 2% per 100 km.
carrozzeria portante
trasmissione diretta

**PIAGGIO
cambia il mondo
in 2ruote**

Publicizing the Vespa

197

The '80s

While less revolutionary with respect to the previous decades, the advertising campaigns in this period played with language and emphasized the freedom of wide, open spaces. "Today I'm the sea", "Today I'm the woods", "I Vespa, you Jane". The copy also highlighted the Vespisti's sense of initiative and efficiency: "Vespa: moves the will to get things done", "Vespa: changes things".

To celebrate Italy's triumph in the 1982 World Cup the patriotic slogan read, "L'Italia s'è Vespa !", a play on the second line of the national anthem "L'Italia s'è desta", "Italy has awakened."

The advertising in this period was less incisive, more tentative. On the one hand there was the market composed of young and trendy consumers while on the other there was a more mature clientele in search of sophisticated user-friendly products.

Piaggio appealed to the younger generations above all through the advertising campaign that early in the year cited Marx rather than March, while it offered the Automatica to the adults with the slogan "From here to there easily".

In general, all the proposals show how much attention Piaggo paid to communications with Pontedera always careful to evaluate everything that was going on around it, from politics through to social themes.

L'Italia s'è !

NUOVE VESPA PK 50 E 125
L'ITALIA S'E' VESPA

Nuove VESPA PK: quattro modelli, tre motori e decine di innovazioni tecniche ed estetiche.
Nuove VESPA PK: una linea compatta tutta in acciaio che conquista un nuovo primato di styling. Le nuove VESPA PK sono docili nei comandi, brillanti nella ripresa, decise in frenata, sicure e confortevoli nella guida. Sono dotate di serie di accensione elettronica, lampeggiatori, bauletto porta oggetti, alloggiamento ruota di scorta,

unica chiave che comanda accensione e bloccasterzo.

LE NUOVE VESPA PK 50 ELECTRONIC, PK 50S ELECTRONIC, PK 125 ELECTRONIC, PK 125S ELECTRONIC 3 CON CILINDRO A TRE TRAVASI, SI AFFIANCANO ALLA GAMMA DELLE VESPA PX PER RIPETERNE IL SUCCESSO E APRIRE UN NUOVO CAPITOLO NELLA STORIA DELLO SCOOTER.

The '90s

The early part of the decade was devoted to the problematic launch of the Cosa. From plays on words, "Quella Cosa della Piaggio" ("Piaggio's Thing"), "Che Cosa la vita" ("What a Thing is life") the campaign moved on to technological aspects: "It has an anti-lock braking circuit but it's not a Mercedes. What is it?" Fortunately, in 1996, the firm moved on to the celebrations for the 50th anniversary of the Vespa and attention was naturally focussed on the brand-new ET4: "It's great to think with your own Vespa!"

The PX was given no advertising support, the intention being to let it gradually fade away from the Piaggio catalogue. It was its clientele that ensured its career continued despite the absence of commercial backing. Low-key campaigns were also run for the small 50 and 125 models that were not very different to their counterparts from the previous decade and therefore difficult to promote with any great enthusiasm.

Scansati baloccone

Per VESPA 50 lo stile non è solo un fatto estetico, non è un optional. È il frutto di un design razionale, il punto di arrivo di una evoluzione che solo una grande azienda come

Piaggio può permettersi. VESPA 50 si differenzia da tutto e da tutti per tre caratteristiche che la rendono unica:
□ le marce, per una guida in grado di dare sempre

una interpretazione personale della strada
□ la carrozzeria autoportante, stampata in un solo blocco, che porta con sé un concetto rivoluzionario per il mondo del due ruote

□ l'acciaio con cui è costruita, certezza di solidità e sicurezza di guida in ogni circostanza. Perché VESPA 50 è un mito che resta.

vespa 50 gelosia d'acciaio con tre marce **PIAGGIO**

Ha il circuito frenante antibloccaggio ma non è una Mercedes. Cos'è?

E' l'unico scooter dotato, a richiesta, del sistema frenante EBC (Electronic Brake Control) che modula la pressione del circuito frenante impedendo il bloccaggio della ruota anteriore e assicurando una frenata efficace e modulare anche alle alte velocità. E' nuovo in tutto.

La sella è lunga e larga, le sospensioni calibrate, la strumentazione tra le più moderne. E' la Nuova Cosa Piaggio. E in più, i clienti Cosa potranno usufruire di un Numero Verde per qualsiasi osservazione legata all'utilizzo del veicolo.

COSA

NUMERO VERDE 1678-69040

La Nuova Cosa.

PIAGGIO

The 2000s

The advertising campaign focussing on the new four-stroke ET4 models that carried the Vespa into the new millennium began in the late Nineties. Pride in the new creation was obvious: "It's great thinking with your own Vespa", with Vespa rhyming with the Italian word "testa" meaning head. It was in these years that the internet became such an all-important part of our lives and the Vespa could even be ordered from the website. The advertising campaign featured the full-page slogan "Download is complete", while alongside a satisfied girl in front of a computer "has just bought her new Vespa between a brioche and a coffee" without even having to visit a dealer. The scooter's strong personality shines through in the campaigns for the successive LX: "Enjoy it" and "Mistreat it". The relative images were painstakingly composed from the points of view of setting and illumination, with a touch of irony provided by the presence of the subjects: in the female version there is an acrobat while in the male image there is a disturbing figure armed with a whip. Poetry and irony instead appeared in the advertising campaign for the Granturismo series: "Even the wind enjoys a caress" and "At 59 you can do without plastic", a play on words and a gentle dig at the other scooters on the market without the benefit of a steel monocoque.

Part four

COMMUNICATION

The Piaggio Calendar

The Calendar

When it first came out it caused a sensation with a certain bishop actually declaring that it was pornographic. In effect, from the outset the Piaggio calendar emphasised the combination of Vespa and beautiful women, the latter usually being scantily clad. It was hardly surprising that in the Fifties this created something of a scandal. In any case, it has to be admitted that Piaggio had a good eye: many of the girls photographed went on to become famous models or actresses.

The first Piaggio calendar appeared in 1951. The girls were portrayed in splendid drawings inspired by the covers of the most popular Italian periodicals of the era such as the *La Domenica del Corriere* or *Grand Hotel*. From 1951 to 1954, the drawings were executed by the celebrated Franco Mosca. From 1955 onwards, the girls instead appeared in photographs. Each edition was based on a different theme, from travel (1951) to sport (1952), from nature to animals… In 1957, the girls and their Vespas were superimposed over drawings, while in 1959 the background was black in order to lend greater emphasis to the subjects.

During the Fifties, Leo Longanesi produced some stunning drawings depicting Vespas with a highly original and particularly sophisticated style.

4. COMMUNICATION

The Piaggio Calendar

DICEMBRE

GIUGNO

enero

1955   1955

GIUGNO

Agosto Piaggio 1990

The '50s

gennaio

agosto

mayo

ottobre

luglio

marzo

julio

D	L	M	M	J	V	S
	1	2	3	4	5	6
7	8	9	10	11	12	13
14	15	16	17	18	19	20
21	22	23	24	25	26	27
28	29	30	31			

The '60s

DICEMBRE

APRILE

GIUGNO

LUGLIO

FEBBRAIO

D	L	M	M	G	V	S
	1	2	3	4	5	6
7	8	9	10	11	12	13
14	15	16	17	18	19	20
21	22	23	24	25	26	27
28	29					

The Piaggio Calendar

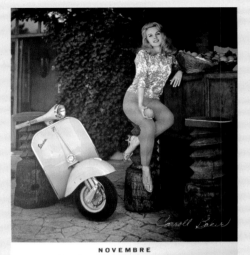

NOVEMBRE

D	L	M	M	G	V	S
					1	2
3	4	5	6	7	8	9
10	11	12	13	14	15	16
17	18	19	20	21	22	23
24	25	26	27	28	29	30

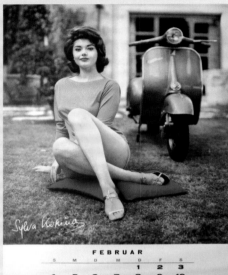

FEBRUAR

S	M	D	M	D	F	S
				1	2	3
4	5	6	7	8	9	10
11	12	13	14	15	16	17
18	19	20	21	22	23	24
25	26	27	28			

MÄRZ

S	M	D	M	D	F	S
				1	2	3
4	5	6	7	8	9	10
11	12	13	14	15	16	17
18	19	20	21	22	23	24
25	26	27	28	29	30	31

APRILE

D	L	M	M	G	V	S
	1	2	3	4	5	6
7	8	9	10	11	12	13
14	15	16	17	18	19	20
21	22	23	24	25	26	27
28	29	30				

Models and actresses

THE ITALIANS

Raffaella Carrà	May 1966
Sylva Koshina	February 1962
Antonella Lualdi	February 1963
Elsa Martinelli	February 1964
Sandra Milo	July 1964
Giorgia Moll	July 1964
Luciana Paluzzi	February 1966
Paola Pitagora	February 1966
Silvana Podestà	March 1962
Stefania Sandrelli	March 1964
Daniela Rocca	September 1963
Catherine Spaak	March1963
Marilù Tolo	September 1965
Ornella Vanoni	November 1962
Serena Vergano	August 1965

FOREIGN STARS

Elga Andersen	January 1966
Ursula Andress	January 1965
Claudine Auger	January 1967
Caroll Baker	January 1963

Geraldine Chaplin	January 1967
Cyd Charisse	January 1967
Joan Collins	December 1966
Mireille Darc	December 1960
Sandra Dee	December 1964
Mylene Demongeot	December 1963
Angie Dickinson	December 1963
Britt Ekland	April 1966
Anna Maria Ferrero	September 1962
Alice & Ellen Kessler	June 1964
Dalhia Lavi	June 1964
Margaret Lee	July 1966
Jayne Mansfield	July 1964
Michele Mercier	July 1964
Pascale Petit	July 1964
Elke Sommer	July 1964
Agnes Spaak	December 1965
Gloria St. Paul	June 1963
Susan Strasberg	February 1965
Marina Vlady	February 1963
Raquel Welch	August 1967
Joan Whelan	August 1967

The Piaggio Calendar

GIUGNO

D	L	M	M	G	V	S
						1
2	3	4	5	6	7	8
9	10	11	12	13	14	15
16	17	18	19	20	21	22
23 30	24	25	26	27	28	29

MARZO

D	L	M	M	G	V	S
					1	2
3	4	5	6	7	8	9
10	11	12	13	14	15	16
17 24 31	18 25	19 26	20 27	21 28	22 29	23 30

NOVEMBER

S	M	D	M	D	F	S
				1	2	3
4	5	6	7	8	9	10
11	12	13	14	15	16	17
18	19	20	21	22	23	24
25	26	27	28	29	30	

MAGGIO

D	L	M	M	G	V	S
		1	2	3	4	
5	6	7	8	9	10	11
12	13	14	15	16	17	18
19	20	21	22	23	24	25
26	27	28	29	30	31	

MARZO

D	L	M	M	G	V	S
1	2	3	4	5	6	7
8	9	10	11	12	13	14
15	16	17	18	19	20	21
22	23	24	25	26	27	28
29	30	31				

DICEMBRE

D	L	M	M	G	V	S
		1	2	3	4	5
6	7	8	9	10	11	12
13	14	15	16	17	18	19
20	21	22	23	24	25	26
27	28	29	30	31		

The '70s

The '80s

217

The '90s

The Piaggio Calendar

The 2000s

Part four

COMMUNICATION

The Vespa and the Arts

The Vespa,
film and television

There are films from the Fifties and Sixties in which the Vespa continuously appears in the typical urban settings of the period. There are, however, also films in which the Vespa plays roles almost as important as those of the stars. The celebrated Roman Holiday (directed by William Wyler), with Gregory Peck and Audrey Hepburn buzzing round Rome on a Vespa is a classic example. Other films in which the Vespa makes a significant appearance include *Poveri ma Belli, Bellezze in Bicicletta, La Notte Brava, Matrimonio all'Italiana, Le Ragazze di Piazza di Spagna, Peccato che sia una Canaglia, Un Amore a Roma, La Bella di Lodi and Mimì Mettallurgico*. In the film *Quadrophenia* by the rock group The Who, the singer Sting, making his film debut, rode a beautiful GS. In Federico Fellini's masterpiece *La Dolce Vita*, Marcello Mastroiani shows off Rome to Anita Ekberg aboard a Vespa. In *American Graffiti*, made in 1970, one of the protagonists arrives at the drive-in aboard his Vespa. In more recent times, Nanni Moretti toured Rome on a Vespa 150 in his *Caro Diario* from 1993.

In 1996 a video was made for use in television advertisements but it was never broadcast. In 2002 a Vespa ET4 instead appeared in the TV ad for the Fanta soft drink and, above all, received important awards for the "Aperitif" TV campaign.

The Vespa and the Arts

Carlo Dapporto e la nuova Vespa 150

226

The Vespa in books, music and painting

It was not just film that underlined the fame achieved by the Vespa. Its popularity may also be gauged by citations in pop songs and even in books, many of which even had the name Vespa in the title.

Among the most important books are *Taccuino della Vespa* (Orio Vergani), *Vespina e le Streghe* (Silvio Ducati), *Storia di una Vespa Gigante e di una Vespa che Potrebbe Essere Grande Ancora* (Aldo Manos), *Il Sole c'é, Maestrina in Trasferta* and *Convalescenza al Mare* (Luigi Brisochi). In France there was *Ma Vespa Ma Femme et Moi* (Daniel Sauvage), while Odette Ferry's *Vacances Romaines* was the basis for the celebrated film. The book by John Steinbeck, *The Short Reign of Pippin IV*, had a Vespa on the cover. The German writer, Peter Roos, described his experience touring Italy on a Vespa in *Vespa Stracciatella*. Also worthy of mention is the comic strip *Le Avventure di Pasqualino* drawn by Jacovitti and published in the early Seventies in the *Corriere dei Piccoli*. There is then a body of travel literature, with numerous books by authors on their return from their adventures. These include, *In Vespa da Milano a Tokyo* by Roberto Patrignani (1964), *La Via delle Indie in Vespa* by Giorgio Caeran (1977) and *In Vespa Oltre l'Orizzonte* by Giorgio Bettinelli (1998).

The Vespa and the Arts

The Vespa and the Arts

The Vespa literature also features the books published by Piaggio itself to celebrate particular occasions or events. A first volume appeared in 1956 to mark the scooter's 10th anniversary. The second volume came out in 1959 and celebrated the first 75 years of the Piaggio company. The was another book in 1979 for the 25th anniversary of the Vespa, while a splendid volume of images by the photographer Tam Fagiuoli with texts by Luca Goldoni was published in 1981. 1994 instead saw the appearance of Tommaso Fanfani's Una Leggenda Verso il Futuro on the occasion of Piaggio's 110th anniversary.

A waltz named after the Vespa and written by Pienno Pataccini was broadcast on Italian radio as early as 1948. Other waltzes followed in 1949: La Vespa (Antola-Fiorita) and Via con la Vespa (Somalvico-Carenzio). The Vespa also appeared on numerous record sleeves including, An Actor's Holiday (Theodore Bikel), Side by Side (Delta Rhythm Boys), Basie Rides Again (Bill Basie), A Little Travelin' Music (Susan Barett), At Play With the Playmates (Playmates), Music for the Sensational Sixties (Don Elliott).

In 1960, the Piaggio Magazine reproduced a painting by Renato Guttuso that depicted a couple (the woman riding side-saddle) seen from behind as they ride away on a Vespa.

The Vespa decorated by Salvador Dalí

Salvador Dalí painted in Surrealist fashion directly on the frame of the scooter belonging to two Spanish students who visited him at Cadaquez on their way from Madrid to Athens. This Vespa was to feature in The Art of the Motorcycle at the Guggenheim Museum in Bilbao in 2000, an exhibition with the century's most significant motorcycles. The two students were Santiago Guillen

and Antonio Veciana. Their Vespa was a 150 built in Spain by Moto Vespa under license from Piaggio. They started on the 25th of July 1962 aiming to complete a round-the-world trip in 80 days, matching Phileas Fogg's feat in the Jules Verne novel. The journey was made by land as far as India, then by plane from Calcutta to San Francisco. Having crossed the USA from coast to coast, the Vespa was flown to London and re-entered Madrid on the 12th of October, exactly 79 days after setting out. They covered 18,950 km with no mechanical problems of note. This journey is described in the book *En 79 Dias, Vuelta al Mundo in Vespa,* published by Doncel with a preface by Dalí himself.

The whole trip was completed with the bodywork decorated by the celebrated artist. The two students had visited Dalí immediately after leaving Madrid, heading for his residence at Port Ligat and it was here that the Vespa 150 was embellished with artistic brushstrokes on the side-panels and the monocoque beneath the saddle.

The Vespa and the Arts

Part five

SPORT AND TOURING

The Vespa and Racing

The Vespa and Racing

The Vespa was being taken to the tracks almost as soon as it was born. In the April of 1947, just a year after it first went on sale, Carlo Masciocchi entered his Vespa in the Gentleman Moto Club of Milan's Primi Passi event. This was a regularity trial held in the valleys above Bergamo and despite the limitations of the Vespa's small engine and a number of falls, the rider celebrated second place at the finish.

The potential of this type of event encouraged Piaggio to create a works team in which the tester Dino Mazzoncini played a leading role.

The Vespa triumphed in numerous events, despite the fact that its technical characteristics made it better suited to city streets than the race track or off-road venues. Among its many victories were those in the Circuit of Florence and the Lakes Trophy in 1948 and in the Circuit of Naples and the Vicenza-Monte Gallio ski and motorbike event in 1949. That same year, Vespa finished second in the gruelling Industry Trophy that brought together three events: the Southern Shield, the 24 Hours and the Mille Miglia. In the first seven Vespas out of seven reached the finish with no penalty points. In the 24 Hours the scooters achieved similar plac-

The Vespa and Racing

ings, while in the Mille Miglia the seven Vespas once again all finished without incurring any penalties. This was a remarkable overall result given that 500 cc motorbikes were also entered.

However, Piaggio's greatest sporting satisfaction came in the Varese International Six Days event in 1951. Of the 218 motorcycles entered for this extremely demanding regularity trial, just 89 finished without incurring penalties. Among these were no less than nine of the ten Vespas that started. 1951 also saw the introduction of single-marque championships that featured such challenging events as the 1,000 km. The success of the championship led to it being repeated in 1952, while the Vespa Three Seas Tour was organized in 1953.

Competitive sporting activities were also organized outside Italy: the European Championship was staged in England in 1960, in Germany in 1961, in Belgium in 1962 and in France in 1964.

Gymkhanas were organized in numerous Italian piazzas and watched by thousands of spectators. Among the specialists was Marzotto, a true acrobat.

The Vespa and Racing

The Vespa and Racing

The Vespa
and record-breaking

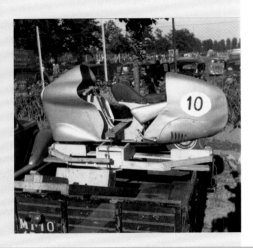

With sporting events proving to be increasingly popular, Piaggio also decided to commit itself to breaking speed records. The Vespa's great rival, the Innocenti-built Lambretta, opened hostilities in 1949 with the conquest of 13 records on the Rome-Ostia autostrada and 36 at the French Monthlèry racing circuit.

A prototype was built at Pontedera that retained links with the production model even though it was fitted with fully streamlined bodywork. The project was led by the engineers Carlo Carbonero and Vittorio Casini. This Vespa lapped Monthlèry in the hands of the riders Mazzoncini, Spadoni and Castiglioni on the 6th of April 1950 and despite strong winds affecting the sessions conquered 17 records.

Piaggio's most significant triumph came in 1951: the breaking of the flying kilometre record, a feat that had enormous publicity value. Vittorio Casini was again responsible for the project, this time flanked by Corradino D'Ascanio himself.

A highly aerodynamic siluro or torpedo-shaped prototype was developed that had virtually nothing in common with the standard Vespa apart from the small-diameter wheels. The engine remained veiled in secrecy for many years. At the time the company merely

Montlhéry, 6ᵗʰ April 1950

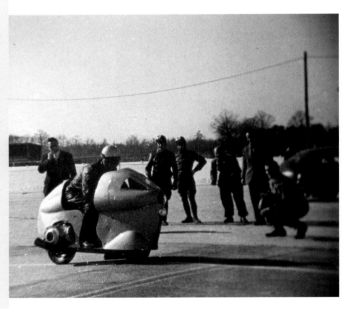

50 km	average kph	134.203
50 miles		134.573
100 km		134.733
100 miles		127.777
500 km		123.463
500 miles		123.919
1000 km		124.306
1 hour		134.054
2 hours		130.794
3 hours		125.713
4 hours		123.376
5 hours		124.065
6 hours		124.636
7 hours		124.056
8 hours		124.274
9 hours		123.434

The Vespa and Racing

said that it was a single-cylinder, two-stroke unit with a "dual cylinder". In reality it was a true twin, with opposing cylinders. It was fed with a mixture of alcohol and oil by two carburettors and cooled by water. In effect, two siluri or torpedoes were constructed, a prototype and the record attempt version. This last differed with respect to the prototype in that it had doors (that acted as airbrakes) and a small spoiler in front of the minuscule windscreen.

Ridden by Dino Mazzoncini, on the 9th of February 1951 the torpedo set a new outright record of no less than 171.102 kph (the average of two runs at 174.418 and 169.910 kph) on the Rome-Ostia autostrada. The result was obtained thanks in part to the studies conducted by Marco Nuti, the head of Piaggio's Technical Innovations department. His engine produced a maximum power output of 21 hp at 9500 rpm, a highly respectable figure and obviously a great advance for a Vespa. Mazzoncini put in a superb performance, especially considering that the road surface was by no means as smooth as that of a racing circuit but full of irregularities (for the record, the measured distance was between the 10th and 11th kilometre posts). At the halfway point there was actually a hump in the asphalt that launched the vehicle into the air for a number of metres.

NOTIZIARIO DEL

Vespista

CLUB · VESPA · D'ITALIA
ROMA

RASSEGNA DI TURISMO, SPORT E TECNICA
A CURA DEL GRUPPO VESPISTI ROMANI

NUMERO UNICO	DIREZIONE E REDAZIONE ROMA - VIA LUCREZIO CARO N. 12A - ROMA	FEBBRAIO 1951

VESPA + MAZONCINI = 171 Km.h

A 174 Km. orari verso la vittoria

The Vespa
and acrobatics

The Piaggio acrobatics team represents a fascinating chapter in the history of the Vespa. Founded in 1955, it was largely composed of the firm's test riders. Each year, these professional Vespisti covered hundreds of thousands of kilometres in all weathers while developing the various models, but their riding abilities were such that a select team was created within the company. Many of the members participated individually in the various organized events (such as the 1,000 kilometres), but Piaggio was also happy for them to ride as team to demonstrate their abilities and the reliability of the Vespa.

Among their various turns, the most spectacular were those in which eight riders balanced on just one Vespa (or five facing backwards) or those in which they rode a Vespa and sidecar with the sidecar's wheel hanging in the air. The team also perfected a series of jumps of a number of metres; launching their Vespas from a ramp over seven barrels. These displays were staged in Italy and abroad, especially in the Far East (India and China) and South America (Brazil, Colombia) and the team continued to perform through to the end of the 1960s.

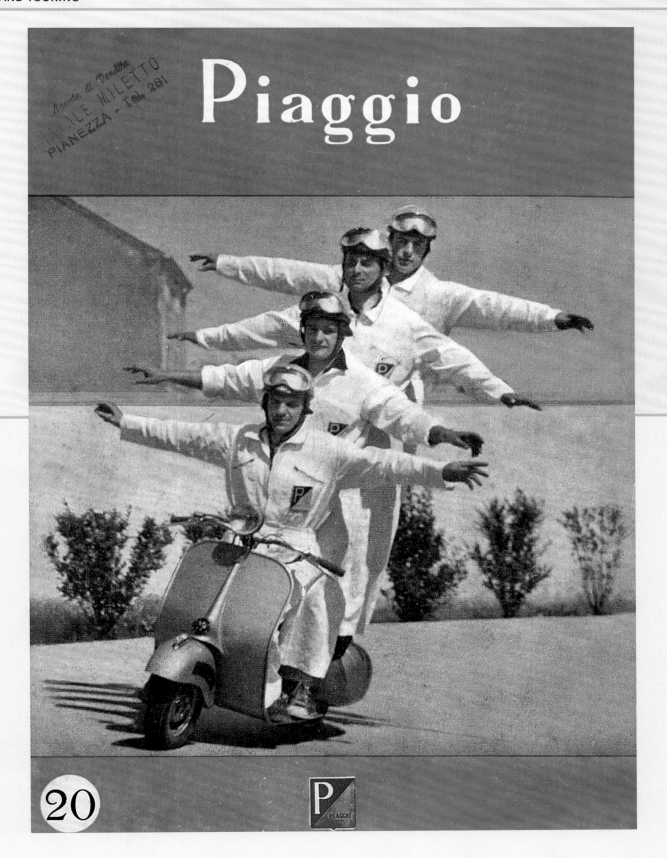

The Vespa
and endurance events

Although it was created above all as an urban vehicle, the Vespa proved to have rare qualities of reliability and robustness that made it the favourite means of transport for numerous adventurers who covered great distances on their scooters.

The first to set out on one of these memorable expeditions was the well-known journalist and rider Roberto Patrignani who crossed Asia solo in 1964 with his Vespa 150. He in fact travelled from Italy to Japan to hand over the trophy offered by the Vespa Club of Europe to the International Olympic Committee. The 13,000 km trip lasted three months and a report on his adventure was published by Patrignani in his book "In Vespa da Milano a Tokyo". Another Vespista-explorer was Giancarlo Nuzzo who, in less than six years, traversed 47 nations and covered over 100,000 miles with his trusty GTR from 1976. Also worthy of mention is Giorgio Caeran's trip with his 200 Rally from Italy to Nepal in 1977, covering 20,000 kilometres in two months.

The Vespista to have undertaken the longest trips is Giorgio Bettinelli who has ridden his scooter to all four corners of the globe and published a richly illustrated account entitled "In Vespa oltre l'orizzonte, 110 mila chilometri attraverso 60 paesi".

Bertinelli's trips are veritable expeditions. In 1992-93 he travelled from Rome to Saigon (24 thousand km, 18 countries, 7 months). In 1994-95 from Alaska to

Left, Antonio Corona with its Vespa Rally 200 on the way of Luxor, Egypt (1980). Below, Roberto Patrignani and the Vespa 150 at the Olympic Games held in Tokyo in 1964.

L'eco dell'impresa

The Vespa and Racing

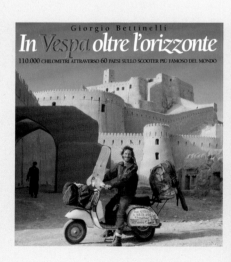

Tierra del Fuego (36 thousand km, 18 countries, 9 months). In 1995-96 from Melbourne, Australia to Cape Town, South Africa (52 thousand km, 23 countries, 1 year). In 1997-2001 from Chile to Australia (144 thousand km, 90 countries, 3 years). His travel stories can also be found in the book "Brum Brum, 254.000 chilometri in Vespa".

Remarkable trips have also been completed by non-Italian Vespisti: in 1953, Pierre Delliere rode from Vietnam to Paris, covering 16 thousand km in 51 days. The same route was also taken by Renè Mourier in 1956, 17 thousand km in 44 days. In 1959, Georges Monneret went from Paris to the Sahara desert with his 150. James Owen instead crossed the Americas, from the United States to Tierra del Fuego. Soren Nielsen drove his Vespa to Greenland. The Englishwoman Betty Warral rode from London to Australia, while the Australian Geoff Dean completed a round-the-world trip. In 1980, four Frenchmen entered their Vespa 200 Rallies in the Paris-Dakar. But the story does not end here: there are those who have gone to sea and taken to the skies with their Vespas.

In 1952, the Frenchman Monneret linked the rear wheel of his Vespa to a propeller via rollers and rode his catamaran scooter across the English Channel from Calais to Dover. In the 1967 film Dick Smart, the protagonist used a Vespa modified by Piaggio together with Alpha Wallis so that it could lift off like a helicopter.

The Vespa and Racing

Part six

THE VESPA CLUB

A successful partnership

In Italy and around the world

Piaggio was not slow to recognize the promotional value of the coordination of the Vespa clubs that had been formed spontaneously ever since the scooter went on sale. The framework was established by Renato Tassinari. A former sub-editor at the Gazzetta dello Sport and subsequently at the Corriere dello Sport, Tassinari was the right man in the right place. In 1948, he was asked to organize the Piaggio stand at the Milan trade fair. Enthusiastic and long-sighted coordinator that he was, Tassinari invented the "silver swarm" and brought together under his direction 2,000 Vespisti from all over Italy.

The success of this initiative encouraged Piaggio to organize the clubs with ever greater efficiency. On the 23rd of October 1949, the Vespa Club d'Italia was officially born with the organization of the first National Conference at Viareggio. The president was Renato Tassinari. On the 9th of December 1951, delegates from the various Italian Vespa clubs attended the conference in Rome where the new publication Vespa Club Italia was presented. Distributed to all members, the periodical kept them informed about the club's various activities. By the end of 1959, the year the Vespa Club d'Italia celebrated its 10th anniversary at Viareg-

6. THE VESPA CLUB

A successful partnership

gio, there were no less than 220 Italian clubs with over 50,000 members. The same city also saw the club celebrate its 20th anniversary in 1969, 30th in 1979 and 40th in 1989…

In 1973 the president of the Vespa Club d'Italia was Manlio Riva, succeeded in 1984 by Roberto Leardi.

An important initiative, the birth of the Historical Register, took place within the ambit of the Legnago conference in the December of 1980. The first curator was Mario Carini, a leading figure in the history of the Vespa in Italy. In 1984, he was succeeded by Luigi Frisinghelli. The aim of the register is that of preserving the historical models and conserving those of particular interest to collectors. In 1985, the first rallies devoted to classic scooters were held at Castiglione della Pescaia (Grosseto) and Grottaferrata (Rome).

In 1984, Christa Solbach of Germany was nominated as President of the International Federation of International Vespa Clubs.

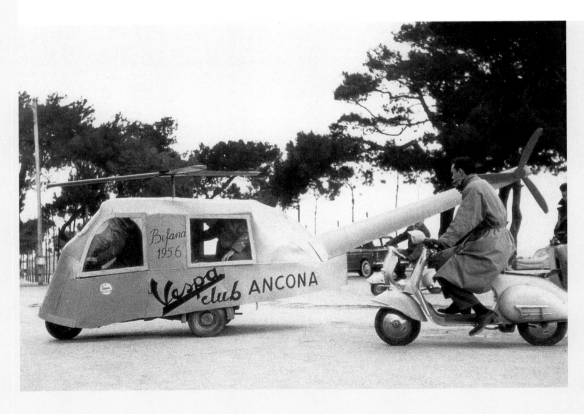

A successful partnership

The rallies

The first Vespa Day was staged on the 6th of May 1953, with no less than 20,000 Vespisti attending rallies in 12 different cities. The success of this initiative encouraged Piaggio to organize a second day in 1956, with 56,000 Vespisti attending in 16 cities.

Eurovespa, the event bringing together Vespisti from throughout Europe was also a great success. In 1955, at San Remo, 13 countries were represented, with the same number being present at Munich in 1956. Over 2,000 Vespisti attended the EuroVespa event in Barcelona in 1957. Subsequently, events were held in

Brussels in 1958, Paris in 1959, Rome in 1960 and Salzburg in 1961.

In more recent times, EuroVespa has been held in Rome in 1981, Reggio Calabria in 1982, Austria in 1983, Verona in 1984, Barcelona in 1986, Switzerland in 1990, San Marino in 1991, Germany in 1992, Abano Terme in 1993, Spain in 1994, San Remo in 1996, Greece in 1997 and Holland in 1998.

A successful partnership

The rallies

Part seven

THE PONTEDERA MUSEUM

The origins of the legend

The historical legacy

The Piaggio Museum

Inaugurated on the 29th of March 2000, the Pontedera museum is a fundamental point of reference in the history of the Vespa. The fact that today we are able to admire this exhibition space is due largely to Giovanni Alberto Agnelli who passed away prematurely in 1997 at just 36 years of age. The Piaggio chairman from 1988, the young Agnelli was the first to propose a cultural project that would promote the company's heritage. The point of departure was the creation of the foundation in 1994 that laid the basis for the collection and cataloguing of the documentation relating to the entire Piaggio story. Heading up and coordinating the foundation since 1998 is Professor Tommaso Fanfani. The museum was established at the company's Pontedera factory in spaces created in the former toolshop. In this way the link between the history of the Vespa and that of the Piaggio company is strengthened. The museum features not only the most important models from the Vespa line-up, but also acknowledges Piaggio's other significant achievements: from aircraft (on the forecourt) to trains. An example of the stainless steel railcar actually "enters" the museum itself. A number of radial aero engines are also on display inside.

The origins of the legend

Naturally, there are examples of racing and record-breaking Vespas, the Ape, the 400 small car and the Moscone outboard motor (with a splendid section). One particularly intriguing exhibit: the one-off prototype Vespa used in the 1967 film Dick Smart complete with a rotary wing. For lovers of the Gilera, there is a mezzanine floor with the most significant historical models, from the unique VT 317 from 1909 to the Paris-Dakar RC 600 from 1991. Also on display is a highly streamlined Gilera record-breaker from 1937.

Vespa production models are well represented by a series of particularly important and well displayed examples. Some are located in a large hall, others are actually mounted in three rows on the wall. The right-hand side of each of these is displayed allowing the engine to be presented and from a distance it almost seems as though you are looking at a magnificent series of models enclosed in their boxes. Only they are, of course, life-size! A visit to the museum is a fascinating and enthralling experience for all Vespa enthusiasts.

The origins of the legend

The Historical Archive is located within the museum and boasts a wealth of documents, drawings, sketches and advertising material. The majority of the over 150,000 documents are from the offices of the Pontedera and Genoa factories. The original nucleus is constituted by the Lanzara Archive, named after the engineer Francesco Lanzara, the director of the factories between 1940 and 1979. Successively the following acquisitions were added: the Legal Documents Archive (foundation deeds and assembly minutes), the General Management Archive (account books and administrative deeds), the Commercial Management Archive (brochures and press reviews), the Iconographical Archive (photographs and films), the Production and Design Archive (research and technical manuals), the Personnel Archive (organization and social activities), the SARPI Archive (marketing between 1948 and 1961) and the Gilera Archive (documentation from Arcore). The Historical Archive located within the Piaggio Museum at Pontedera is named after Antonella Bechi Piaggio, the mother of Giovanni Alberto Agnelli. An appropriate acknowledgement for the historical resource containing all the most important documentation regarding the Vespa.

The origins of the legend

The catalogue

È UN PRODOTTO DELLA PIAGGIO & C. -

Bella da capo a coda.

VESPA
PK 125 XL

The '40s

98
125

Presentation
Golf Club, Rome, March 1946
Milan Trade Fair, April 1946

Price
L. 55,000

Production
1,399 examples

Colours
grey (Max Meyer 8003M) - maroon

Frame numbers
V 98 1001 - V 98 2399

ENGINE	
CYLINDERS/CYCLE	single/2-stroke
DISPLACEMENT	98 cc
BORE AND STROKE	50 x 50 mm
COMPRESSION RATIO	6.5:1
POWER/REVS	3.3 hp/ 4500 rpm
TORQUE/REVS	n.a.
COOLING	forced air
INDUCTION SYSTEM	deflector piston/single port
FUEL SYSTEM	Dell'Orto carburettor T2 16/17 - Ta 17 (17 mm)
OIL/FUEL RATIO	5%
IGNITION	flywheel - magneto
STARTING	kick-start lever
CLUTCH	multiplate, oil-bath
GEARBOX	3 speeds, grip-shift
FRAME, WHEELS, SUSPENSION, BRAKES	
FRAME	monocoque
FRONT SUSPENSION	swing arm with spiral spring
REAR SUSPENSION	rubber buffers
FINAL DRIVE	direct
WHEELS	interchangeable, cantilevered with split rim
FRONT BRAKE	124 mm drum
REAR BRAKE	124 mm drum
TYRES	3.50 x 8 front 3.50 x 8 rear
DIMENSIONS/WEIGHT	
LENGTH	1655 mm
WIDTH	700 mm
SADDLE HEIGHT	700 mm
WHEELBASE	1170 mm
FUEL TANK	5 litres
WEIGHT	60 kg
DECLARED PERFORMANCE	
MAXIMUM SPEED	60 kph
ACCELERATION	n.a.
FUEL CONSUMPTION	50 km/l

The 98 is the most significant of all the Vespa models as it was the very first to go on sale. From the very outset, the 98 brought to light those characteristics that were to remain virtually unchanged for the first fifty years of the scooter's history: monocoque frame, side-mounted engine, direct final drive and interchangeable wheels. The 98 model was officially presented to the general public at the Milan Trade Fair in the April of 1946 and immediately attracted great interest. It had previously only been seen by a restricted circle of people at the Golf Club of Rome, just a month earlier. Piaggio presented the new scooter as a "utilitarian light motorcycle" in order to reassure clients with regard to the protection offered by the sheet-metal body. The first examples to leave the Pontedera factory were delivered in the spring and were priced at 55,000 lire. Technically, the 98 was not significantly different to the 1945 prototype that preceded it: in practice the only major variation concerned the cooling which, instead of relying on a natural flow of air through the side-panel louvres, used a forced air system with a fan. In order to test this feature, D'Ascanio introduced talcum powder into the manifold, an empirical but effective method that the staff then present recall because it left them covered in white powder. Piaggio's clientele appreciated above all the Vespa's ease of use, the weather protection it offered, its reliability and its cleanness but also the elegance of the new vehicle. The presence of a spare wheel gave added peace of mind when travelling on the poor roads of post-war years in Italy. The kick-start lever was particularly easy to use and allowed anyone to ride the Vespa. The defects found with the 98 were mainly concerned with the limited comfort provided by the very ineffective front suspension. Rather than being fitted with a coil spring like subsequent models, the 98 had just a pair of small spiral springs.

To all intents and purposes, there was no rear suspension, rider comfort being entrusted to the saddle springs. The gearbox, actuated by four metal rods

also required perfecting. When the rods became loose, changes were more difficult and they had to be adjusted. Vibration was fairly well damped, but at times could cause the kick-start lever to fall off. As there was no stand, the original Vespa had to be leant over on one side.

The first version of the 98 model may be distinguished from the second series by its particularly large front mudguard with deep sides that were fitted with removable panels to facilitate wheel changing. Other details: the exhaust had a straight tail-pipe, the saddle had cylindrical springs, the rear light was pear-shaped, the kick-start lever was straight, the front suspension had a spiral with a curl, the side-panels were

Presentation
no official presentation

Price
L. 76,000

Production
15,680 examples

Colours
grey (Max Meyer 8000M)

Frame numbers
V98 2400 - V98 18079

The 98 was subjected to numerous detail improvements: the front mudguard lost its removable panels in favour of the normal type (from frame 2400). The silencer was of the square type (frame 2280). The saddle spring was conical (frame 3800). The side-panels had a sealing gasket and a knob (frame 1150). The straight kick-start lever and the pear-shaped rear light were retained.
Minor improvements continued to be made to the model: a curved rather than straight kick-start lever was adopted to facilitate starting (frame 5779), a round rear light was fitted (frame 5740) and a flat spiral front suspension spring was adopted (frame 5600). The last examples had an aluminium alloy rather than steel engine support mount.

Presentation
no official presentation

Price
L. 118,000

Production
about 35,000 examples

Colours
met. green (Max Meyer 6000M)

Frame numbers
V1T 01 - n.a.

While the 98 was reasonably successful in terms of sales, with the Vespa 125 of 1948 we may talk about a boom. The public was no longer as diffident as it was at the presentation in 1946, while the 125 was a decisive step forwards with respect to the earlier model. The most significant change concerned the improved comfort deriving from coil spring suspension on both wheels. The scooter still lacked dampers to control the springs, but compared with the 98 the ride was considerably improved. Performance was far better, with sharper acceleration and a maximum speed that was increased from 60 to 70 kph. The first examples were fitted with the same ancillary components as the earlier 98 and still lacked a stand. Only later was a side stand fitted. The engine of the early examples featured radial finning which subsequently became vertical. The rod gear change system of the 98 was retained, but instead of being fully external it was run through a central tunnel just behind the brake pedal. This first series featured two eyelets that allowed a padlock to be fitted at the centre of the leg-shield to lock the handlebars. The hook for hanging a bag below the saddle appeared for the first time, while the saddle itself was fitted with a spring at the front for the first time. The fuel tap was fitted with a reserve position. The engine kill button was located below the saddle. A round rear light made by Feme was fitted. The final examples had a segment-shaped rather than round switch unit. The first examples still lacked a stand, but a side

ENGINE

CYLINDERS/CYCLE	single/2-stroke
DISPLACEMENT	124.79 cc
BORE AND STROKE	56.5 x 49.8 mm
COMPRESSION RATIO	6.5:1
POWER/REVS	3.3 hp/ 4500 rpm
TORQUE/REVS	n.a.
COOLING	forced air
INDUCTION SYSTEM	deflector piston/ single transfer port
FUEL SYSTEM	Dell'Orto TA 17 - TA 17B (17 mm) carburettor
OIL/FUEL RATIO	5%
IGNITION	flywheel - magneto
STARTING	kick-start lever
CLUTCH	multiplate, oil-bath
GEARBOX	3 speeds, grip-shift

FRAME, WHEELS, SUSPENSION, BRAKES

FRAME	monocoque
FRONT SUSPENSION	trailing arm with coil spring
REAR SUSPENSION	coil spring and damper
FINAL DRIVE	direct
WHEELS	interchangeable, cantilevered with split rim
FRONT BRAKE	124 mm drum
REAR BRAKE	124 mm drum
TYRES	3.50 x 8 front 3.50 x 8 rear

DIMENSIONS/WEIGHT

LENGTH	1655 mm
WIDTH	790 mm
SADDLE HEIGHT	790 mm
WHEELBASE	1130 mm
FUEL TANK	5 litres
WEIGHT	77.5 kg

DECLARED PERFORMANCE

MAXIMUM SPEED	70 kph
ACCELERATION	n.a.
FUEL CONSUMPTION	100 km/2 l

PIAGGIO & C.
GENOVA

stand was later fitted while only the final examples had a centre stand with curled ends. Frame numbers were initially stamped below the central saddle spring and subsequently moved to the edge of the carburettor hatch and then the left-hand side of the frame below the toolbox. A quick-release fuel cap was fitted. Compared with the 98, the single front suspension strut was moved from the left- to the right-hand side, a configuration that was to remain unchanged throughout the Vespa's subsequent production history. This model aroused considerable interest among a public that it has to be said had given the 98 a lukewarm reception. The first rallies began to be held and the scooter's enormous commercial success began to take shape.

Presentation
no official presentation

Price
L. 138,000

Production
about 52,000 examples

Colours
met. green (Max Meyer 6000M)

Frame numbers
included between 001 and 104096

The second series "rod-model" featured a number of modifications with respect to the first version. The most important concerned the gearbox control system that instead of using the rigid elements with joints, boasted a mixed system of rods and flexible cables. A light-switch unit with an engine kill button was fitted to the handlebars. With regard to the engine, the fan cover and the cylinder barrel shroud were new. The exhaust silencer was initially a boxy shape and subsequently a flatter rhomboid. The first examples had the engine kill button beneath the saddle.

Presentation
no official presentation

Price
L. 154,000

Production
about 17,000 examples

Colours
met. green (Max Meyer 6000M)

Frame numbers
V15T 104096

The third series rod-model was distinguished from the earlier version by the different body styling with no reinforcing rib.
The side-panels were completely smooth. Rather than riveted, the headlight was bolted on.
The stand was fitted with two rubber feet. The exhaust was oval in shape and chrome-plated.

The '50s

125
125 U
125 Sport
125 Sei Giorni
150
150 GS

Presentation
30 December 1950, SARPI, Milan

Price
L. 168,000

Production
147,723 examples
V30T: 75,887 examples
V33T; 71,836 examples

Colours
met. green (Max Meyer 6002M)

Frame numbers
V30T: 104097 - V33T: 251820

ENGINE

CYLINDERS/CYCLE	single/2-stroke
DISPLACEMENT	124.79 cc
BORE AND STROKE	56.5 x 49.8 mm
COMPRESSION RATIO	6.5:1
POWER/REVS	4.5 hp/ 4500 rpm
TORQUE/REVS	n.a.
COOLING	forced air
INDUCTION SYSTEM	deflector piston/ single transfer port
FUEL SYSTEM	Dell'Orto TA 17B carburettor (17 mm)
OIL/FUEL RATIO	5%
IGNITION	flywheel - magneto
STARTING	kick-start lever
CLUTCH	multiplate, oil-bath
GEARBOX	3 speeds, grip-shift

FRAME, WHEELS, SUSPENSION, BRAKES

FRAME	monocoque
FRONT SUSPENSION	swing arm with coil spring and damper
REAR SUSPENSION	coil spring and damper
FINAL DRIVE	direct
WHEELS	interchangeable, cantilevered with split rim
FRONT BRAKE	124 mm drum
REAR BRAKE	126 mm drum
TYRES	3.50 x 8 front 3.50 x 8 rear

DIMENSIONS/WEIGHT

LENGTH	1680 mm
WIDTH	790 mm
SADDLE HEIGHT	790 mm
WHEELBASE	1160 mm
FUEL TANK	5 litres
WEIGHT	82 kg

DECLARED PERFORMANCE

MAXIMUM SPEED	70 kph
ACCELERATION	n.a.
FUEL CONSUMPTION	100 km/2 l

The 125 was constantly improved with a new version being launched in 1951 with a fundamental change to the transmission system. The rigid control rods (with all their problems of play) were eliminated in favour of Bowden cables. The gear change was significantly improved and the Vespa was easier to use. Greater comfort was also provided by a damper alongside the coil spring of the front suspension, which also guaranteed improved handling. The already low level of vibration was further reduced by new flexible supports at the handlebars. In terms of styling, the 125 from 1951 was distinguished by a rectangular rather than round rear light. The saddle was also changed, with foam rubber padding being introduced. The passenger enjoyed greater comfort as the running-boards were extended by 10 cm meaning they no longer had to stretch their legs. The 1951 version may be recognised by its bolt-on adjustable headlight rather than the earlier version riveted to the mudguard. The rear light was rectangular. The kick-start lever was in light alloy with a rubber pedal crank. The saddle was dark green. The silencer was located centrally, with the tail-pipe on the right on the first version (V30T) and on the left on the second (V33T).

Presentation
Milan Show 1952

Price
L. 150,000

Production
175,014 examples
VM1T: 84,870 examples
VM2T: 90,144 examples

Colours
solid grey (Max Meyer 15048)

Frame numbers
1953: VM1T 01001 - 085870
1954: VM2T 085871 - 0176014

The 125 from 1953 was the first with a right-hand side-panel that was full rather than cut away around the cooling fan as had been the case with the previous versions. This innovation resulted in cleaner and more attractive styling. Part of the merit was due to the new "square" engine with its 54 mm bore and stroke.
The design had been thoroughly revised and provided significantly improved performance.
The power output rose but without compromising fuel consumption thanks to the new configuration with opposing ports.
The new dimensions of the engine allowed it to be fully enclosed within the right-hand side-panel.

The steering column shroud was widened and reinforced.
A 105 rather than a 95 mm headlight was fitted for the first time. Both the clutch and the gear change mechanism (gears and cruciform) were reinforced. The carburettor was enlarged to 18 mm. The fan cover had a new design and was painted the same colour as the bodywork. The central section of the frame was strengthened. The fuel tank capacity was increased to 6.25 litres. The platform featured 9 rubber strips. The VM2T was fitted with a new electrical system that satisfied the new Highway Code requirement for sidelights. The light switch unit was changed, with a further position being added.

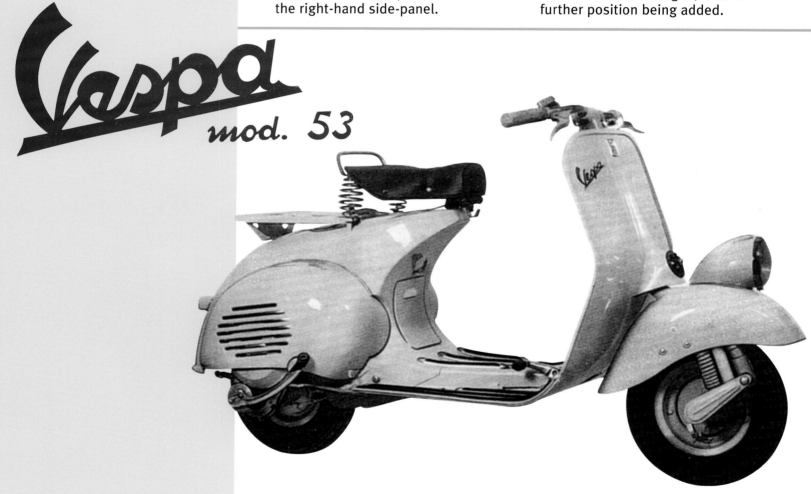

Presentation
no official presentation

Price
L. 145,000

Production
124,600 examples
VN1T: 49,100 examples
VN2T: 75,500 examples

Colours
VN1T: grey (Max Meyer 15048)
VN2T: grey (Max Meyer 15081)

Frame numbers
1954: VN1T 01001 - 023000,
1955: VN1T 023001 - 050100,
1956: VN2T 050101 - 096569,
1957: VN2T 096570 - 0125600

The third series was less well-equipped to distinguish it further from the 150. The last examples had a Y-shaped fan cover. The platform featured 7 rubber strips. The rear damper had a biconical coil spring like that of the 150. The kick-start lever had anti-slip grooves. The rear brake pedal was in unpolished aluminium. The front suspension had no hubcap. The Vespa script on the leg-shield was painted dark green. The Piaggio badge was in relief and for the first time lacked the "Genova" script. The leg-shield of the 2nd version (VN2T) wrapped around further and the saddle was larger. The saddle springs were painted dark green instead of being chromed. The saddle had a grab-handle for the passenger.

Presentation	
Milan Show 1952	
Price	
L. 130,000	
Production	
6,000 examples	
Colours	
solid green (Max Meyer 12986334)	
Frame numbers	
VU1T 1001 - 7001	

The U designation of this 125 model stood for Utilitarian. Despite a price far more inviting than that of the standard 125, the series failed to find favour with the clientele. The specification was too spartan and the U was never appreciated as the extremely economical vehicle it truly was. To cut costs numerous details changed. The front suspension damper was eliminated, as was the chrome-plating, the engine cover was lightened, the front mudguard and the right-hand side-panel were cut down. Just one of the changes adopted for reasons of economy proved to be efficacious and was to become a feature of the Vespa range: the headlight was located on the handlebars rather than the front mudguard. There were few creature comforts: the rubber brake pedal and kick-start lever covers were eliminated as were the rubber feet on the stand, replaced by a small pressed steel grille. The saddle was smaller. The side-panels were fixed with exposed screws and gaskets. The Vespa script on the leg-shield was painted instead of chromed. The U's lack of success is perhaps indicative of the improved economic condition of scooter users at that time.

ENGINE

CYLINDERS/CYCLE	single/2-stroke
DISPLACEMENT	124.79 cc
BORE AND STROKE	56.5 x 49.8 mm
COMPRESSION RATIO	6.5:1
POWER/REVS	4.5 hp/ 4500 rpm
TORQUE/REVS	n.a.
COOLING	forced air
INDUCTION SYSTEM	deflector piston/ single transfer port
FUEL SYSTEM	Dell'Orto TA 17B carburettor (17 mm)
OIL/FUEL RATIO	5%
IGNITION	flywheel - magneto
STARTING	kick-start lever
CLUTCH	multiplate, oil-bath
GEARBOX	3 speeds

FRAME, WHEELS, SUSPENSION, BRAKES

FRAME	monocoque
FRONT SUSPENSION	trailing arm with coil spring but no damper
REAR SUSPENSION	coil spring and damper
FINAL DRIVE	direct
WHEELS	interchangeable, cantilevered with split rim
FRONT BRAKE	124 mm drum
REAR BRAKE	126 mm drum
TYRES	3.50 x 8 front 3.50 x 8 rear

DIMENSIONS/WEIGHT

LENGTH	1680 mm
WIDTH	790 mm
SADDLE HEIGHT	775 mm
WHEELBASE	1160 mm
FUEL TANK	6.5 litres
WEIGHT	78 kg

DECLARED PERFORMANCE

MAXIMUM SPEED	70 kph
ACCELERATION	n.a.
FUEL CONSUMPTION	100 km/2 l

Vespa mod. 53 u

Presentation	
no official presentation	
Price	
L. 460,000	
Production	
n.a.	
Colours	
white, green	
Frame numbers	
from CLXI to CCLX	

The Sport series was characterised by a particularly aggressive appearance. The most significant element was the enlarged fuel tank located behind the saddle. The earliest models had a simple rectangular shape, gradually rounded to a more aerodynamic form. With respect to the standard models, the Sport also had slimmer lines: the handlebars were narrower, the leg-shield was more aerodynamic and the platform was raised. Other details: the carburettor hatch was domed, the silencer was modified internally but remained outwardly identical to that of the standard model. The spare wheel was located in the centre of the platform to provide the rider's knees with greater support. A model with such a sporting character was born out of the desire to demonstrate what could be achieved with an essentially utilitarian machine. Thanks to its experimental department, Piaggio succeeded in developing a Vespa capable of significant results in trials events as well as on city street circuits.

ENGINE	
CYLINDERS/CYCLE	single/2-stroke
DISPLACEMENT	124.2 cc
BORE AND STROKE	54 x 54 mm
COMPRESSION RATIO	7.5:1
POWER/REVS	7 hp/6750 rpm
TORQUE/REVS	n.a.
COOLING	forced air
INDUCTION SYSTEM	domed piston
FUEL SYSTEM	Dell'Orto SSI 23C carburettor (23 mm)
OIL/FUEL RATIO	10%
IGNITION	flywheel - magneto
STARTING	kick-start lever
CLUTCH	multiplate, oil-bath
GEARBOX	3 speeds, grip-shift
FRAME, WHEELS, SUSPENSION, BRAKES	
FRAME	monocoque
FRONT SUSPENSION	trailing arm with coil spring and damper
REAR SUSPENSION	coil spring and damper
FINAL DRIVE	direct
WHEELS	interchangeable, cantilevered with split rim
FRONT BRAKE	124 mm drum
REAR BRAKE	126 mm drum
TYRES	3.50 x 8 front 3.50 x 8 rear
DIMENSIONS/WEIGHT	
LENGTH	1680 mm
WIDTH	630 mm
SADDLE HEIGHT	790 mm
WHEELBASE	1160 mm
FUEL TANK	11 litres
WEIGHT	95 kg
DECLARED PERFORMANCE	
MAXIMUM SPEED	95 kph
ACCELERATION	n.a.
FUEL CONSUMPTION	100 km/4.5 l

Presentation
no official presentation
Price
L. 500,000
Production
300 examples
Colours
green
Frame numbers
n.a.

ENGINE	
CYLINDERS/CYCLE	single/2-stroke
DISPLACEMENT	124.2 cc
BORE AND STROKE	54 x 54 mm
COMPRESSION RATIO	7.5:1
POWER/REVS	7 hp/6750 rpm
TORQUE/REVS	n.a.
COOLING	forced air
INDUCTION SYSTEM	domed piston
FUEL SYSTEM	Dell'Orto SSI 23C carburettor (23 mm)
OIL/FUEL RATIO	10%
IGNITION	flywheel - magneto
STARTING	kick-start lever
CLUTCH	multiplate, oil-bath
GEARBOX	3 speeds, grip-shift
FRAME, WHEELS, SUSPENSION, BRAKES	
FRAME	monocoque
FRONT SUSPENSION	trailing arm with coil spring and damper
REAR SUSPENSION	coil spring and damper
FINAL DRIVE	direct
WHEELS	interchangeable, cantilevered with split rim
FRONT BRAKE	124 mm drum
REAR BRAKE	126 mm drum
TYRES	3.50 x 8 front 3.50 x 8 rear
DIMENSIONS/WEIGHT	
LENGTH	1680 mm
WIDTH	630 mm
SADDLE HEIGHT	790 mm
WHEELBASE	1160 mm
FUEL TANK	11 litres
WEIGHT	95 kg
DECLARED PERFORMANCE	
MAXIMUM SPEED	95 kph
ACCELERATION	n.a.
FUEL CONSUMPTION	100 km/4.5 l

The Sei Giorni (Six Days) model is one of the most significant in Vespa production. Highly sought-after by collectors, it is a special case in that it was produced in limited numbers (around 300 examples) and destined for competitive trials. The most demanding event in those years was the "Sei Giorni Internazionale" and Piaggio decided to construct a Vespa specifically prepared for the competition. Along with Corradino D'Ascanio, the engineers Carbonero and Casini worked on the project after having previously developed the record-breaking models. The Testing Department worked on numerous components to make this Vespa as reliable and robust as possible in view of the particularly gruelling demands of the event. First and foremost, the engine was significantly uprated with the maximum speed of the trials scooter rising from the 65 kph of the standard model to 95 kph. The Dell'Orto carburettor was specially manufactured for the Sei Giorni. Further modifications concerned the ignition advance (controlled via a handlebar lever), the clutch (reinforced), the exhaust pipe (with expansion

chambers), the crankcase (cast in sand rather than die cast), the mating of the crankcase with the cylinder barrel (via four rather than three studs). With regard to the frame, the modifications also affected the bodywork with a more aerodynamic leg-shield, the platform shaped to accentuate leans and the right-hand side-panel enlarged to accommodate the new engine.

The front hub was reinforced and the fuel capacity was increased with a second tank behind the saddle. This tank had a foam rubber pad to allow the rider to take up a more aerodynamic position. The wheels had reinforcing bolts and could be fitted as necessary with 8 or 10" tyres. There was a spare wheel, mounted vertically in the centre of the platform. The trial held in the September of 1951 involved both off-road sections in the valleys above Bergamo and track sessions at Monza (complete with the pavé-surfaced Parabolica corner). Initially offered a cool reception by

competitors, the Sei Giorni Vespas soon began to attract interest, especially from an almost incredulous public. The overall results testified to the overwhelming success of the model: of the ten examples entered, nine finished and won gold medals while just one failed to be classified due to a fall. This memorable result encouraged Piaggio to produce a limited, and highly expensive, series of the Sei Giorni that was sold at almost four times the normal price.

Presentation
Milan Show 1954
Price
L. 148,000
Production
131,735 examples
VL1T: 16,000 examples
VL2T: 76,100 examples
VL3T: 39,635 examples
Colours
solid grey (Max Meyer 15048)
Frame numbers
1954: VL1T 1001 – 17000
1955: VL2T 17001 – 93101
1956: VL3T 63101 – 132737

ENGINE

CYLINDERS/CYCLE	single/2-stroke
DISPLACEMENT	145.6 cc
BORE AND STROKE	57 x 57 mm
COMPRESSION RATIO	6.3:1
POWER/REVS	5.5 hp/ 5000 rpm
TORQUE/REVS	n.a.
COOLING	forced air
INDUCTION SYSTEM	flat piston/2 transfer ports, opposing ports
FUEL SYSTEM	Dell'Orto carburettor, 1954/1955:TA 18D (18 mm), 1956: MA 19C, 1957/1958: MA 19D (19 mm)
OIL/FUEL RATIO	5%
IGNITION	flywheel - magneto
STARTING	kick-start lever
CLUTCH	multiplate, oil-bath
GEARBOX	3 speeds, grip-shift

FRAME, WHEELS, SUSPENSION, BRAKES

FRAME	monocoque
FRONT SUSPENSION	trailing arm with coil spring and damper
REAR SUSPENSION	coil spring and damper
FINAL DRIVE	direct
WHEELS	interchangeable, cantilevered with split rim
FRONT BRAKE	125 mm drum
REAR BRAKE	127 mm drum
TYRES	3.50 x 8 front 3.50 x 8 rear

DIMENSIONS/WEIGHT

LENGTH	1700 mm
WIDTH	785 mm
SADDLE HEIGHT	790 mm
WHEELBASE	1165 mm
FUEL TANK	6.5 litres
WEIGHT	92 kg

DECLARED PERFORMANCE

MAXIMUM SPEED	80 kph
ACCELERATION	n.a.
FUEL CONSUMPTION	100 km/2.2 l

In contrast with the 125, the 150 was fitted with the higher headlight from the outset. Piaggio introduced this model in order to offer a slight increase in performance, but above all to allow the Vespa to be ridden on the "autostrada". The first series was produced with exposed handlebars and only in 1957 was a cast aluminium headset introduced. The 150 was very well received by the public and the displacement became a feature of the Vespa range with various series produced alongside the 125 models. A speedometer was standard equipment and the brake drums were finned. The first models (VL1T) lacked a battery. The second version (VL2T) had a battery located behind the left-hand side-panel. The third version (VL3T) had a saddle with a single spring. The headlight shape and the profile of the rubber strips on the platform changed. The headlight featured a pronounced brow.

| **Presentation** |
| Milan Show 1956 |
| **Price** |
| L. 165,000 |
| **Production** |
| 98,700 examples |
| **Colours** |
| grey – met. blue (Max Meyer 15028) |
| **Frame numbers** |
| VB1T 1001 – VB1T 99700 |

The most important styling modification concerned the fairing of the handlebars with a one-piece cast headset within which ran the cables. A speedometer was fitted as standard. The headlight had a chromed bezel. The saddle was dark blue and the Vespa script on the leg-shield was chrome-plated. With the new handlebars, this model acquired a more elegant and attractive personality. The styling was sleeker, an aspect that was a great success with the public.

Presentation
Milan Show 1954

Price
L. 178,000

Production
12,300 examples

Colours
met. Aluminium grey
(Max Meyer 15005)

Frame numbers
VS1T 001001 - 0013300

ENGINE

CYLINDERS/CYCLE	single/2-stroke
DISPLACEMENT	145.6 cc
BORE AND STROKE	57 x 57 mm
COMPRESSION RATIO	6.7:1
POWER/REVS	8 hp/7500 rpm
TORQUE/REVS	n.a.
COOLING	forced air
INDUCTION SYSTEM	flat piston/ 2 ports
FUEL SYSTEM	Dell'Orto carburettor UB 23 S3 (23 mm)
OIL/FUEL RATIO	6%
IGNITION	flywheel - magneto
STARTING	kick-start lever
CLUTCH	multiplate, oil-bath
GEARBOX	4 speeds, grip-shift

FRAME, WHEELS, SUSPENSION, BRAKES

FRAME	monocoque
FRONT SUSPENSION	trailing arm with coil spring and damper
REAR SUSPENSION	coil spring and damper
FINAL DRIVE	direct
WHEELS	interchangeable, cantilevered with split rim
FRONT BRAKE	150 mm drum
REAR BRAKE	150 mm drum
TYRES	3.50 x 10 front 3.50 x 10 rear

DIMENSIONS/WEIGHT

LENGTH	1700 mm
WIDTH	700 mm
SADDLE HEIGHT	800 mm
WHEELBASE	1180 mm
FUEL TANK	12 litres (VS1) 9.5 (VS2-5)
WEIGHT	104 kg

DECLARED PERFORMANCE

MAXIMUM SPEED	100 kph
ACCELERATION	n.a.
FUEL CONSUMPTION	100 km/3 l

The GS is one of the most important models in Vespa production and one of the most sought-after by collectors. This is due to its particularly interesting technical and stylistic features. The styling was highly individual with very tall and voluminous side-panels, a consequence of the new engine that had the carburettor mounted directly above the cylinder. The GS was an immediate success and soon became the Vespisti's dream machine. There were numerous firsts with this model: the four-speed gearbox, 10" wheels and the die cast headset with incorporated speedometer. But this was not all: performance was particularly lively with respect to the traditional 150, the power output rose from 5.4 to no less than 8 hp. At this point the Vespisti could reach the all-important 100 kph and keep up with the light motorcycles of the era. The new engine was characterised with a number of features experimented on the Sei Giorni: it had a square configuration with bore and stroke dimensions of 57 mm, an induction system with opposing ports, a flat piston with no deflector and a carburettor mounted directly on the cylinder barrel. Given that performance had reached a certain level, the other components were also uprated: the clutch was fitted with stronger spring drives and larger plates, the brakes had a ring in centrifugal cast iron, the suspension had longer travel with variable rate biconical springs and dual action hydraulic dampers.
The fuel tank capacity was increased to no less than 12 litres.

SERBATOIO SUPPLEMENTARE PER

DESCRIZIONE

Il serbatoio supplementare di miscela appositamente studiato per consentire agli utenti della Vespa G.S. una maggiore indipendenza dalle stazioni di rifornimento carburanti, è costruito in lamierino d'acciaio rinforzato e viene fissato direttamente alla ruota di scorta mediante un prigioniero con relativa piastrina circolare e dado. Il suo montaggio e rimontaggio è quindi molto agevole e può essere eseguito assai rapidamente.

E' munito di un'unica apertura, chiusa con tappo a vite, attraverso la quale si effettua il riempimento ed il successivo travaso della miscela nel serbatoio normale interno alla scocca.

Il suo peso a secco, tenuto conto della buona robustezza, è sufficientemente limitato (2,5 kg.) e la sua capacità è di 5 lt.

S. A. R. P. I.

RAPPRESENTANTE GENERALE ESCLUSIVA PER LA VENDITA
————— G E N O V A —————
VIALE DELLE BRIGATE PARTIGIANE, 12 — TELEFONI 580.641 · 42 · 43

Prezzo di vendita al pubblico **L. 3.000** + **I. G. E.**

Presentation
Milan Show 1956

Price
L. 194,000

Production
30,040 examples

Colours
met. aluminium grey
(Max Meyer 15005)

Frame numbers
1956: VS2T 0013301 - 0023310
1957: VS3T 0023311 - 0035310
1958: VS4T 0035311 - 0047350

The second series GS was distinguished by the passage of the cables inside the headset. The speedometer was white. The ignition switch was flat. The saddle had a new, rounder shape. The leg-shield was trimmed with stainless steel edging. The exhaust manifold was attached to the cylinder barrel with an aluminium bezel rather than a clip. The fuel tank filler cap was secured with a wing nut. The VS3T version had a flat battery that could be located within the tool bag. The VS4T version had a new rear light fixture incorporating a brake light, as required by the Highway Code. The engine cover was secured by a curved aluminium clasp.

Presentation
Milan Show 1958

Price
L. 205,000

Production
80,000 examples

Colours
met. aluminium grey
(Max Meyer 15005)

Frame numbers
VS5T 0047351 - 00127350

The third series of the GS was distinguished by the new wheel design that revealed the extensive finning of the brake drums. The wheels were anchored with 5 rather than 4 studs. The speedometer was of a new fan-shaped design with a scale reading up to 120 kph. The trim on the upper part of the mudguard was slimmer and profiled. The front mudguard had a beaded edge. In the first version the rear light is identical to that of the previous series, subsequently a larger unit with a chromed body was fitted. The badge on the leg-shield was in plastic. The final models carried the frame number below the tool bag on the rear left-hand side.

The '60s

50 N
50 L
50 S
50 Super Sprint
90
90 SS
125
125 Super
125 GT
125 Nuova
150
150 GL
150 Super
150 Sprint
160 GS
180 Super Sport
180 Rally

Presentation	
Milan Show 1963	
Price	
L. 98,000	
Production	
50 N: 189.977 examples	
50 N allungata: 83,299 examples	
Colours	
green (Max Meyer 12986301)	
yellow (Max Meyer 12982902)	
grey (Max Meyer 12988710)	
red (Max Meyer 12985847)	
blue (Max Meyer 12987400)	
Frame numbers	
50 N: V5A1T 1001-190977	
50 N allungata: V5A1T 200001-283299	

ENGINE

CYLINDERS/CYCLE	single/2-stroke
DISPLACEMENT	49.8 cc
BORE AND STROKE	38.4 43 mm
COMPRESSION RATIO	7.2:1
POWER/REVS	1.5 hp/ 4500 rpm
TORQUE/REVS	n.a.
COOLING	forced air
INDUCTION SYSTEM	rotary valve
FUEL SYSTEM	Dell'Orto carburettor (16 mm)
OIL/FUEL RATIO	2%
IGNITION	flywheel - magneto
STARTING	kick-start lever
CLUTCH	multiplate, oil-bath
GEARBOX	3 speeds, grip-shift

FRAME, WHEELS, SUSPENSION, BRAKES

FRAME	monocoque
FRONT SUSPENSION	trailing arm with coil spring and damper
REAR SUSPENSION	coil spring and damper
FINAL DRIVE	direct
WHEELS	interchangeable, cantilevered with split rim
FRONT BRAKE	125 mm drum
REAR BRAKE	125 mm drum
TYRES	2.75 x 9 front 2.75 x 9 rear

DIMENSIONS/WEIGHT

LENGTH	1655 mm 50 allungata: 1655 mm
WIDTH	700 mm
SADDLE HEIGHT	700 mm
WHEELBASE	1166 mm 50 allungata: 1175 mm
FUEL TANK	5.3 litres
WEIGHT	66 kg

DECLARED PERFORMANCE

MAXIMUM SPEED	40 kph
ACCELERATION	n.a.
FUEL CONSUMPTION	1.5 l/100 km

With various versions offered, the first Vespa 50 was a success, above all among the youngest riders. Its displacement and power output of just 1.5 hp made it ideal for Italian fourteen-year-olds who were allowed to ride it without any licence. Compared with the larger displacement models, the 50 had a smaller frame and, above all, side-panels integrated with the rest of the bodywork. The gearbox had three speeds. The engine was accessed via a hinged panel set into the side-panel itself. The headlight was round with no bezel. The speedometer was offered as an accessory and positioned in the centre of the headset in a round housing otherwise covered by a rubber plug. The front suspension had a single damper and integral spring. The wheels had a 9" diameter. The script on the leg-shield was dark blue but from 1 October 1967 it was finished in black. From the same year the 50 N was produced with an elongated frame.

Presentation
Milan Show 1966

Price
L. 105,000

Production
50 N: 30,932 examples
50 N allungata: 87,063 examples

Colours
apple green (Max Meyer 12986302)
turquoise (Max Meyer 12680110)

Frame numbers
50 L: V5A1T 500001-530932
50 L allungata: V5A1T 540001-637063

The L was a more lavishly appointed version of the N. The leg-shield had aluminium edging, the scripts on the leg-shield and above the rear light were in relief, the front mudguard was fitted with decorative trim, the rubber strips on the platform had aluminium profiles, the saddle was fitted with a front hook and the headlight had a stainless steel bezel. The L had front suspension featuring a dual-action hydraulic damper. From 1967 it was produced with the elongated frame.

ENGINE

CYLINDERS/CYCLE	single/2-stroke
DISPLACEMENT	49.8 cc
BORE AND STROKE	38.4 43 mm
COMPRESSION RATIO	7.2:1
POWER/REVS	1.5 hp/ 4500 rpm
TORQUE/REVS	n.a.
COOLING	forced air
INDUCTION SYSTEM	rotary valve
FUEL SYSTEM	Dell'Orto carburettor (16 mm)
OIL/FUEL RATIO	2%
IGNITION	flywheel - magneto
STARTING	kick-start lever
CLUTCH	multiplate, oil-bath
GEARBOX	3 speeds, grip-shift

FRAME, WHEELS, SUSPENSION, BRAKES

FRAME	monocoque
FRONT SUSPENSION	trailing arm with coil spring and damper
REAR SUSPENSION	coil spring and damper
FINAL DRIVE	direct
WHEELS	interchangeable, cantilevered with split rim
FRONT BRAKE	125 mm drum
REAR BRAKE	125 mm drum
TYRES	2.75 x 9 front 2.75 x 9 rear

DIMENSIONS/WEIGHT

LENGTH	1655 mm 50 allungata: 1655 mm
WIDTH	700 mm
SADDLE HEIGHT	700 mm
WHEELBASE	1166 mm 50 allungata: 1175 mm
FUEL TANK	5.3 litres
WEIGHT	66 kg

DECLARED PERFORMANCE

MAXIMUM SPEED	40 kph
ACCELERATION	n.a.
FUEL CONSUMPTION	1.5 l/100 kph

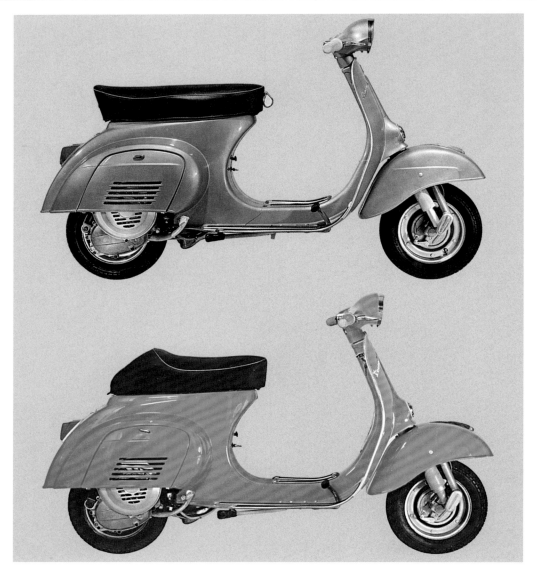

50 S

V5SA1T

1963-1968

Presentation
Milan Show 1963

Price
L. 112,000

Production
29.900 examples

Colours
amethyst grey (Max Meyer 12988710)

Frame numbers
V5SA1T 1101-31000

The 50 S series was destined for export markets. It had a two-seater saddle and was fitted with 10" tyres. The rear light was finished in the same colour as the body. The gearbox had four speeds. This was a model that, despite a displacement of just 50 cc, was a lively performer thanks to its 2.5 hp engine. It could even carry a passenger. For this reason it did not satisfy the Italian legislation of the time and was destined for European markets, in particular Germany.

DAS FAHRZEUG FÜR DIE GANZE FAMILIE

ENGINE	
CYLINDERS/CYCLE	single/2-stroke
DISPLACEMENT	49.8 cc
BORE AND STROKE	38.4 43 mm
COMPRESSION RATIO	7.2:1
POWER/REVS	2.5 hp/ 5800 rpm
TORQUE/REVS	n.a.
COOLING	forced air
INDUCTION SYSTEM	rotary valve
FUEL SYSTEM	Dell'Orto carburettor (16 mm)
OIL/FUEL RATIO	2%
IGNITION	flywheel - magneto
STARTING	kick-start lever
CLUTCH	multiplate, oil-bath
GEARBOX	4 speeds, grip-shift
FRAME, WHEELS, SUSPENSION, BRAKES	
FRAME	monocoque
FRONT SUSPENSION	trailing arm with coil spring and damper
REAR SUSPENSION	coil spring and damper
FINAL DRIVE	direct
WHEELS	interchangeable, cantilevered with split rim
FRONT BRAKE	125 mm drum
REAR BRAKE	125 mm drum
TYRES	3.00 x 10 front 3.10 x 10 rear
DIMENSIONS/WEIGHT	
LENGTH	1630 mm
WIDTH	610 mm
SADDLE HEIGHT	745 mm
WHEELBASE	1166 mm
FUEL TANK	5.3 litres
WEIGHT	66 kg
DECLARED PERFORMANCE	
MAXIMUM SPEED	60 kph
ACCELERATION	n.a.
FUEL CONSUMPTION	1.8 l/100 km

Die VESPA 50 S ist eine zeitgemäße VESPA-Fortentwicklung. Sie vereinigt in sich 20jährige VESPA-Tradition und die Fertigungs-Erfahrung von fast 3 Millionen VESPA-Rollern.

Millionenfach bewährte Technik und praktische Eleganz

25. Sep. 1966

Ab 16 Jahren zu fahren ·

Führerschein IV
Steuerfrei

Der ideale Roller für die ganze Familie!

50 Super Sprint

Presentation
Milan Show 1963

Price
export markets only

Production
2,525 examples

Colours
white (Max Meyer 12985178)

Frame numbers
V5SS1T 1001-3525

The 50 SS series, destined for export markets, was characterised by a two-seater saddle with an opening, hinged front section. It was the 50 cc version of the 90 SS and it had an elongated and chromed exhaust and the spare wheel located vertically on the platform and topped by a glovebox. From 1971 the SS was renamed as the Sprinter (V5SS2T).

ENGINE

CYLINDERS/CYCLE	single/2-stroke
DISPLACEMENT	49.8 cc
BORE AND STROKE	38.4 x 43 mm
COMPRESSION RATIO	7.2:1
POWER/REVS	3.7 hp/ 7000 rpm
TORQUE/REVS	n.a.
COOLING	forced air
INDUCTION SYSTEM	rotary valve
FUEL SYSTEM	Dell'Orto carburettor (16 mm)
OIL/FUEL RATIO	2%
IGNITION	flywheel - magneto
STARTING	kick-start lever
CLUTCH	multiplate, oil-bath
GEARBOX	4 speeds, grip-shift

FRAME, WHEELS, SUSPENSION, BRAKES

FRAME	monocoque
FRONT SUSPENSION	trailing arm with coil spring and damper
REAR SUSPENSION	coil spring and damper
FINAL DRIVE	direct
WHEELS	interchangeable, cantilevered with split rim
FRONT BRAKE	125 mm drum
REAR BRAKE	125 mm drum
TYRES	3.00 x 10 front 3.00 x 10 rear

DIMENSIONS/WEIGHT

LENGTH	1655 mm
WIDTH	550 mm
SADDLE HEIGHT	745 mm
WHEELBASE	1166 mm
FUEL TANK	5.6 litres
WEIGHT	81 kg

DECLARED PERFORMANCE

MAXIMUM SPEED	70 kph
ACCELERATION	n.a.
FUEL CONSUMPTION	2.2 l/100 km

Presentation	
Milan Show 1963	
Price	
L. 121,000	
Production	
24,000 examples	
Colours	
dark blue (Max Meyer 12987220)	
Frame numbers	
V9A1T 1001-25000	

Destined mainly for export markets, the Vespa 90 was virtually identical to the 50 cc version. The details that distinguished it were the 10" diameter wheels and the more powerful electrical system with a main-beam headlight and a brake light. The leg-shield was fitted with aluminium edge trim, the front suspension had the dual-action damper and the script on the leg-shield was in dark blue, like the single saddle. A two-seater saddle was optional. This rather unsuccessful model did form the basis for the very muscular Super Sprint.

ENGINE

CYLINDERS/CYCLE	single/2-stroke
DISPLACEMENT	88.5 cc
BORE AND STROKE	47x51 mm
COMPRESSION RATIO	7.2:1
POWER/REVS	7.2 hp/ 5250 rpm
TORQUE/REVS	n.a.
COOLING	forced air
INDUCTION SYSTEM	rotary valve
FUEL SYSTEM	Dell'Orto carburettor (16 mm)
OIL/FUEL RATIO	2%
IGNITION	flywheel - magneto
STARTING	kick-start lever
CLUTCH	multiplate, oil-bath
GEARBOX	3 speeds, grip-shift

FRAME, WHEELS, SUSPENSION, BRAKES

FRAME	monocoque
FRONT SUSPENSION	trailing arm with coil spring and damper
REAR SUSPENSION	coil spring and damper
FINAL DRIVE	direct
WHEELS	interchangeable, cantilevered with split rim
FRONT BRAKE	125 mm drum
REAR BRAKE	150 mm drum
TYRES	3.00 x 10 front 3.00 x 10 rear

DIMENSIONS/WEIGHT

LENGTH	1650 mm
WIDTH	610 mm
SADDLE HEIGHT	745 mm
WHEELBASE	1160 mm
FUEL TANK	5 litres
WEIGHT	73 kg

DECLARED PERFORMANCE

MAXIMUM SPEED	80 kph
ACCELERATION	n.a.
FUEL CONSUMPTION	1.8 l/100 km

Presentation
Milan Show 1965

Price
L. 137,000

Production
5,309 examples

Colours
cobalt blue (Max Meyer 12680983)
red (Max Meyer 22685850)

Frame numbers
V9SS1T 1001-6309

ENGINE

CYLINDERS/CYCLE	single/2-stroke
DISPLACEMENT	88.5 cc
BORE AND STROKE	47 x 51 mm
COMPRESSION RATIO	8.7:1
POWER/REVS	6 hp/ 6000 rpm
TORQUE/REVS	n.a.
COOLING	forced air
INDUCTION SYSTEM	rotary valve
FUEL SYSTEM	Dell'Orto carburettor (16 mm)
OIL/FUEL RATIO	2%
IGNITION	flywheel - magneto
STARTING	kick-start lever
CLUTCH	multiplate, oil-bath
GEARBOX	4 speeds, grip-shift

FRAME, WHEELS, SUSPENSION, BRAKES

FRAME	monocoque
FRONT SUSPENSION	trailing arm with coil spring and damper
REAR SUSPENSION	coil spring and damper
FINAL DRIVE	direct
WHEELS	interchangeable, cantilevered with split rim
FRONT BRAKE	125 mm drum
REAR BRAKE	150 mm drum
TYRES	3.00 x 10 front 3.00 x 10 rear

DIMENSIONS/WEIGHT

LENGTH	1650 mm
WIDTH	550 mm
SADDLE HEIGHT	745 mm
WHEELBASE	1160 mm
FUEL TANK	5 litres
WEIGHT	77 kg

DECLARED PERFORMANCE

MAXIMUM SPEED	93 kph
ACCELERATION	0-70 kph: 12.7 sec.
FUEL CONSUMPTION	2.6 l/100 km

While the sporting Vespa of the Fifties was clearly the Sei Giorni, the Super Sprint was its heir in the Sixties. Small, compact and with high performance, it was sharply differentiated with respect to its sister models. Its styling left little to the imagination with regard to its sporting vocation. Even the bodywork was cut-down to make it particularly sleek. The handlebars were also narrower. However, in order to reinforce this sporting image, Piaggio came up with a styling feature that made this model unique: the spare wheel was mounted vertically in the centre of the platform and was topped with a false fuel tank (in reality a glovebox) with a chest pad like those fitted to racing motorcycles. In this way the rider was invited to lean forwards as low as possible, just as one would do when trying to obtain maximum performance. Another component that characterised the SS was the chrome-plated and elongated exhaust, very different in shape to the one fitted to the other models. Its particularly whistling exhaust note led many owners of the later 125 Primavera to adopt this modification. The 90 SS's performance was interesting but less dramatic than its image promised: it could achieve a maximum speed of just over 90 kph. However, the appeal of this so un-Vespa-like Vespa was irresistible to sixteen-year-olds and all those who enjoyed riding sports scooters. This was demonstrated in the races for which it was entered, from the Giro d'Italia to circuit races at Imola and Vallelunga, not to speak of the gymkhanas in which the SS dominated thanks to its extraordinary manoeuvrability. Between 1971 and 1974, 3,515 examples of the celebrated "Gruppo Piloti Sportivi" special version were constructed (V9SS2T), distinguished by the absence of the spare wheel and the glovebox.

Presentation
Milan Show 1959

Price
L. 122,000

Production
115,431 examples
VNA1T: 67,031 examples
VNA2T: 48,400 examples

Colours
VNA1T: solid grey (Max Meyer 15046)
VNA2T: beige (Max Meyer 15099)

Frame numbers
1957: VNA1T 001001-068031
1958: VNA2T 068032-116431

ENGINE

CYLINDERS/CYCLE	single/2-stroke
DISPLACEMENT	123.7 cc
BORE AND STROKE	54 x 54 mm
COMPRESSION RATIO	6.5:1
POWER/REVS	4.5 HP/ 5000 rpm
TORQUE/REVS	n.a.
COOLING	forced air
INDUCTION SYSTEM	flat piston/ 2 transfer ports, opposing ports
FUEL SYSTEM	Dell'Orto UA 16 S1 carburettor (16 mm)
OIL/FUEL RATIO	5%
IGNITION	flywheel - magneto
STARTING	kick-start lever
CLUTCH	multiplate, oil-bath
GEARBOX	3 speeds

FRAME, WHEELS, SUSPENSION, BRAKES

FRAME	monocoque
FRONT SUSPENSION	trailing arm with coil spring and damper
REAR SUSPENSION	coil spring and damper
FINAL DRIVE	direct
WHEELS	interchangeable, cantilevered with split rim
FRONT BRAKE	125 mm drum
REAR BRAKE	127 mm drum
TYRES	3.50 x 8 front 3.50 x 8 rear

DIMENSIONS/WEIGHT

LENGTH	1655 mm
WIDTH	790 mm
SADDLE HEIGHT	700 mm
WHEELBASE	1130 mm
FUEL TANK	6.5 litres
WEIGHT	80 kg

DECLARED PERFORMANCE

MAXIMUM SPEED	75 kph
ACCELERATION	n.a.
FUEL CONSUMPTION	1.8 l/100 km

The 1958 version of the 125 was recognisable by its high, handlebar-mounted headlight. This configuration had only previously been seen on the budget U model from 1953 and then on the 150 models. Henceforth the headlight was to remain in this position. The headset was composed of two half-shells. Other styling features that characterised this series included the ribbing on the side-panels and the slots, all of the same length, corresponding to the air intake. For the first time the frame was composed of two half shells welded together with a central reinforcing rib. The engine cover was removable.

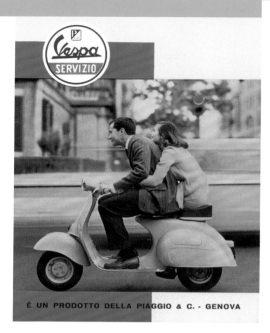

È UN PRODOTTO DELLA PIAGGIO & C. - GENOVA

vespizzatevi!

Vespa 125

MOTORE: a 2 tempi - 125 cc. - 4,5 CV.

CAMBIO: a tre velocità.

ALIMENTAZIONE: a gravità con miscela benzina/olio - capacità del serbatoio litri 7,7 compresa riserva.

TELAIO: a guscio in lamiera di acciaio stampata.

RUOTE: intercambiabili: pneumatici da 3,5 x 8" a bassa pressione.

IMPIANTO ELETTRICO: Accensione: mediante bobina alta tensione del volano - magnete. Illuminazione: alimentata in c.a. direttamente da due bobine B.T. del volano-magnete.

VELOCITA': 75 Km. all'ora.

CONSUMO: 1 litro ogni 55 Km.

PESO: Kg. 81.

Presentation
Milan Show 1959

Price
L. 122,000

Production
122.547 examples
VNB1T: 88,849 examples
VNB2T: 33,698 examples

Colours
light blue (Max Meyer 12988840)

Frame numbers
1959: VNB1T 01001-89850
1960: VNB2T 01001-34699

The headset was still composed of two half-shells. In order to meet the requirements of the new Highway Code this model was fitted with a brake light and a suitably uprated electrical system. The most important modification concerned the new engine using the rotary valve induction system and the possibility of running on a 2% rather than a 5% fuel/oil mixture. The carburettor was located on the crankcase rather than on the cylinder barrel. The reduced oil percentage was due to the fact that with the induction system the mixture was sprayed directly on the conrod assembly, thus lubricating the bearings. The intake port in the crankcase was actuated on each rotation by the opening and closing of the left-hand crankshaft counterweight. The advantages were: more flexible power delivery, less coking and lower running costs. The gearbox had three speeds. The VNB1 version had a carburettor with no choke and an optional speedometer. The VNB2T version had a choke and a standard speedometer.

ENGINE	
CYLINDERS/CYCLE	single/2-stroke
DISPLACEMENT	123.7 cc
BORE AND STROKE	52.5 x 57 mm
COMPRESSION RATIO	7.2:1
POWER/REVS	4.5 HP/ 5000 rpm
TORQUE/REVS	n.a.
COOLING	forced air
INDUCTION SYSTEM	flat piston/ 2 transfer ports, opposing ports
FUEL SYSTEM	Dell'Orto SI 20/15 carburettor (20 mm)
OIL/FUEL RATIO	2%
IGNITION	flywheel - magneto
STARTING	kick-start lever
CLUTCH	multiplate, oil-bath
GEARBOX	3 speeds
FRAME, WHEELS, SUSPENSION, BRAKES	
FRAME	monocoque
FRONT SUSPENSION	trailing arm with coil spring and damper
REAR SUSPENSION	coil spring and damper
FINAL DRIVE	direct
WHEELS	interchangeable, cantilevered with split rim
FRONT BRAKE	124 mm drum
REAR BRAKE	126 mm drum
TYRES	3.50 x 8 front 3.50 x 8 rear
DIMENSIONS/WEIGHT	
LENGTH	1655 mm
WIDTH	790 mm
SADDLE HEIGHT	700 mm
WHEELBASE	1130 mm
FUEL TANK	6.5 litres
WEIGHT	80 kg
DECLARED PERFORMANCE	
MAXIMUM SPEED	75 kph
ACCELERATION	n.a.
FUEL CONSUMPTION	1.8 l/100 km

È UN PRODOTTO DELLA PIAGGIO & C. - GENOVA

LA NUOVA 125 A DISTRIBUZIONE ROTANTE

La Vespa 125 nella sua edizione 1960 è caratterizzata da un motore sostanzialmente nuovo, analogo a quello già adottato con successo dalla Vespa 150. Esso raccoglie la specifica esperienza della Piaggio sui 2 tempi e introduce un nuovo sistema di distribuzione i cui risultati consentono l'impiego di miscela meno costosa, la riduzione delle spese di manutenzione, unite alla massima elasticità del motore.

Per valutare i benefici che la distribuzione rotante porta direttamente al funzionamento termo-dinamico del motore, occorre fissare l'attenzione sul fatto che la curva di potenza ottenuta è particolarmente piatta; ciò, come è noto, rende il motore atto a funzionare su di un largo campo di giri e ad adeguarsi automaticamente, con lievi variazioni di velocità, alle variazioni di resistenza al moto del veicolo (vento contrario, pendenza ecc.).

La riduzione della percentuale di olio sulla miscela ed il notevole effetto raffreddante a cui è sottoposto tutto il complesso pistone-cilindro rendono praticamente insignificante la formazione di incrostazioni con conseguente economia d'esercizio da parte degli utenti.

La lunghezza del condotto di aspirazione è ridottissima e quindi la resistenza al passaggio del gas è quella del solo carburatore. Si ottengono quindi i vantaggi del diagramma di aspirazione corretto: coppia motrice elevata ai bassi regimi e quindi motore molto elastico.

Le pendenze che si incontrano normalmente nelle strade di comunicazione, si superano agevolmente in 3ª anche con due persone a bordo; la 2ª porta velocemente su qualsiasi salita; la 1ª è solo una marcia di spunto adatta ai fondi cattivi ed ai fuori strada.

SOSPENSIONI

La sospensione anteriore è realizzata mediante molla conica elicoidale ed ammortizzatore idraulico a doppio effetto. La sospensione posteriore è munita di molla biconica elicoidale a flessibilità variabile e di ammortizzatore idraulico coassiale a doppio effetto.

COMANDI

I comandi sono razionalmente riuniti sul manubrio. A sinistra vi è la leva della frizione (1) e il comando cambio (2); a destra la leva del freno anteriore (4), la manopola del gas (5) e il gruppo commutatore-deviatore (3), clacson e bottone di massa. La nuova 125 viene fornita con contachilometri incorporato (6).

ILLUMINAZIONE

Nel proiettore anteriore è montata una lampada biluce da 6 V. 25/25 W. con posizione abbagliante, anabbagliante e luce di città. L'impianto elettrico è completato dalla lampadina d'illuminazione contachilometri, dal fanalino posteriore, dalla luce targa e dalla luce Stop.

Presentation
Milan Show 1961

Price
L. 127,000

Production
101,784 examples
VNB3T: 55,695 examples
VNB4T: 46,089 examples

Colours
light grey (Max Meyer 15210)

Frame numbers
1961: VNB3T 034700-090395
1962: VNB4T 0903396-0136485

The second series was recognisable by the headset design, now a one-piece cast aluminium component. The rear light was chromed rather than painted. The brake pedal had an anti-slip rubber cover. The leg-shield featured aluminium edging. The gearbox again had three speeds. The VNB3T version lacked trim elements on the side-panels and was not fitted with a battery. The VNB4T version had squared-off rear bodywork allowing a number plate to be attached and was fitted with two aluminium trim elements on the side-panels.

La Vespa 125 mod. 1962
vanta nei confronti dei modelli precedenti ulteriori perfezionamenti tecnici nel gruppo motore e migliorie di carattere estetico-funzionale

Il manubrio è stato migliorato sia da un punto di vista estetico che strutturale. Il faro di maggiore diametro è dotato di elevate caratteristiche fotometriche

Guida comoda facile e protetta

Le ruote piccole rendono assai maneggevole il veicolo e ne aumentano il comfort di marcia

Lo scooter più venduto nel mondo

Presentation
Milan Show 1963

Price
L. 138,000

Production
76,677 examples
VNB5T: 42,239 examples
VNB6T: 34,438 examples

Colours
grey (Max Meyer 12988710)

Frame numbers
1963: VNB5T 01001-043240
1965: VNB6T 01001-037028

The most important modification introduced with the third series was the new four-speed gearbox. The VNB5T version featured body-coloured painted wheels and a small, round rear light. The VNB6T version had wheels finished in aluminium silver and a larger, square rear light. The script on the leg-shield was in relief. The possibility of using a 2% fuel-oil mixture and the introduction of the four-speed gearbox made this model attractive to a broad clientele. The Vespa was always up-to-date and its popularity was reflected in its commercial success.

125 Super

VNC1T

1965-1969

Presentation
Milan Show 1965

Price
L. 145,000

Production
24,146 examples

Colours
light green (Max Meyer 12986303) –
white (Max Meyer 12983412)

Frame numbers
VNC1T 1001-025146

This budget model retained the 8" wheels but was to be the last Vespa to use them. The bodywork was modified and updated thanks to the sleeker and more angular styling also seen on the GL. The leg-shield featured aluminium edging. The speedometer had an oval face, while the headlight was round and had no bezel. It is a particular model which matches an updated styling with the old diameter wheels. It is not appreciated by the market and was replaced by the GT model.

ENGINE

CYLINDERS/CYCLE	single/2-stroke
DISPLACEMENT	123.4 cc
BORE AND STROKE	52.5 x 57 mm
COMPRESSION RATIO	7.7:1
POWER/REVS	7.4 hp/ 5000 rpm
TORQUE/REVS	n.a.
COOLING	forced air
INDUCTION SYSTEM	rotary valve
FUEL SYSTEM	Dell'Orto SI 20/15 carburettor (15 mm)
OIL/FUEL RATIO	2%
IGNITION	flywheel - magneto
STARTING	kick-start lever
CLUTCH	multiplate, oil-bath
GEARBOX	4 speeds, grip-shift

FRAME, WHEELS, SUSPENSION, BRAKES

FRAME	monocoque
FRONT SUSPENSION	trailing arm with coil spring and damper
REAR SUSPENSION	coil spring and damper
FINAL DRIVE	direct
WHEELS	interchangeable, cantilevered with split rim
FRONT BRAKE	125 mm drum
REAR BRAKE	127 mm drum
TYRES	3.50 x 8 front 3.50 x 8 rear

DIMENSIONS/WEIGHT

LENGTH	1740 mm
WIDTH	670 mm
SADDLE HEIGHT	700 mm
WHEELBASE	1200 mm
FUEL TANK	7.5 litres
WEIGHT	87 kg

DECLARED PERFORMANCE

MAXIMUM SPEED	85 kph
ACCELERATION	0-75kph :18.5 sec.
FUEL CONSUMPTION	100 km/2,1 l

Presentation
Milan Show 1966

Price
L. 152,000

Production
51,582 examples

Colours
grey-blue (Max Meyer 12987305)

Frame numbers
VNL2T 30001-81582

This model was distinguished principally by its 10" wheels. The performance was improved thanks to a higher compression ratio. A trapezoidal headlight was fitted. The transformation was now complete: the bodywork was even more modern (thanks in part to the new headlight) and the wheels were larger in diameter. The teenage public at which the scooter was aimed showed their appreciation of its innovative styling and notable performance, both key elements in its great success.

ENGINE

CYLINDERS/CYCLE	single/2-stroke
DISPLACEMENT	123 cc
BORE AND STROKE	52.5 x 57 mm
COMPRESSION RATIO	7.7:1
POWER/REVS	6.27 hp/ 4500 rpm
TORQUE/REVS	n.a.
COOLING	forced air
INDUCTION SYSTEM	rotary valve
FUEL SYSTEM	Dell'Orto SI 20/17D carburettor (17 mm)
OIL/FUEL RATIO	2%
IGNITION	flywheel - magneto
STARTING	kick-start lever
CLUTCH	multiplate, oil-bath
GEARBOX	4 speeds, grip-shift

FRAME, WHEELS, SUSPENSION, BRAKES

FRAME	monocoque
FRONT SUSPENSION	trailing arm with coil spring and damper
REAR SUSPENSION	coil spring and damper
FINAL DRIVE	direct
WHEELS	interchangeable, cantilevered with split rim
FRONT BRAKE	125 mm drum
REAR BRAKE	127 mm drum
TYRES	3.50 x 10 front 3.50 x 10 rear

DIMENSIONS/WEIGHT

LENGTH	1770 mm
WIDTH	670 mm
SADDLE HEIGHT	810 mm
WHEELBASE	1200 mm
FUEL TANK	7.5 litres
WEIGHT	89 kg

DECLARED PERFORMANCE

MAXIMUM SPEED	88 kph
ACCELERATION	0-75 kph: 18.5 sec.
FUEL CONSUMPTION	100 km/2,1 l

311

Presentation
Milan Show 1965

Price
L. 128,000

Production
17,100 examples

Colours
met. light blue (Max Meyer 12680110)

Frame numbers
VMA1T 01001 - 018100

The 125 that appeared in 1965 was based on the small frame initially conceived for the 50. For the first time, the frame featured side-panels welded to the main body. Access to the engine was via a lateral hatch. The engine was also new and for the first time featured a cylinder angled at 45° rather than horizontal. 10" wheels were fitted to a 125 model for the first time. A single-or two-seater saddle could be fitted.
The front suspension featured a coil-over damper. While this was an interesting model it was relatively unsuccessful due to its weak performance. To make amends, Piaggio introduced the Primavera version, which thanks to its sparkling performance was enormously successful.

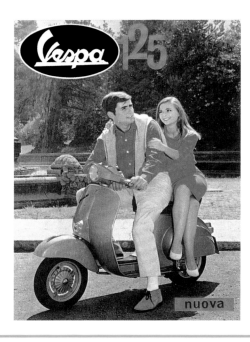

ENGINE

CYLINDERS/CYCLE	single/2-stroke
DISPLACEMENT	121.16 cc
BORE AND STROKE	55 x 51 mm
COMPRESSION RATIO	7.2.1
POWER/REVS	4.8 hp/ 4500 rpm
TORQUE/REVS	n.a.
COOLING	forced air
INDUCTION SYSTEM	rotary valve
FUEL SYSTEM	Dell'Orto SHB 16/16 carburettor (16 mm)
OIL/FUEL RATIO	2%
IGNITION	flywheel - magneto
STARTING	kick-start lever
CLUTCH	multiplate, oil-bath
GEARBOX	4 speeds, grip-shift

FRAME, WHEELS, SUSPENSION, BRAKES

FRAME	monocoque
FRONT SUSPENSION	trailing arm with coil spring and damper
REAR SUSPENSION	coil spring and damper
FINAL DRIVE	direct
WHEELS	interchangeable, cantilevered with split rim
FRONT BRAKE	125 mm drum
REAR BRAKE	127 mm drum
TYRES	3.00 x 10 front 3.50 x 10 rear

DIMENSIONS/WEIGHT

LENGTH	1650 mm
WIDTH	670 mm
SADDLE HEIGHT	780 mm
WHEELBASE	1160 mm
FUEL TANK	5.6 litres
WEIGHT	76 kg

DECLARED PERFORMANCE

MAXIMUM SPEED	80 kph
ACCELERATION	n.a.
FUEL CONSUMPTION	100 km/2 l

Presentation
Milan Show 1965

Price
L. 148,000

Production
348,812 examples

Colours
met. blue (Max Meyer 15067)

Frame numbers
VBA1T 1001 - 125040

The 150 actually adopted the rotary valve induction system that allowed a 2% fuel/oil mixture to be run before the 125. The carburettor was located on the crankcase rather than on the cylinder barrel. The reduced oil percentage was due to the fact that with the induction system the mixture was sprayed directly on the conrod assembly, thus lubricating the bearings. The intake port in the crankcase was actuated on each rotation by the opening and closing of the left-hand crankshaft counterweight. The advantages were significant: more flexible power delivery, less coking and lower running costs.

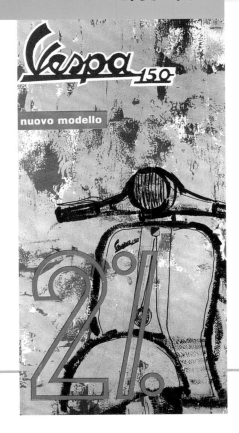

ENGINE

CYLINDERS/CYCLE	single/2-stroke
DISPLACEMENT	145.5 cc
BORE AND STROKE	57 x 57 mm
COMPRESSION RATIO	6.5:1
POWER/REVS	5.5 hp/ 5000 rpm
TORQUE/REVS	n.a.
COOLING	forced air
INDUCTION SYSTEM	rotary valve
FUEL SYSTEM	Dell'Orto SI 20/17 carburettor (20 mm)
OIL/FUEL RATIO	2%
IGNITION	flywheel - magneto
STARTING	kick-start lever
CLUTCH	multiplate, oil-bath
GEARBOX	3 speeds, grip-shift

FRAME, WHEELS, SUSPENSION, BRAKES

FRAME	monocoque
FRONT SUSPENSION	trailing arm with coil spring and damper
REAR SUSPENSION	coil spring and damper
FINAL DRIVE	direct
WHEELS	interchangeable, cantilevered with split rim
FRONT BRAKE	125 mm drum
REAR BRAKE	127 mm drum
TYRES	3.50 x 8 front 3.50 x 8 rear

DIMENSIONS/WEIGHT

LENGTH	1770 mm
WIDTH	710 mm
SADDLE HEIGHT	780 мм
WHEELBASE	1185 mm
FUEL TANK	7.7 litres
WEIGHT	83 kg

DECLARED PERFORMANCE

MAXIMUM SPEED	80 kph
ACCELERATION	n.a.
FUEL CONSUMPTION	100 km/2 l

Presentation
Milan Show 1960
Price
L. 153,000
Production
280,148 examples
VBB1T: 145,000 examples
VBB2T: 134,147 examples
Colours
blue (Max Meyer 12680890)
Frame numbers
1960-62: VBB1T 1001-146000
1962-67: VBB2T 146001-280148

The side-panels were fitted with decorative trim. The gearbox had four speeds. The rear section of the VBB1T version was rounded. The VBB2T version had a squared-off rear end to allow for the fitting of a number plate. The battery was removed from the electrical system.

The engine running a 2% oil-fuel mixture was particularly well received thanks to its smoother power delivery. Less coking was also an important advantage. The 8" wheels remained, however, and clients had to move up to the luxurious GL for those with a 10" diameter.

Presentation
Milan Show 1965

Price
L. 148,000

Production
348,812 examples

Colours
met. blue (Max Meyer 15067)

Frame numbers
VBA1T 1001 - 125040

As the GL (Gran Lusso) designation suggests, this model was aimed at the more demanding enthusiasts. The styling was updated with a sleeker front mudguard and chrome trim elements emphasising the sophisticated finish. The headset had a rectangular form, while the headlight was trapezoidal with a chromed bezel. The wheels were enlarged to 10" with the front mudguard also being larger to suit. The steering column shroud formed a single element with the leg-shield which itself was finished with aluminium edging. The Vespa GL script had a new graphic style and was finished in dark blue.

ENGINE

CYLINDERS/CYCLE	single/2-stroke
DISPLACEMENT	145.5 cc
BORE AND STROKE	57 x 57 mm
COMPRESSION RATIO	7.2:1
POWER/REVS	6 hp/5000 rpm
TORQUE/REVS	n.a.
COOLING	forced air
INDUCTION SYSTEM	rotary valve
FUEL SYSTEM	Dell'Orto SI 20/17 carburettor (20 mm)
OIL/FUEL RATIO	2%
IGNITION	flywheel - magneto
STARTING	kick-start lever
CLUTCH	multiplate, oil-bath
GEARBOX	4 speeds, grip-shift

FRAME, WHEELS, SUSPENSION, BRAKES

FRAME	monocoque
FRONT SUSPENSION	trailing arm with coil spring and damper
REAR SUSPENSION	coil spring and damper
FINAL DRIVE	direct
WHEELS	interchangeable, cantilevered with split rim
FRONT BRAKE	125 mm drum
REAR BRAKE	127 mm drum
TYRES	3.50 x 10 front 3.50 x 10 rear

DIMENSIONS/WEIGHT

LENGTH	1770 mm
WIDTH	675 mm
SADDLE HEIGHT	800 mm
WHEELBASE	1200 mm
FUEL TANK	7.5 litres
WEIGHT	97 kg

DECLARED PERFORMANCE

MAXIMUM SPEED	90 kph
ACCELERATION	n.a.
FUEL CONSUMPTION	100 km/2,4 l

Presentation
Milan Show 1965

Price
L. 150,000

Production
553,808 examples

Colours
blue (Max Meyer 12987210)

Frame numbers
VBC1T 1001-554808

As with the 125 Super produced at the same time, this 150 model retained the 8" wheels and was commercially unsuccessful in Italy due to its rather awkward styling.

The headlight was round. This Vespa was destined above all for export markets where it was offered for sale through to the end of the Seventies. The combination of updated bodywork styling and small diameter wheels began to pall and the public showed that it preferred the 10" rims, but the combination of a Vespa 150 with 10" wheels was only available in the form of the Sprint model.

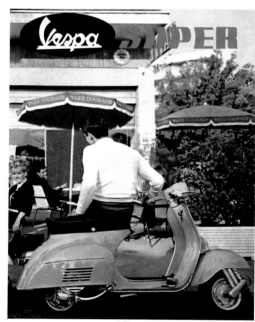

ENGINE

CYLINDERS/CYCLE	single/2-stroke
DISPLACEMENT	145.5 cc
BORE AND STROKE	57 x 57 mm
COMPRESSION RATIO	7.4:1
POWER/REVS	7.7 hp/ 5000 rpm
TORQUE/REVS	n.a.
COOLING	forced air
INDUCTION SYSTEM	rotary valve
FUEL SYSTEM	Dell'Orto SI 20/15 D carburettor (20 mm)
OIL/FUEL RATIO	2%
IGNITION	flywheel - magneto
STARTING	kick-start lever
CLUTCH	multiplate, oil-bath
GEARBOX	4 speeds, grip-shift

FRAME, WHEELS, SUSPENSION, BRAKES

FRAME	monocoque
FRONT SUSPENSION	trailing arm with coil spring and damper
REAR SUSPENSION	coil spring and damper
FINAL DRIVE	direct
WHEELS	interchangeable, cantilevered with split rim
FRONT BRAKE	125 mm drum
REAR BRAKE	127 mm drum
TYRES	3.50 x 8 front 3.50 x 8 rear

DIMENSIONS/WEIGHT

LENGTH	1740 mm
WIDTH	670 mm
SADDLE HEIGHT	800 mm
WHEELBASE	1200 mm
FUEL TANK	7.5 litres
WEIGHT	87 kg

DECLARED PERFORMANCE

MAXIMUM SPEED	90 kph
ACCELERATION	0-75 kph: 17.5 sec.
FUEL CONSUMPTION	100 km/2,2 l

Presentation	
Milan Show 1965	
Price	
L. 160,000	
Production	
121,068 examples	
VLB1T: 119,546	
VLB2T: 1522	
Colours	
met. grey-blue (Max Meyer 12680110)	
Frame numbers	
1965: VLB1T 01001-1205477	
1967: VLB2T 050001-051523	

ENGINE

CYLINDERS/CYCLE	single/2-stroke
DISPLACEMENT	145.5 cc
BORE AND STROKE	57 x 57 mm
COMPRESSION RATIO	7.5:1
POWER/REVS	7.7 hp/ 5000 rpm
TORQUE/REVS	n.a.
COOLING	forced air
INDUCTION SYSTEM	rotary valve
FUEL SYSTEM	Dell'Orto SI 20/17 C carburettor (20 mm)
OIL/FUEL RATIO	2%
IGNITION	flywheel - magneto
STARTING	kick-start lever
CLUTCH	multiplate, oil-bath
GEARBOX	4 speeds, grip-shift

FRAME, WHEELS, SUSPENSION, BRAKES

FRAME	monocoque
FRONT SUSPENSION	trailing arm with coil spring and damper
REAR SUSPENSION	coil spring and damper
FINAL DRIVE	direct
WHEELS	interchangeable, cantilevered with split rim
FRONT BRAKE	125 mm drum
REAR BRAKE	127 mm drum
TYRES	3.50 x 10 front 3.50 x 10 rear

DIMENSIONS/WEIGHT

LENGTH	1770 mm
WIDTH	670 mm
SADDLE HEIGHT	810 mm
WHEELBASE	1200 mm
FUEL TANK	7.6 litres
WEIGHT	89 kg

DECLARED PERFORMANCE

MAXIMUM SPEED	95 kph
ACCELERATION	0-75 kph: 17.5 sec.
FUEL CONSUMPTION	100 km/2,8 l

The 150 Sprint model replaced the GL and boasted notable performance. The revised styling was so successful that it remained untouched for many years. A trapezoidal headlight was fitted and the front mudguard and the side-panels were embellished with trim strips. The styling was modern, with polished embellishments that helped slim the lines. The wheels had 10" rims. A four-speed gearbox was fitted. The Sprint offered notable performance and it enjoyed such commercial success that it was to remain in the Piaggio catalogue in virtually unchanged form throughout the first half of the 1970s.

Presentation
Milan Show 1961

Price
L. 175,000

Production
29,000 examples

Colours
light grey (Max Meyer 12988714)

Frame numbers
VSB1T 1001-029970

The heir to the GS 150, the 160 was distinguished by its modern and sleeker styling. The front suspension was also changed, with the spring incorporating the damper. The brakes had symmetrical rims. The side-panels were removable. The spare wheel was located behind the left-hand side-panel. The saddle was upholstered in light grey. The rear section had a hinged panel concealing a tool bag. In spite of the improvements, the model failed to win place in the enthusiasts' hearts as the GS 150 had done.

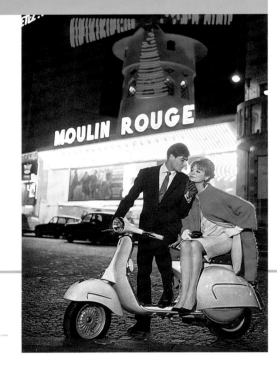

ENGINE

CYLINDERS/CYCLE	single/2-stroke
DISPLACEMENT	158.5 cc
BORE AND STROKE	58 x 60 mm
COMPRESSION RATIO	7.3:1
POWER/REVS	8.2 hp/ 6500 rpm
TORQUE/REVS	n.a.
COOLING	forced air
INDUCTION SYSTEM	opposing ports
FUEL SYSTEM	Dell'Orto SI 27/23 (23 mm)
OIL/FUEL RATIO	2%
IGNITION	flywheel - magneto
STARTING	kick-start lever
CLUTCH	multiplate, oil-bath
GEARBOX	4 speeds, grip-shift

FRAME, WHEELS, SUSPENSION, BRAKES

FRAME	monocoque
FRONT SUSPENSION	trailing arm with coil spring and damper
REAR SUSPENSION	coil spring and damper
FINAL DRIVE	direct
WHEELS	interchangeable, cantilevered with split rim
FRONT BRAKE	170 mm drum
REAR BRAKE	170 mm drum
TYRES	3.50 x 10 front 3.50 x 10 rear

DIMENSIONS/WEIGHT

LENGTH	1795 mm
WIDTH	710 mm
SADDLE HEIGHT	780 mm
WHEELBASE	1220 mm
FUEL TANK	9 litres
WEIGHT	110 kg

DECLARED PERFORMANCE

MAXIMUM SPEED	100 kph
ACCELERATION	n.a.
FUEL CONSUMPTION	100 km/2,9 l

Presentation
Milan Show 1963

Price
L. 181,000

Production
31,00 examples

Colours
light grey (Max Meyer 12988714)

Frame numbers
VSB1T 0030001 - 0061000

The 2nd series GS 160 was recognisable by the glovebox behind the leg-shield. The accessory replaced the tool bag located behind the rear hatch provided with the previous version. The two-seater saddle was upholstered in black. The presence of the new glovebox made this GS highly attractive for all those not wishing to fit a luggage rack. The generously sized lid allowed relatively large objects to be carried that would not have fitted through the previous version's small hatch.

319

Presentation
Milan Show 1964

Price
L. 182,000

Production
35,700 examples

Colours
(Max Meyer 12985850)
white (Max Meyer 12981715)
blue (Max Meyer 12987220)

Frame numbers
VSC1T 001001-0036700

As a replacement for the GS 160, Piaggio introduced a significantly better performing 180 model. Known as the Super Sport, its maximum speed of 105 kph made it the fastest scooter of the period. The styling was more square-cut and more modern, embellished with a number of features from the GL (such as the trapezoidal headlight). Compared with the 160, the rear suspension was lower and the headset was raised by lengthening the steering column. The side panels and the front mudguard were more angular and had aluminium trim strips. The 180 SS was the last Vespa to use a piston ported engine configuration as the successive 180 Rally adopted the rotary valve.

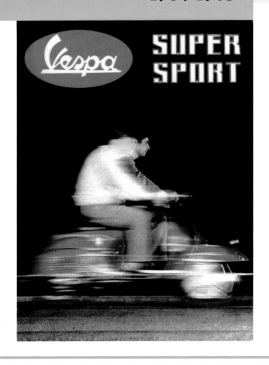

ENGINE

CYLINDERS/CYCLE	single/2-stroke
DISPLACEMENT	181.1 cc
BORE AND STROKE	62 x 60 mm
COMPRESSION RATIO	8:1
POWER/REVS	10 hp/6250 rpm
TORQUE/REVS	n.a.
COOLING	forced air
INDUCTION SYSTEM	opposing ports
FUEL SYSTEM	Dell'Orto carburettor (23 mm)
OIL/FUEL RATIO	5%
IGNITION	flywheel - magneto
STARTING	kick-start lever
CLUTCH	multiplate, oil-bath
GEARBOX	4 speeds, grip-shift

FRAME, WHEELS, SUSPENSION, BRAKES

FRAME	monocoque
FRONT SUSPENSION	trailing arm with coil spring and damper
REAR SUSPENSION	coil spring and damper
FINAL DRIVE	direct
WHEELS	interchangeable, cantilevered with split rim
FRONT BRAKE	150 mm drum
REAR BRAKE	150 mm drum
TYRES	3.50 x 10 front 3.50 x 10 rear

DIMENSIONS/WEIGHT

LENGTH	1770 mm
WIDTH	690 mm
SADDLE HEIGHT	810 mm
WHEELBASE	1230 mm
FUEL TANK	9 litres
WEIGHT	105 kg

DECLARED PERFORMANCE

MAXIMUM SPEED	105 kph
ACCELERATION	n.a.
FUEL CONSUMPTION	100 km/2,8 l

Presentation
Milan Show 1968

Price
L. 187,000

Production
26,495 examples

Colours
yellow (Max Meyer 12982902)
orange (Max Meyer 12982916)

Frame numbers
VSD1T 001001-0027495

The 180 Rally replaced the earlier SS and boasted improvements to both the engine and the frame. The engine was very different and more up-to-date given that it used a rotary valve rather than the piston ported configuration. In terms of styling, the new 180 had a large round headlight and a longer, more comfortable saddle. The speedometer had a black dial. The glovebox mounted behind the leg-shield was of a new design. The side-panels had a more up-to-date look with no trim and were fitted with black gaskets where they met the frame. The handlebar grips were also black. The brake and clutch levers had ball ends for safety. The early examples had a chrome-plated rear light with subsequent models adopting a square unit with a black housing. The exhaust silencer was also new.

ENGINE

CYLINDERS/CYCLE	single/2-stroke
DISPLACEMENT	180.7 cc
BORE AND STROKE	63.5 x 57 mm
COMPRESSION RATIO	8:1
POWER/REVS	10.4 hp/5700 rpm
TORQUE/REVS	n.a.
COOLING	forced air
INDUCTION SYSTEM	rotary valve
FUEL SYSTEM	Dell'Orto carburettor (20 mm)
OIL/FUEL RATIO	2%
IGNITION	flywheel - magneto
STARTING	kick-start lever
CLUTCH	multiplate, oil-bath
GEARBOX	4 speeds, grip-shift

FRAME, WHEELS, SUSPENSION, BRAKES

FRAME	monocoque
FRONT SUSPENSION	trailing arm with coil spring and damper
REAR SUSPENSION	coil spring and damper
FINAL DRIVE	direct
WHEELS	interchangeable, cantilevered with split rim
FRONT BRAKE	150 mm drum
REAR BRAKE	150 mm drum
TYRES	3.50 x 10 front 3.50 x 10 rear

DIMENSIONS/WEIGHT

LENGTH	1770 mm
WIDTH	660 mm
SADDLE HEIGHT	810 mm
WHEELBASE	1230 mm
FUEL TANK	8.2 litres
WEIGHT	102 kg

DECLARED PERFORMANCE

MAXIMUM SPEED	105 kph
ACCELERATION	n.a.
FUEL CONSUMPTION	100 km/2,8 l

The '70s

50 R
50 Special
50 Elestart
125 Primavera
125 Primavera ET3
125 GTR
125 TS
150 Sprint Veloce
200 Rally

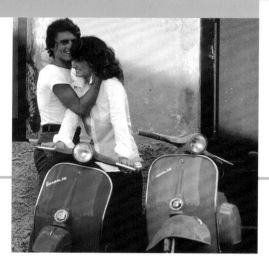

The R version of the 50 was the most economical model in the series. It was distinguished by 9" wheels with self-ventilating drums and a steering column shroud in the same colour as the body. The scripts were set diagonally. The gearbox had three speeds.

Presentation
Milan Show 1969

Price
L. 119,000

Production
about 420,000 examples, complete "R" series: 868,760 examples

Colours
red (Max Meyer 12985806)
blue (Max Meyer 12987275)
light blue (12987402)
yellow (Max Meyer 12982902)

Frame numbers
V5A1T 700001-893568

ENGINE
CYLINDERS/CYCLE	single/2-stroke
DISPLACEMENT	49.8 cc
BORE AND STROKE	38.4 43 mm
COMPRESSION RATIO	7.5:1
POWER/REVS	1.5 hp/ 4500 rpm
TORQUE/REVS	n.a.
COOLING	forced air
INDUCTION SYSTEM	rotary valve
FUEL SYSTEM	Dell'Orto SHB 16/10 carburettor (16 mm)
OIL/FUEL RATIO	2%
IGNITION	flywheel - magneto
STARTING	kick-start lever
CLUTCH	multiplate, oil-bath
GEARBOX	3 speeds, grip-shift

FRAME, WHEELS, SUSPENSION, BRAKES
FRAME	monocoque
FRONT SUSPENSION	trailing arm with coil spring and damper
REAR SUSPENSION	coil spring and damper
FINAL DRIVE	direct
WHEELS	interchangeable, cantilevered with split rim
FRONT BRAKE	125 mm drum
REAR BRAKE	135 mm drum
TYRES	2.75 x 9 front 2.75 x 9 rear

DIMENSIONS/WEIGHT
LENGTH	1655 mm
WIDTH	610 mm
SADDLE HEIGHT	745 mm
WHEELBASE	1175 mm
FUEL TANK	5.2 litres
WEIGHT	67 kg

DECLARED PERFORMANCE
MAXIMUM SPEED	40 kph
ACCELERATION	n.a.
FUEL CONSUMPTION	1.5 l/100 km

324

Presentation
Milan Show 1975

Price
L. 269,000

Production
about 448,000 examples,
complete "R" series: 868,760

Colours
red (Max Meyer 12985806)
blue (Max Meyer 12987275)
light blue (12987402)
yellow (Max Meyer 12982902)

Frame numbers
V5A1T-938761

The 2nd series of the R model featured a number of detail modifications. The saddle was equipped with a hook. The scripts were set horizontally. The gearbox had 3 speeds. At this time there was a strong craze for 50 cc scooters and mopeds among Italian teenagers and this model satisfied their desires with a lightweight offering an excellent price/quality ratio. While the performance was modest, all the appeal of the Vespa scooter remained intact with this series.

The Special was the better-equipped version of the Vespa 50. Compared with the R version of the same period, the main differences were the headset and headlight assembly (square), the finned hubs and the more up-to-date rear light. In stylistic terms it was distinguished by the steering column shroud finished in a colour contrasting with the bodywork. The scripts were set diagonally. The gearbox had three speeds. From 1972, the V5B1T version was fitted with 10" wheels.

Presentation
Milan Show 1969

Price
L. 132,000

Production
189,682 examples
V5A2T: 95,012; V5B1T: 94,670

Colours
white (Max Meyer 12981715)
red (Max Meyer 12985806)
blue (Max Meyer 12987275)
light blue (12987402)
yellow (Max Meyer 12982902)

Frame numbers
1969: V5A2T 1001-96013
1972: V5B1T 1001-95671

ENGINE

CYLINDERS/CYCLE	single/2-stroke
DISPLACEMENT	49.8 cc
BORE AND STROKE	38.4 43 mm
COMPRESSION RATIO	7.5:1
POWER/REVS	1.5 hp/ 4500 rpm
TORQUE/REVS	n.a.
COOLING	forced air
INDUCTION SYSTEM	rotary valve
FUEL SYSTEM	Dell'Orto SHB 16/10 carburettor (16 mm)
OIL/FUEL RATIO	2%
IGNITION	flywheel - magneto
STARTING	kick-start lever
CLUTCH	multiplate, oil-bath
GEARBOX	3 speeds, grip-shift

FRAME, WHEELS, SUSPENSION, BRAKES

FRAME	monocoque
FRONT SUSPENSION	trailing arm with coil spring and damper
REAR SUSPENSION	coil spring and damper
FINAL DRIVE	direct
WHEELS	interchangeable, cantilevered with split rim
FRONT BRAKE	125 mm drum
REAR BRAKE	135 mm drum
TYRES	3.00 x 10 front 3.00 x 10 rear

DIMENSIONS/WEIGHT

LENGTH	1655 mm
WIDTH	610 mm
SADDLE HEIGHT	745 mm
WHEELBASE	1175 mm
FUEL TANK	5.2 litres
WEIGHT	72 kg

DECLARED PERFORMANCE

MAXIMUM SPEED	40 kph
ACCELERATION	n.a.
FUEL CONSUMPTION	1.5 l/100 km

50 Special

2ⁿᵈ series   **V5B3T**   **1975-1983**

Presentation
Milan Show 1975

Price
L. 289,000

Production
563,955 examples

Colours
white (Max Meyer 12981715)
red (Max Meyer 12985806)
blue (Max Meyer 12987275)
light blue (12987402)
yellow (Max Meyer 12982902)

Frame numbers
V5B3T 1001-565056

ENGINE

CYLINDERS/CYCLE	single/2-stroke
DISPLACEMENT	49.8 cc
BORE AND STROKE	38.4 43 mm
COMPRESSION RATIO	7.5:1
POWER/REVS	1.5 hp/ 4500 rpm
TORQUE/REVS	n.a.
COOLING	forced air
INDUCTION SYSTEM	rotary valve
FUEL SYSTEM	Dell'Orto SHB 16/10 carburettor (16 mm)
OIL/FUEL RATIO	2%
IGNITION	flywheel - magneto
STARTING	kick-start lever
CLUTCH	multiplate, oil-bath
GEARBOX	4 speeds, grip-shift

FRAME, WHEELS, SUSPENSION, BRAKES

FRAME	monocoque
FRONT SUSPENSION	trailing arm with coil spring and damper
REAR SUSPENSION	coil spring and damper
FINAL DRIVE	direct
WHEELS	interchangeable, cantilevered with split rim
FRONT BRAKE	125 mm drum
REAR BRAKE	135 mm drum
TYRES	3.00 x 10 front 3.00 x 10 rear

DIMENSIONS/WEIGHT

LENGTH	1655 mm
WIDTH	610 mm
SADDLE HEIGHT	745 mm
WHEELBASE	1175 mm
FUEL TANK	5.2 litres
WEIGHT	72 kg

DECLARED PERFORMANCE

MAXIMUM SPEED	40 kph
ACCELERATION	n.a.
FUEL CONSUMPTION	1.5 l/100 km

The 2nd series of the Special was distinguished by the more modern script set horizontally rather than diagonally. Thanks to the new 10" wheels, the Special's handling was significantly improved and all it lacked was a more user-friendly gearbox. With the introduction of the new four-speed 'box the model was all but perfect and became the dream machine of untold fourteen-year-olds: it was attractive and rode well.

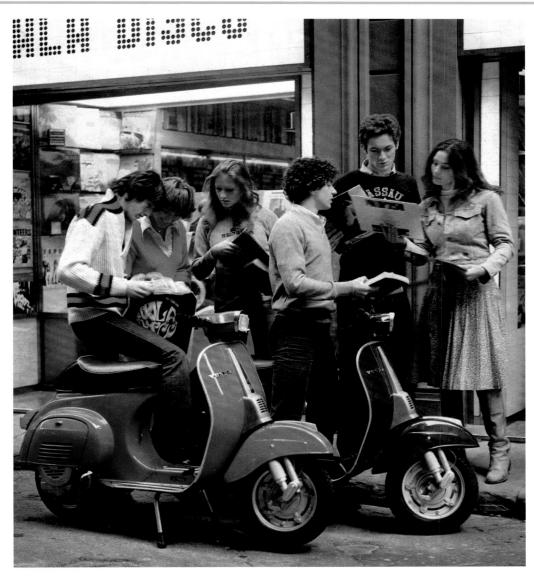

Presentation
Milan Show 1969

Price
L. 162,000

Production
7,373 examples
V5A3T: 4,707
V5B2T: 2,666

Colours
yellow (Max Meyer 12982933)
white (Max Meyer 12981715)
red (Max Meyer 12985847)

Frame numbers
1969: V5A3T 1001-5708
1972: V5B2T 1001-3667

ENGINE

CYLINDERS/CYCLE	single/2-stroke
DISPLACEMENT	49.8 cc
BORE AND STROKE	38.4 43 mm
COMPRESSION RATIO	7.5:1
POWER/REVS	1.5 hp/ 4500 rpm
TORQUE/REVS	n.a.
COOLING	forced air
INDUCTION SYSTEM	rotary valve
FUEL SYSTEM	Dell'Orto SHB 16/10 carburettor (16 mm)
OIL/FUEL RATIO	2%
IGNITION	flywheel - magneto battery (12V)
STARTING	electric
CLUTCH	multiplate, oil-bath
GEARBOX	3 speeds, grip-shift

FRAME, WHEELS, SUSPENSION, BRAKES

FRAME	monocoque
FRONT SUSPENSION	trailing arm with coil spring and damper
REAR SUSPENSION	coil spring and damper
FINAL DRIVE	direct
WHEELS	interchangeable, cantilevered with split rim
FRONT BRAKE	125 mm drum
REAR BRAKE	135 mm drum
TYRES	3.00 x 10 front 3.00 x 10 rear

DIMENSIONS/WEIGHT

LENGTH	1655 mm
WIDTH	610 mm
SADDLE HEIGHT	745 mm
WHEELBASE	1175 mm
FUEL TANK	5.2 litres
WEIGHT	76 kg

DECLARED PERFORMANCE

MAXIMUM SPEED	40 kph
ACCELERATION	n.a.
FUEL CONSUMPTION	1.5 l/100 km

Even though the Vespa had always been extremely easy to start, Piaggio launched a version equipped with electric starting that was aimed above all at its female clientele. In contrast with the Special, the spare wheel could only be located behind the leg-shield given that the left-hand side-panel was occupied by the batteries. The ignition key slot was in the centre of the headset. The gearbox had three speeds.

50 Elestart

2nd series   **V5B4T**   **1975-1976**

The only mechanical modification introduced with the 2nd series of the 50 Elestart was the four-speed gearbox. The scripts were set horizontally. In this period electric starting was the height of sophistication. It was at least 20 years ahead of its time and was seen as an accessory suitable only for girls. The four-speed gearbox was not enough to attract the male clientele who opted for the 50 Special.

Presentation
Milan Show 1975

Price
L. 330,000

Production
432 examples

Colours
yellow (Max Meyer 12982933)
white (Max Meyer 12981715)
red (Max Meyer 12985847)

Frame numbers
V5B4T 1101-1533

ENGINE

CYLINDERS/CYCLE	single/2-stroke
DISPLACEMENT	49.8 cc
BORE AND STROKE	38.4 43 mm
COMPRESSION RATIO	7.5:1
POWER/REVS	1.5 hp/ 4500 rpm
TORQUE/REVS	n.a.
COOLING	forced air
INDUCTION SYSTEM	rotary valve
FUEL SYSTEM	Dell'Orto SHB 16/10 carburettor (16 mm)
OIL/FUEL RATIO	2%
IGNITION	flywheel - magneto battery (12V)
STARTING	electric
CLUTCH	multiplate, oil-bath
GEARBOX	4 speeds, grip-shift

FRAME, WHEELS, SUSPENSION, BRAKES

FRAME	monocoque
FRONT SUSPENSION	trailing arm with coil spring and damper
REAR SUSPENSION	coil spring and damper
FINAL DRIVE	direct
WHEELS	interchangeable, cantilevered with split rim
FRONT BRAKE	125 mm drum
REAR BRAKE	135 mm drum
TYRES	3.00 x 10 front 3.00 x 10 rear

DIMENSIONS/WEIGHT

LENGTH	1655 mm
WIDTH	610 mm
SADDLE HEIGHT	745 mm
WHEELBASE	1175 mm
FUEL TANK	5.2 litres
WEIGHT	76 kg

DECLARED PERFORMANCE

MAXIMUM SPEED	40 kph
ACCELERATION	n.a.
FUEL CONSUMPTION	1.5 l/100 km

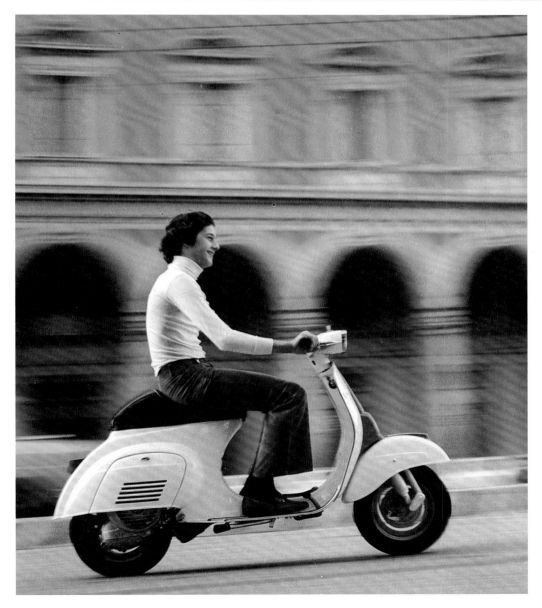

Presentation
Milan Show 1967

Price
L. 137,000 (1968)

Production
around 185,000 examples

Colours
white (Max Meyer 12981715)
met. brown
(Max Meyer 12685130)
met. light blue, met. grey

Frame numbers
VMA2T 020001-205000

The Vespa Primavera was an enormous success. During the years in which it was produced it was the dream machine of sixteen-year-olds attracted by its clean styling and notable performance. Compared with the 125 GTR, it had the same size engine in a smaller and more modern frame. With respect to the Nuova 125, it was distinguished by the hook in front of the saddle. The major difference was the more powerful new engine that provided a 10 kph increase in the maximum speed and sharper acceleration. That the Primavera remained on sale in virtually unchanged form for no less than 15 years speaks volumes for the stregth.

ENGINE

CYLINDERS/CYCLE	single/2-stroke
DISPLACEMENT	121.2 cc
BORE AND STROKE	55 x 51 mm
COMPRESSION RATIO	8.2:1
POWER/REVS	5.6 hp/ 5500 rpm
TORQUE/REVS	n.a.
COOLING	forced air
INDUCTION SYSTEM	rotary valve
FUEL SYSTEM	Dell'Orto SHB 19/19 carburettor (19 mm)
OIL/FUEL RATIO	2%
IGNITION	flywheel - magneto
STARTING	kick-start lever
CLUTCH	multiplate, oil-bath
GEARBOX	4 speeds, grip-shift

FRAME, WHEELS, SUSPENSION, BRAKES

FRAME	monocoque
FRONT SUSPENSION	trailing arm with coil spring and damper
REAR SUSPENSION	coil spring and damper
FINAL DRIVE	direct
WHEELS	interchangeable, cantilevered with split rim
FRONT BRAKE	125 mm drum
REAR BRAKE	150 mm drum
TYRES	3.00 x 10 front 3.00 x 10 rear

DIMENSIONS/WEIGHT

LENGTH	1665 mm
WIDTH	670 mm
SADDLE HEIGHT	750 mm
WHEELBASE	1180 mm
FUEL TANK	5.6 litres
WEIGHT	76 kg

DECLARED PERFORMANCE

MAXIMUM SPEED	88 kph
ACCELERATION	n.a.
FUEL CONSUMPTION	2 l/100 km

of the design. The 1st series was distinguished by the scripts set diagonally on the bodywork and the rear light painted the same colour as the body. The Primavera was popular above all among the young people of the time who identified this model in particular with the slogan "He Who Vespas Eats the Apples".

It was a perfect vehicle, transmitting appeal and innovation. It was a hit with teenagers who appreciated its great manoeuvrability and bright performance. It was also very popular with girls who liked its compact dimensions and the highly elegant styling.

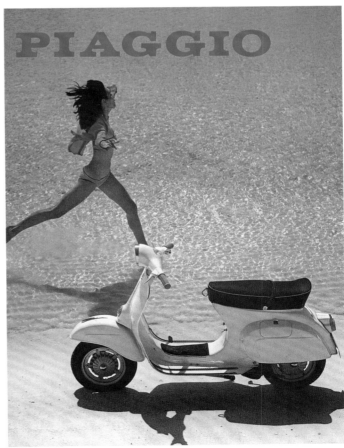

331

125 Primavera

2ⁿᵈ series

VMA2T

1974-1977

Presentation
no official presentation

Price
L. 264,000

Production
around 35,329 examples

Colours
white (Max Meyer 12981715)
met. brown
(Max Meyer 12685130)
met. light blue, met. grey

Frame numbers
VMA2T-240329-205001

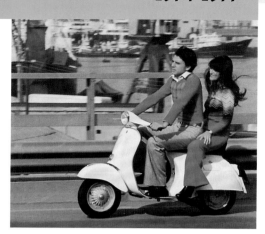

The 2nd series Primavera presented a few styling modifications with respect to the 1st series: the handlebar grips were shaped differently and were black rather than grey. The scripts on the leg-shield and at the rear were set horizontally rather than diagonally. The small, painted rear light was identical to that of the 1st series. The success of this Vespa continued unabated and the changes made to the formula were truly minimal.

Presentation
no official presentation

Price
L. 426,000

Production
around 40,000 examples

Colours
white (Max Meyer 12981715)
met. brown
(Max Meyer 12685130)
met. light blue, met. grey

Frame numbers
VMA2T-0240329

The final Primavera series was characterised by instrumentation with a black dial and a larger, transparent rear light (the same unit fitted to the ET3). The scripts were set horizontally. This series suffered somewhat from the presence of the ET3, especially among young people who were far keener on the version offering greater performance. The styling changes failed to update the model effectively.

Presentation
Milan Show 1975

Price
L. 487,000

Production
144,211 examples

Colours
light blue (Max Meyer 22680108)
blue (Max Meyer 12987228)
orange red (Max Meyer 12985632)

Frame numbers
VMB1T 1101-145312

ENGINE
CYLINDERS/CYCLE	single/2-stroke
DISPLACEMENT	121.2 cc
BORE AND STROKE	55 x 51 mm
COMPRESSION RATIO	9.5:1
POWER/REVS	6 hp/ 5500 rpm
TORQUE/REVS	n.a.
COOLING	forced air
INDUCTION SYSTEM	rotary valve
FUEL SYSTEM	Dell'Orto carburettor (19 mm)
OIL/FUEL RATIO	2%
IGNITION	flywheel - magneto
STARTING	kick-start lever
CLUTCH	multiplate, oil-bath
GEARBOX	4 speeds, grip-shift

FRAME, WHEELS, SUSPENSION, BRAKES
FRAME	monocoque
FRONT SUSPENSION	trailing arm with coil spring and damper
REAR SUSPENSION	coil spring and damper
FINAL DRIVE	direct
WHEELS	interchangeable, cantilevered with split rim
FRONT BRAKE	125 mm drum
REAR BRAKE	150 mm drum
TYRES	3.00 x 10 front 3.00 x 10 rear

DIMENSIONS/WEIGHT
LENGTH	1665 mm
WIDTH	670 mm
SADDLE HEIGHT	750 mm
WHEELBASE	1180 mm
FUEL TANK	5.6 litres
WEIGHT	78 kg

DECLARED PERFORMANCE
MAXIMUM SPEED	90 kph
ACCELERATION	400 m from standing start: 22.9 sec.
FUEL CONSUMPTION	2 l/100 km

334

The ET3 ("Elettronica Travasi 3" or "Electronic 3 Ports") was the sporting version of the Primavera. Thanks to its more powerful engine and new exhaust it offered greater performance. Another modification concerned the electronic ignition adopted in place of the flywheel magneto, with the unit being located in the consequentially less capacious left-hand side-panel. The ET3 was more sporting in appearance, with new trim on the front mudguard and on the side-panels, picking up on the styling of the 200 Rally. Further detail changes concerned the ignition key on the headset, the saddle in denim-effect plastic and the elongated black exhaust (like that of the 90 SS).

Presentation
Milan Show 1968

Price
L. 175,000

Production
51,788 examples

Colours
green (Max Meyer 22680108)
orange (Max Meyer 12985811)
light blue (Max Meyer 22987230)

Frame numbers
VNL2T 100001-151788

With the GTR model (the R stood for "Rinnovato" or "Revised") Piaggio doubled up the 125 range: the GTR continued the evolution of the "large" frame series, with the "small" frame being reserved for the Primavera. The GTR retained the same bodywork as the contemporary 150 Sprint Veloce and 200 Rally models, but could be ridden at 16 years of age. Compared with the preceding 125 series, it was distinguished by the new, larger headlight (130 mm diameter) with a chromed bezel.

ENGINE	
CYLINDERS/CYCLE	single/2-stroke
DISPLACEMENT	123.4 cc
BORE AND STROKE	52.5 x 57 mm
COMPRESSION RATIO	7.8:1
POWER/REVS	7.8 HP/ 5000 rpm
TORQUE/REVS	n.a.
COOLING	forced air
INDUCTION SYSTEM	rotary valve
FUEL SYSTEM	Dell'Orto carburettor (20 mm)
OIL/FUEL RATIO	2%
IGNITION	flywheel - magneto
STARTING	kick-start lever
CLUTCH	multiplate, oil-bath
GEARBOX	4 speeds, grip-shift
FRAME, WHEELS, SUSPENSION, BRAKES	
FRAME	monocoque
FRONT SUSPENSION	trailing arm with coil spring and damper
REAR SUSPENSION	coil spring and damper
FINAL DRIVE	direct
WHEELS	interchangeable, cantilevered with split rim
FRONT BRAKE	160 mm drum
REAR BRAKE	160 mm drum
TYRES	3.50x10 front 3.50x10 rear
DIMENSIONS/WEIGHT	
LENGTH	1770 mm
WIDTH	670 mm
SADDLE HEIGHT	810 mm
WHEELBASE	1200 mm
FUEL TANK	8 litres
WEIGHT	93 kg
DECLARED PERFORMANCE	
MAXIMUM SPEED	92 kph
ACCELERATION	n.a.
FUEL CONSUMPTION	2 l/100 kph

Presentation
Milan Show 1975

Price
L. 411,600

Production
28,704 examples

Colours
brown (Max Meyer 12985875)
 green (Max Meyer 12986380)

Frame numbers
VNL3T 1101-29804

The TS 125 (Turismo Speciale) replaced the GTR of the same displacement. Very similar to the GTR, it was distinguished by a more modern style with no trim on the front mudguard and side-panels. The saddle was slightly different, with a hint of a tail. A glovebox was fitted as standard behind the leg-shield. The script on the leg-shield was set horizontally.

ENGINE

CYLINDERS/CYCLE	single/2-stroke
DISPLACEMENT	123.4 cc
BORE AND STROKE	52.5 x 57 mm
COMPRESSION RATIO	8:1
POWER/REVS	8 hp/ 5600 rpm
TORQUE/REVS	n.a.
COOLING	forced air
INDUCTION SYSTEM	rotary valve
FUEL SYSTEM	Dell'Orto SI 20/20 carburettor (20 mm)
OIL/FUEL RATIO	2%
IGNITION	flywheel - magneto
STARTING	kick-start lever
CLUTCH	multiplate, oil-bath
GEARBOX	4 speeds, grip-shift

FRAME, WHEELS, SUSPENSION, BRAKES

FRAME	monocoque
FRONT SUSPENSION	trailing arm with coil spring and damper
REAR SUSPENSION	coil spring and damper
FINAL DRIVE	direct
WHEELS	interchangeable, cantilevered with split rim
FRONT BRAKE	150 mm drum
REAR BRAKE	150 mm drum
TYRES	3.50 x 10 front 3.50 x 10 rear

DIMENSIONS/WEIGHT

LENGTH	1770 mm
WIDTH	670 mm
SADDLE HEIGHT	810 mm
WHEELBASE	1230 mm
FUEL TANK	7.5 litres
WEIGHT	101 kg

DECLARED PERFORMANCE

MAXIMUM SPEED	93 kph
ACCELERATION	n.a.
FUEL CONSUMPTION	2 l/100 km

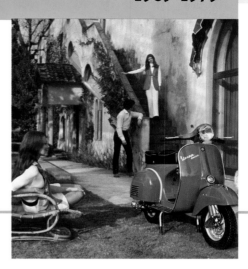

To all intents and purposes the Sprint was a larger-displacement version of the 125 GTR and retained the same styling configuration. The new headlight had a diameter of 130 mm and a chromed bezel. The new hexagonal Piaggio badge was set in the centre of the headset. The rear light had a body-coloured housing.

Presentation
Milan Show 1968
Price
L. 165,000
Production
218,119 examples
Colours
met. grey
(Max Meyer 129801039)
white (Max Meyer 12987230)
green (Max Meyer 12986307)
red (12985847)
blue (Max Meyer 12987275)
Frame numbers
VLB1T 0150001-368,120

ENGINE

CYLINDERS/CYCLE	single/2-stroke
DISPLACEMENT	145.5 cc
BORE AND STROKE	57 x 57 mm
COMPRESSION RATIO	8:1
POWER/REVS	8.5 hp/ 5800 rpm
TORQUE/REVS	n.a.
COOLING	forced air
INDUCTION SYSTEM	rotary valve
FUEL SYSTEM	Dell'Orto SI 20/20 carburettor (20 mm)
OIL/FUEL RATIO	2%
IGNITION	flywheel - magneto
STARTING	kick-start lever
CLUTCH	multiplate, oil-bath
GEARBOX	4 speeds, grip-shift

FRAME, WHEELS, SUSPENSION, BRAKES

FRAME	monocoque
FRONT SUSPENSION	trailing arm with coil spring and damper
REAR SUSPENSION	coil spring and damper
FINAL DRIVE	direct
WHEELS	interchangeable, cantilevered with split rim
FRONT BRAKE	150 mm drum
REAR BRAKE	150 mm drum
TYRES	3.50 x 10 front 3.50 x 10 rear

DIMENSIONS/WEIGHT

LENGTH	1770 mm
WIDTH	670 mm
SADDLE HEIGHT	810 mm
WHEELBASE	1200 mm
FUEL TANK	7.5 litres
WEIGHT	95 kg

DECLARED PERFORMANCE

MAXIMUM SPEED	97 kph
ACCELERATION	n.a.
FUEL CONSUMPTION	2.2 l/100 km

Presentation
no official presentation

Price
L. 187,000

Production
41,275 examples

Colours
orange (Max Meyer 12985875)
met. grey
(Max Meyer 12988200)
red (Max Meyer 12985806)

Frame numbers
VSE1T 001001-0010300
VSE1T 0010301-0042275

ENGINE
CYLINDERS/CYCLE	single/2-stroke
DISPLACEMENT	197.97 cc
BORE AND STROKE	66.5 x 57 mm
COMPRESSION RATIO	8.2:1
POWER/REVS	12.5 HP/ 5700 rpm
TORQUE/REVS	n.a.
COOLING	forced air
INDUCTION SYSTEM	rotary valve
FUEL SYSTEM	Dell'Orto carburettor (24 mm)
OIL/FUEL RATIO	2%
IGNITION	electronic
STARTING	kick-start lever
CLUTCH	multiplate, oil-bath
GEARBOX	4 speeds, grip-shift

FRAME, WHEELS, SUSPENSION, BRAKES
FRAME	monocoque
FRONT SUSPENSION	trailing arm with coil spring and damper
REAR SUSPENSION	coil spring and damper
FINAL DRIVE	direct
WHEELS	interchangeable, cantilevered with split rim
FRONT BRAKE	150 mm drum
REAR BRAKE	150 mm drum
TYRES	3.50x10 front 3.50x10 rear

DIMENSIONS/WEIGHT
LENGTH	1770 mm
WIDTH	670 mm
SADDLE HEIGHT	810 mm
WHEELBASE	1230 mm
FUEL TANK	8.5 litres
WEIGHT	106 kg

DECLARED PERFORMANCE
MAXIMUM SPEED	97 kph
ACCELERATION	0-80 kph: 10.7 sec.
FUEL CONSUMPTION	2.8 l/100 km

The 200 Rally had the largest engine of any Vespa produced up to that point. It was actually a development of the Rally 180 and was equipped with electronic ignition. It was distinguished visually by the presence of white stripes on the sides, sporting graphics that were well suited to the new and particularly lively Rally which with its good performance was a worthy heir to the GS 150. The first series had a n engine kill button located beneath the hook. On request, a version was available with separate lubrication and relative oil tank. The brochure emphasised the model's excellent performance: maximum speed 110 kph, a standing start kilometre in 42 seconds with an exit speed of 100 kph. The second series was distinguished from the first one by the ignition key over the head-lamp.

The '80s

50 PK - PK S
50 PK S Automatica
50 PK XL - PK XLS
50 PK XL Plurimatic
50 PK Rush
125 PK - PK S
125 PK S Automatica
125 PK ETS
125 PK XL - PK XLS
125 PK XL Plurimatic
125 PX
125 PX-E
125 PX Arcobaleno
125 PX-T5
150 PX
150 PX-E
150 PX-E Arcobaleno
200 PE
200 PX-E Arcobaleno

Presentation
Cologne Show 1982
Price
PK: L. 1,148,000
PK/S: L. 1,365,000
Production
PK: 16,411 examples
PK/S: 220,477 examples
Colours
white, red, blue, green
Frame numbers
PK 50: V5X1T 1101-17512
PK/S: V5X2T 1101-221578

The Vespa 50 for the '80s was the PK series: a twin to the larger PK 125. With respect to earlier 50 models, the PK was distinguished by a new frame with angular styling. The riding position was more comfortable with greater distance between the handlebars, saddle and platform. The welds were no longer visible thanks to the edges rolled inwards on the frame and mudguard half-shells. The centre section of the platform was covered with a broad strip of anti-slip rubber. The light alloy headset had a removable centre section for easy access to the internal components. The side-panel covering the engine had a completely smooth, hinged hatch with no louvres. The PK (V5X1T) version was the base model. The PK S (V5X2T) was more sophisticated and

boasted a standard glovebox behind the leg-shield and indicators. From 1985, the versions were designated as respectively the XL (V5X3T) and the XLS (V5S2T) with a number of styling changes to the frontal aspect and the saddle. The angular lines, very different to those of the 1970s failed to attract the same kind of success.

ENGINE	
CYLINDERS/CYCLE	single/2-stroke
DISPLACEMENT	49.79 cc
BORE AND STROKE	38.4 x 43 mm
COMPRESSION RATIO	9:1
POWER/REVS	1.5 hp/ 4500 rpm
TORQUE/REVS	n.a.
COOLING	forced air
INDUCTION SYSTEM	rotary valve
FUEL SYSTEM	Dell'Orto carburettor (19 mm)
OIL/FUEL RATIO	2%
IGNITION	flywheel - magneto
STARTING	kick-start lever
CLUTCH	multiplate, oil-bath
GEARBOX	4 speeds, grip-shift
FRAME, WHEELS, SUSPENSION, BRAKES	
FRAME	monocoque
FRONT SUSPENSION	trailing arm with coil spring and damper
REAR SUSPENSION	coil spring and damper
FINAL DRIVE	direct
WHEELS	interchangeable, cantilevered with split rim
FRONT BRAKE	125 mm drum
REAR BRAKE	150 mm drum
TYRES	3.00 x 10 front 3.00 x 10 rear
DIMENSIONS/WEIGHT	
LENGTH	1675 mm
WIDTH	700 mm
SADDLE HEIGHT	790 mm
WHEELBASE	1175 mm
FUEL TANK	5.8 litres
WEIGHT	70 kg
DECLARED PERFORMANCE	
MAXIMUM SPEED	40 kph
ACCELERATION	n.a.
FUEL CONSUMPTION	2 l/100 km

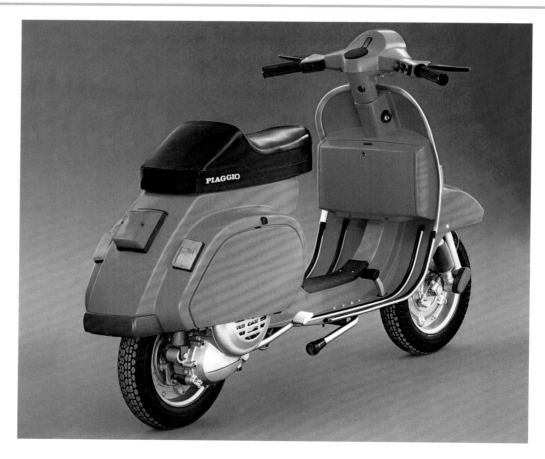

50 PK S Automatica

VA51T-VA52T

1984-1986

Presentation
Cologne Show 1984

Price
L. 1,960,000

Production
2,121 examples

Colours
white, red, blue

Frame numbers
VAS1T 3000001 - 30021.2

The automatic version of the 50 PK was practically identical to the base model with the obvious exception of the automatic gearbox. The left-hand lever controlled the rear brake rather than the clutch, which meant the floor pedal was eliminated. Another minor difference was that the side-panel hatches had louvres rather than being smooth. A glovebox was fitted as standard behind the leg-shield. The engine featured reed valve induction. 80 and 100 cc versions were also produced for export markets. From 1987, the Vespa 50 PK S Automatica (VA51T) evolved into the Plurimatic version (VA52T) to which only minor styling modifications were made.

nuova vespa 50
automatica

Questo depliant è dedicato a te, che ami la libertà, il presente, l'allegria e la magia dell'aria che ti viene incontro, perché annuncia una Vespa nata per te: la nuova Magica Vespa Magic.
Piaggio dedica a te il suo nuovo cambio automatico e la sua linea fresca, essenziale, elegante che ti accompagna nel tuo mondo senza chiederti niente: via la targa, via la patente.

Presentation
Milan Show 1985

Price
L. 1,688,000

Produzione
192,418 examples

Colours
white, red, blue, green

Frame numbers
V5X3T 001101-00193519
XL Elestart: V5X3T3000001-3010706

The PK series was not successful and to compensate Piaggio introduced the PK XL series that improved certain aspects but aggravated others. The styling of the steering shroud and the glovebox behind the leg-shield was more fluid, but the part beneath the saddle and the angular rear light remained awkward. The wheel covers were unpopular. Among the technical improvements were the replacement of the flywheel magneto points with updated electronic ignition. The instrumentation was more comprehensive and now included a fuel level gauge.

Presentation
Cologne Show 1985

Price
L. 1,960,000

Production
XL Plurimatic: 18,396 examples
XLS Plurimatic: 1,569 examples

Colours
white, red, blue

Frame numbers
XL Plurimatic : VA52T 1101-4989
XLS Plurimatic : VA53T 1101-1670

The automatic version of the PK XL was not very well received by the 14-year-olds at whom it was aimed. The automatic transmission worked well, but the styling was unpopular; attempts were made to soften it. The steering shroud and the glovebox behind the leg-shield benefited, but the part beneath the saddle remained ill at ease with the rest of the bodywork. The slotted wheel covers were also unpopular. The electronic ignition replacing the obsolete flywheel magneto points was a welcome step forward. The instrumentation was improved.

Presentation
Milan Show 1987

Price
L. 1,722,000

Production
61,069 examples

Colours
red, white

Frame numbers
V5X4T 1101-62170

With this series of the PK, the company could take advantage of the new regulations that eliminated the restriction of the power output of 1.5 hp. Acceleration from a standing start was improved. Another important innovation concerned the anti-dive front suspension. The Rush was appreciated for its lively engine. A 46% increase in power impressed the younger clientele. But the styling was still unpopular, especially the conspicuous section beneath the saddle and the black finish to certain components.

Le nuove
Vespa 50 RUSH
pungono di più.

Presentation
Cologne Show 1982

Price
PK 125: L. 1,760,000
PK 125 S: L. 1,840,000

Production
PK 125: 7,278 examples
PK 125 S: 61,505 examples

Colours
white, red, green

Frame numbers
PK 125: VMX1T 1101-8378
PK 125 S: VMX5T 1101-62606

The 125 PK was faced with the difficult task of replacing the highly successful 125 Primavera model. Both had the so-called small frame, shared with the 50 models, but the new PK had far more angular styling and was less popular. Comfort was instead improved with more space between headset, saddle and platform. The welding was less conspicuous with the edges of the side-panels and the front mudguard rolled inwards rather than being superimposed. The headset had a removable centre section to improve access to interior. The engine cover hatch was smooth with no louvres. The PK (VMX1T) was the base version. The PK S version (VMX5T) was more sophisticated and fitted with a standard glovebox behind the leg-shield and indicators. From 1986, the versions were unified in the XL version (VMX6T) with a number of styling modifications at the front and to the saddle. PK 80 and PK 100 versions were also produced for export markets.

ENGINE	
CYLINDERS/CYCLE	single/2-stroke
DISPLACEMENT	121.1 cc
BORE AND STROKE	55 x 51 mm
COMPRESSION RATIO	9.25:1
POWER/REVS	6.8 hp/ 5600 rpm
TORQUE/REVS	0.95 kgm-70 kph
COOLING	forced air
INDUCTION SYSTEM	rotary valve
FUEL SYSTEM	Dell'Orto carburettor (19 mm)
OIL/FUEL RATIO	2%
IGNITION	electronic
STARTING	kick-start lever
CLUTCH	multiplate, oil-bath
GEARBOX	4 speeds, grip-shift
FRAME, WHEELS, SUSPENSION, BRAKES	
FRAME	monocoque
FRONT SUSPENSION	trailing arm with coil spring and damper
REAR SUSPENSION	coil spring and damper
FINAL DRIVE	direct
WHEELS	interchangeable, cantilevered with split rim
FRONT BRAKE	150 mm drum
REAR BRAKE	150 mm drum
TYRES	3.00 x 10 front 3.00 x 10 rear
DIMENSIONS/WEIGHT	
LENGTH	1675 mm
WIDTH	700 mm
SADDLE HEIGHT	790 mm
WHEELBASE	1175 mm
FUEL TANK	5.8 litres
WEIGHT	88 kg
DECLARED PERFORMANCE	
MAXIMUM SPEED	90 kph
ACCELERATION	n.a.
FUEL CONSUMPTION	2 l/100 km

Presentation
Milan Show 1983

Price
PK/S Automatica: L. 2,015,000

Produzione
PK/S Automatica: 10,024 examples

Colours
blue, grey

Frame numbers
PK/S Automatica: VAM1T 1101-3366

The 125 Automatica was absolutely innovative: the very first Vespa with automatic transmission. Structurally, the model was the same as the 125 PK S that, in contrast with the base PK, was fitted with a three-port engine for improved performance. Rather than having different positions numbered according to the gear selected, the left-hand handlebar grip had just two, the first corresponding to neutral and the second to drive. The left-hand lever no longer controlled the clutch but the rear brake. This meant that the brake pedal on the platform was eliminated for the first time. Compared with the other PK models, the indicators were larger, the side-panel hatches had louvres and the leg-shield had black edging. A glovebox was fitted as standard. The oil tank

ENGINE	
CYLINDERS/CYCLE	single/2-stroke
DISPLACEMENT	121.1 cc
BORE AND STROKE	55 x 51 mm
COMPRESSION RATIO	10.5:1
POWER/REVS	7.5 hp/ 6200 rpm
TORQUE/REVS	n.a.
COOLING	forced air
INDUCTION SYSTEM	reed valve
FUEL SYSTEM	Dell'Orto carburettor (20 mm)
OIL/FUEL RATIO	2%
IGNITION	electronic
STARTING	kick-start lever
CLUTCH	centrifugal
GEARBOX	continuously variable
FRAME, WHEELS, SUSPENSION, BRAKES	
FRAME	monocoque
FRONT SUSPENSION	trailing arm with coil spring and damper
REAR SUSPENSION	coil spring and damper
FINAL DRIVE	direct
WHEELS	interchangeable, cantilevered with split rim
FRONT BRAKE	150 mm drum
REAR BRAKE	150 mm drum
TYRES	3.00 x 10 front 3.00 x 10 rear
DIMENSIONS/WEIGHT	
LENGTH	1675 mm
WIDTH	700 mm
SADDLE HEIGHT	790 mm
WHEELBASE	1175 mm
FUEL TANK	5.8 litres
WEIGHT	88 kg
DECLARED PERFORMANCE	
MAXIMUM SPEED	90 kph
ACCELERATION	n.a.
FUEL CONSUMPTION	2.4 l/100 km

usually located under the saddle was eliminated. Compared with the manual transmission PK, the major difference concerned the engine which was completely revised. This was apparent visually, with a different configuration visible below the right-hand side-panel. The Automatica engine had a higher compression ratio, a fuel system featuring a larger carburettor and (for the first time) a reed valve induction system rather than the classic flywheel rotary valve. The automatic transmission featured a clutch engaged via the expansion of three centrifugal masses and a trapezoidal belt with a pair of pulleys, the sides of which drew together or separated as the gear ratio varied via a hydraulic actuator in relation to engine speed. There was also a supplementary control to engage a low gear should greater torque be required. While this was an extremely advanced design, it was excessively complicated. From 1987, the Automatic version (VAM1T) evolved into the Plurimatic (VVM1T0) with minor styling modifications and the elimination of the hydraulic device that was the one true defect of the Automatica. While it was technically sophisticated, it was expensive, absorbed power and was fragile, but from the point of view of riding pleasure it was virtually perfect: the Automatica was fun and the passage from a model with a manual gearbox made all other versions seem obsolete. In any case, it was a very important step forward: within a few years there would be no scooters available with manual transmission; except for the Vespa PX!

Presentation
Milan Show 1983

Price
L. 1,847,000

Production
11,711 examples

Colours
red, grey/black stripes

Frame numbers
VMS1T 1101-12811

The ETS was a sporting version of the 125 PK series. It was distinguished by the new, more compact headset, the saddle with a hint of a tail and silk-screened script, the black and silver trim on the front mudguard and the side-panels (somewhat similar to that of the very sporty Rally 200), the black fan housing, the rounded and larger glovebox behind the leg-shield and the elongated exhaust silencer. Furthermore, the steering column shroud was slimmer and pointed, which required the horn to placed to one side on the leg-shield. The crankshaft was strengthened, the intake port was enlarged and the exhaust port and carburettor were improved. The braking performance was also improved thanks to the new floating cams and the anti-dive system applied to the front suspension.

ENGINE	
CYLINDERS/CYCLE	single/2-stroke
DISPLACEMENT	121.1 cc
BORE AND STROKE	55 x 51 mm
COMPRESSION RATIO	9.5:1
POWER/REVS	8.5 hp/ 6000 rpm
TORQUE/REVS	n.a.
COOLING	forced air
INDUCTION SYSTEM	rotary valve
FUEL SYSTEM	Dell'Orto carburettor (20 mm)
OIL/FUEL RATIO	2%
IGNITION	electronic
STARTING	kick-start lever, electric
CLUTCH	multiplate, oil-bath
GEARBOX	4 speeds, grip-shift
FRAME, WHEELS, SUSPENSION, BRAKES	
FRAME	monocoque
FRONT SUSPENSION	trailing arm with coil spring and damper
REAR SUSPENSION	coil spring and damper
FINAL DRIVE	direct
WHEELS	interchangeable, cantilevered with split rim
FRONT BRAKE	150 mm drum
REAR BRAKE	150 mm drum
TYRES	3.00 x 10 front 3.00 x 10 rear
DIMENSIONS/WEIGHT	
LENGTH	1675 mm
WIDTH	700 mm
SADDLE HEIGHT	790 mm
WHEELBASE	1175 mm
FUEL TANK	5.8 litres
WEIGHT	88 kg
DECLARED PERFORMANCE	
MAXIMUM SPEED	97 kph
ACCELERATION	n.a.
FUEL CONSUMPTION	2.4 l/100 km

Presentation
Milan Show 1985

Price
L. 1,847,000

Production
53,750 examples

Colours
red, grey/black stripes

Frame numbers
VMX6T 1101-54751

The PK series failed to find favour with the public. Its styling was far from that of the PX and was excessively angular. To improve the appearance of the model numerous detail modifications were made, giving rise to the PK XL series. Certain aspects, such as the frontal appearance were improved. The new steering shroud and the glovebox located behind the leg-shield had rounded lines more in keeping with the rest of the bodywork. In contrast, other elements aggravated the situation, such as the section beneath the saddle that was uncoordinated and excessively conspicuous. Even the slotted wheel covers came in for criticism. Plaudits were instead gained by the electronic ignition system that replaced the traditional points. Despite the advertising campaign claiming that "Attractive from head to tail", the XL series was one of the least successful of those produced over the years. The styling improved significantly with the successive rounder and more harmonious PK FL2 series.

Bella da capo a coda.

VESPA PK 125 XL

Presentation
Milan Show 1987

Price
PK: n.a.
Elestart: n.a.

Production
n.a.

Colours
n.a.

Frame numbers
VVM1T 1101-20103
Elestart; VVM1T 3000001-3001582

The Plurimatic retained the automatic transmission, in a simplified form. The hydraulic system was replaced with a mechanical centrifugal device. Thanks to the reduced power absorption, lower fuel consumption was achieved without compromising low-speed response. However, the styling was never popular. The more rounded front end with the new steering shroud and the glovebox behind the leg-shield contrasted with an uncoordinated and conspicuous under-saddle section.

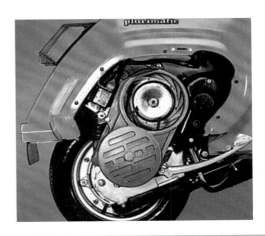

ENGINE

CYLINDERS/CYCLE	single/2-stroke
DISPLACEMENT	121.1 cc
BORE AND STROKE	55 x 51 mm
COMPRESSION RATIO	9.25:1
POWER/REVS	6.8 hp/ 5600 rpm
TORQUE/REVS	0.95 kgm-70 kph
COOLING	forced air
INDUCTION SYSTEM	rotary valve
FUEL SYSTEM	Dell'Orto carburettor (19 mm)
OIL/FUEL RATIO	2%
IGNITION	electronic
STARTING	kick-start lever
CLUTCH	multiplate, oil-bath
GEARBOX	automatic

FRAME, WHEELS, SUSPENSION, BRAKES

FRAME	monocoque
FRONT SUSPENSION	trailing arm with coil spring and damper
REAR SUSPENSION	coil spring and damper
FINAL DRIVE	direct
WHEELS	interchangeable, cantilevered with split rim
FRONT BRAKE	150 mm drum
REAR BRAKE	150 mm drum
TYRES	3.00 x 10 front 3.00 x 10 rear

DIMENSIONS/WEIGHT

LENGTH	1675 mm
WIDTH	700 mm
SADDLE HEIGHT	790 mm
WHEELBASE	1175 mm
FUEL TANK	5.8 litres
WEIGHT	88 kg

DECLARED PERFORMANCE

MAXIMUM SPEED	90 kph
ACCELERATION	n.a.
FUEL CONSUMPTION	2 l/100 km

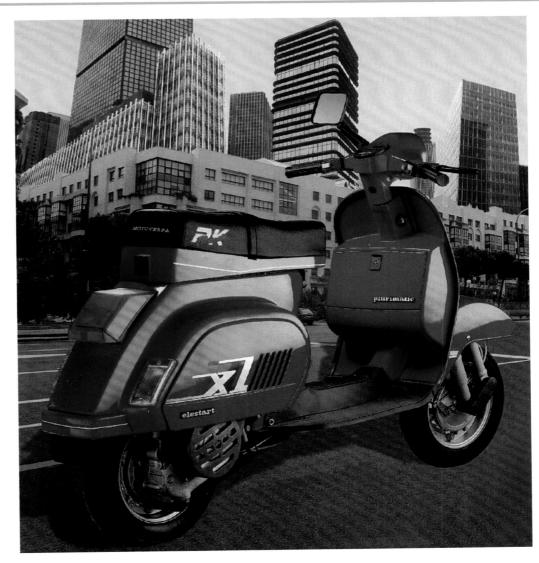

Presentation
Milan Show 1977

Price
L. 767,000

Production
197,147 examples

Colours
white (12981715)
light blue (7002M)

Frame numbers
VNX1T 1101-198248

ENGINE	
CYLINDERS/CYCLE	single/2-stroke
DISPLACEMENT	123.4 cc
BORE AND STROKE	52.5 x 57 mm
COMPRESSION RATIO	8.2:1
POWER/REVS	8 hp/ 5600 rpm
TORQUE/REVS	1.25 kgm/ 3800 rpm
COOLING	forced air
INDUCTION SYSTEM	rotary valve
FUEL SYSTEM	Dell'Orto carburettor (20 mm)
OIL/FUEL RATIO	2%
IGNITION	flywheel magneto
STARTING	kick-start lever, electric
CLUTCH	multiplate, oil-bath
GEARBOX	4 speeds, grip-shift

FRAME, WHEELS, SUSPENSION, BRAKES	
FRAME	monocoque
FRONT SUSPENSION	trailing arm with coil spring and damper
REAR SUSPENSION	coil spring and damper
FINAL DRIVE	direct
WHEELS	interchangeable, cantilevered with split rim
FRONT BRAKE	150 mm drum
REAR BRAKE	150 mm drum
TYRES	3.50 x 10 front 3.50 x 10 rear

DIMENSIONS/WEIGHT	
LENGTH	1760 mm
WIDTH	695 mm
SADDLE HEIGHT	800 mm
WHEELBASE	1235 mm
FUEL TANK	8 litres
WEIGHT	80 kg

DECLARED PERFORMANCE	
MAXIMUM SPEED	95 kph
ACCELERATION	n.a.
FUEL CONSUMPTION	33 km/l

The Vespa PX was enormously successful and has remained in production from its presentation in 1978 through into the 3rd millennium. Known as "Nuova linea", or "New Style", it immediately succeeded in conquering a large share of the market thanks to its revised styling. Creating a new Vespa 125/150/200 range with more modern styling compared with the earlier series (125 TS, 150 Sprint Veloce and 200 Rally) was an extremely difficult task. While the design needed updating, it was important not to lose touch with the history and evolution of the earlier models. The result was a success that went beyond all expectations. The PX was everything that was positive about the large frame models, revised and improved. The modified styling was above all in the front mudguard, the headset and the side-panels which all had a more modern appearance. The steering column shroud, rear light and saddle were also all new. The instrumentation was large and circular. The glovebox behind the leg-shield was more angular while its door was flat. Indicators were available as an optional extra for the first time: the models thus equipped had a new electrical system using alternating current, with an electronic regulator maintaining a constant voltage as the loading varied. A significant improvement in roadholding was achieved with the new suspension that avoided the nose-diving under braking that plagued all the earlier models: here the damper was anchored to the brake backing plate and fixed to the trailing arm in correspondence with the wheel hub. The new suspension was distinguished from the traditional layout by the presence of two rather than three elements pivoting on the wheel. Suspension travel was increased from 70 to 90 mm. This version of the PX remained in production for four years before evolving into the PX-E with electronic ignition. PX 80 and PX 100 versions were produced for export markets.

Presentation
Milan Show 1981

Price
L. 1,343,000

Production
134,300 examples

Colours
white, light blue, red

Frame numbers
VNX2T 1101-135401

A number of innovations were introduced with this second series of the PX. The ignition was now electronic. To avoid theft of the side-panels, the release levers were located beneath the saddle. The wheel hub dimension was increased from 19 to 22 mm.
For the last time, the fuel tap retained the traditional reserve position, while on the later model the instrumentation included a fuel level gauge. The series enjoyed exceptional and well deserved success.

Presentation
Milan Show 1983

Price
L. 2,221,000

Production
149,444 examples

Colours
white
light blue
red

Frame numbers
PX Arcobaleno: VNX2T 135402-284846

The Arcobaleno featured a number of variations with respect to the preceding series: the front brake was more efficient thanks to the self-centring of the pads, the steering lock used the same key as the ignition, the headlight was more powerful, the wiring was fitted in sections to facilitate maintenance, the glovebox behind the leg-shield was larger, the saddle was more anatomical and padded, the central platform was larger, the headset had more comprehensive instrumentation including a fuel gauge.

The saddle had a square panel on the seat, the glovebox was more capacious, the trim on the mudguard was larger, the rear light was more rounded, and the leg-shield was edged in plastic. The horn grille was square.
From 1984, in the Elestart versions, the PX was also equipped with the electrical starting, with the battery inside the spare tyre's housing. This innovation was appreciated from many customers and made this PX version of the Vespa really complete, nearly perfect.

Presentation
Sestrière 1985

Price
L. 2,821,000

Production
36,060 examples
Elestart: 5012 examples

Colours
red

Frame numbers
125 PX/T5: VNX5T 1101-37161
125 PX/T5 Elestart: VNX5T 3000001-
3005013

The T5 ("5 Travasi" or "5 Ports") was the sports version of the PX 125. It was also known as the Pole Position: the name of a Piaggio trophy competition that saw a Vespa assigned to the fastest drivers in Formula 1 qualifying: for the record, Nelson Piquet took no less than 9 scooters home. The styling changes included a more sculpted front mudguard, the steering column shroud with a more pointed black grille, the headset was fitted with a small windscreen and larger instrumentation (it was the first Vespa fitted with a digital LCD rev-counter). The wheels were fitted with covers, a black spoiler was located beneath the platform and the engine was faired. A small tray was set onto the top of the glovebox. The saddle had seats at slightly different heights. The modifications made to increase the power output focussed on the domed combustion chamber and the squish band with five ports, two firsts for the Vespa. Compared with the PX, the bore and stroke were different, the stroke being

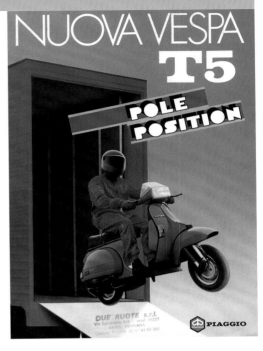

shorter. The intake and exhaust configurations were revised, the finning was more extensive, the carburettor was larger and the crankshaft was strengthened. The maximum power increased from 8 to 11 hp.

ENGINE

CYLINDERS/CYCLE	single/2-stroke
DISPLACEMENT	123.4 cc
BORE AND STROKE	52.5 x 57 mm
COMPRESSION RATIO	11.3:1
POWER/REVS	11 hp/6700 rpm
TORQUE/REVS	1.3 kgm/ 6200 rpm
COOLING	forced air
INDUCTION SYSTEM	5 ports
FUEL SYSTEM	Dell'Orto SI 24/24 carburettor (20 mm)
OIL/FUEL RATIO	2%
IGNITION	flywheel magneto
STARTING	kick-start lever, electric
CLUTCH	multiplate, oil-bath
GEARBOX	4 speeds, grip-shift

FRAME, WHEELS, SUSPENSION, BRAKES

FRAME	monocoque
FRONT SUSPENSION	trailing arm with coil spring and damper
REAR SUSPENSION	coil spring and damper
FINAL DRIVE	direct
WHEELS	interchangeable, cantilevered with split rim
FRONT BRAKE	150 mm drum
REAR BRAKE	150 mm drum
TYRES	3.50 x 10 front 3.50 x 10 rear

DIMENSIONS/WEIGHT

LENGTH	1760 mm
WIDTH	695 mm
SADDLE HEIGHT	800 mm
WHEELBASE	1235 mm
FUEL TANK	8 litres
WEIGHT	110 kg

DECLARED PERFORMANCE

MAXIMUM SPEED	108 kph
ACCELERATION	n.a.
FUEL CONSUMPTION	37 km/l

Presentation
Milan Show 1977

Price
L. 823,000

Production
345,301 examples

Colours
white, green, beige

Frame numbers
VLX1T 1101-346402

The 150 was a strong seller and the most well balanced of the three displacements in the new series. It was equipped with a more powerful and more flexible engine than the 125, which allowed more pleasant and relaxed cruising. With respect to the 200, that had considerably higher fuel consumption, the 150 was less thirsty and above all required fewer fuel stops as with the same sized tank it had a much greater range. The side-panels detached with special levers fixed to the lower part of the frame. To prevent thefts, the levers were later located

ENGINE	
CYLINDERS/CYCLE	single/2-stroke
DISPLACEMENT	149.56 cc
BORE AND STROKE	57.8 x 57 mm
COMPRESSION RATIO	8.2:1
POWER/REVS	8.8 hp/5700 rpm
TORQUE/REVS	1.3 0-70 kph
COOLING	forced air
INDUCTION SYSTEM	rotary valve
FUEL SYSTEM	Dell'Orto carburettor (20 mm)
OIL/FUEL RATIO	2%
IGNITION	flywheel magneto
STARTING	kick-start lever, electric
CLUTCH	multiplate, oil-bath
GEARBOX	4 speeds, grip-shift

FRAME, WHEELS, SUSPENSION, BRAKES	
FRAME	monocoque
FRONT SUSPENSION	trailing arm with coil spring and damper
REAR SUSPENSION	coil spring and damper
FINAL DRIVE	direct
WHEELS	interchangeable, cantilevered with split rim
FRONT BRAKE	150 mm drum
REAR BRAKE	150 mm drum
TYRES	3.50 x 10 front 3.50 x 10 rear

DIMENSIONS/WEIGHT	
LENGTH	1760 mm
WIDTH	695 mm
SADDLE HEIGHT	800 mm
WHEELBASE	1235 mm
FUEL TANK	8 litres
WEIGHT	80 kg

DECLARED PERFORMANCE	
MAXIMUM SPEED	100 kph
ACCELERATION	n.a.
FUEL CONSUMPTION	34 km/l

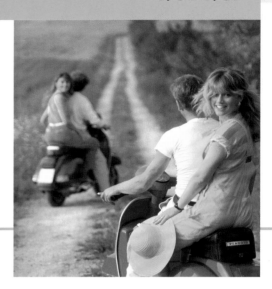

Presentation
Milan Show 1981

Price
L. 823,000

Production
206,007 examples

Colours
white, green, beige

Frame numbers
PX/E: VLX1T 346403-552410

Numerous innovations were introduced with this 2nd series of the PX. The ignition was electronic and the ignition key unit was relocated to the back of the headlight. To avoid theft of the side-panels, the release levers were located beneath the saddle. The 150 continued to sell well. Its perfect intermediate positioning between the 125 and the thirsty 200 made it versatile for urban and extra-urban use.

ENGINE	
CYLINDERS/CYCLE	single/2-stroke
DISPLACEMENT	149.56 cc
BORE AND STROKE	57.8 x 57 mm
COMPRESSION RATIO	8.2:1
POWER/REVS	8.8 hp/5700 rpm
TORQUE/REVS	1.3 0-70 kgm
COOLING	forced air
INDUCTION SYSTEM	rotary valve
FUEL SYSTEM	Dell'Orto carburettor (20 mm)
OIL/FUEL RATIO	2%
IGNITION	flywheel magneto
STARTING	kick-start lever, electric
CLUTCH	multiplate, oil-bath
GEARBOX	4 speeds, grip-shift

FRAME, WHEELS, SUSPENSION, BRAKES	
FRAME	monocoque
FRONT SUSPENSION	trailing arm with coil spring and damper
REAR SUSPENSION	coil spring and damper
FINAL DRIVE	direct
WHEELS	interchangeable, cantilevered with split rim
FRONT BRAKE	150 mm drum
REAR BRAKE	150 mm drum
TYRES	3.50 x 10 front 3.50 x 10 rear

DIMENSIONS/WEIGHT	
LENGTH	1760 mm
WIDTH	695 mm
SADDLE HEIGHT	800 mm
WHEELBASE	1235 mm
FUEL TANK	8 litres
WEIGHT	80 kg

DECLARED PERFORMANCE	
MAXIMUM SPEED	100 kph
ACCELERATION	n.a.
FUEL CONSUMPTION	34 km/l

Presentation
Milan Show 1983

Price
L. 2,441,000

Production
203,232 examples

Colours
white, green, beige

Frame numbers
PX Arcobaleno: VLX1T 600001-803233

The Arcobaleno version presented the following variations with respect to the base PX: the front brake was more efficient thanks to the self-centring of the pads, the steering lock used the same key as the ignition, the headlight was more powerful, the wiring was fitted in sections to facilitate maintenance, the glovebox behind the leg-shield was larger, the saddle was more anatomical and padded, the central platform was larger, the headset had more comprehensive instrumentation including a fuel gauge. The saddle had a square panel on the seat, the glovebox was more capacious, the trim on the mudguard was larger, the rear light was more rounded, and the leg-shield was edged in plastic. The horn grille was square.

Presentation
Milan Show 1977

Price
L. 908,000

Production
158,999 examples

Colours
white, grey, red

Frame numbers
VSX1T 1101-160.000

The 200 version of the PX was virtually identical to the 125 model with the exception of the displacement. There were few differences: electronic ignition and spare wheel were standard equipment. The ignition key was on the headset. In contrast with the 125 and 150 series, fitted with electronic ignition only in 1981 with the model name changing from PX to PX-E, the 200 was born with the electronic system and baptised as the PE. In order to unify the range, it became the PX-E with the later version.

ENGINE	
CYLINDERS/CYCLE	single/2-stroke
DISPLACEMENT	197.97 cc
BORE AND STROKE	66.8 x 57 mm
COMPRESSION RATIO	8.2:1
POWER/REVS	12 hp/5700 rpm
TORQUE/REVS	1.6 kgm/4300 rpm
COOLING	forced air
INDUCTION SYSTEM	rotary valve
FUEL SYSTEM	Dell'Orto carburettor (24 mm)
OIL/FUEL RATIO	2%
IGNITION	electronic
STARTING	kick-start lever, electric
CLUTCH	multiplate, oil-bath
GEARBOX	4 speeds, grip-shift
FRAME, WHEELS, SUSPENSION, BRAKES	
FRAME	monocoque
FRONT SUSPENSION	trailing arm with coil spring and damper
REAR SUSPENSION	coil spring and damper
FINAL DRIVE	direct
WHEELS	interchangeable, cantilevered with split rim
FRONT BRAKE	150 mm drum
REAR BRAKE	150 mm drum
TYRES	3.50 x 10 front 3.50 x 10 rear
DIMENSIONS/WEIGHT	
LENGTH	1760 mm
WIDTH	695 mm
SADDLE HEIGHT	800 mm
WHEELBASE	1235 mm
FUEL TANK	8 litres
WEIGHT	90 kg
DECLARED PERFORMANCE	
MAXIMUM SPEED	110 kph
ACCELERATION	n.a.
FUEL CONSUMPTION	28 km/l

Presentation
Milan Show 1983

Price
L. 2,894,000

Production
124,578 examples

Colours
white, grey, red

Frame numbers
VSX1T 300001-424579

The Arcobaleno version presented the following variations with respect to the base PX: the front brake was more efficient thanks to the self-centring of the pads, the steering lock used the same key as the ignition, the headlight was more powerful, the wiring was fitted in sections to facilitate maintenance, the glovebox behind the leg-shield was larger, the saddle was more anatomical and padded, the central platform was larger, the headset had more comprehensive instrumentation including a fuel gauge.

The '90s

50 PK N
50 PK N Speedmatic
50 PK FL2
50 PK FL2 Speedmatic
125 PK FL2
125 PK FL2 Plurimatic
125 Cosa
125 Cosa 2
150 Cosa
150 Cosa 2
200 Cosa
200 Cosa 2
125 PX - PX Classic
125 PX Disco
150 PX - PX Classic
150 PX Disco
200 PX - PX Classic
200 PX Disco

Presentation
Milan Show 1989
Price
lire 2,150,000
Production
43,478 examples
Colours
green, white
Frame numbers
V5X5T 1101-44579

This version of the Vespa 50 was characterised by a tapering, almost pointed mudguard and leg-shield design. Compared with earlier models, the major variations were as follows: choke lever on the headset, electrical switchgear clearly on view, saddle with non-slip upholstery, electric starting. The blue-faced instrumentation was large and comprehensive (including a fuel gauge) and located in the black central section of the headset. The wheels featured perforated discs. The glovebox behind the leg-shield had an indent for the ignition key.

The fuel tap in the frame compartment was new. The engine featured rotary valve induction and a cast-iron cylinder.

ENGINE	
CYLINDERS/CYCLE	single/2-stroke
DISPLACEMENT	49.8 cc
BORE AND STROKE	38.4 x 43 mm
COMPRESSION RATIO	8.8:1
POWER/REVS	2.2 hp/5000 rpm
TORQUE/REVS	0.3 kgm/3650 rpm
COOLING	forced air
INDUCTION SYSTEM	rotary valve
FUEL SYSTEM	Dell'Orto SHB 16/12 carburettor (12 mm)
OIL/FUEL RATIO	2%
IGNITION	electronic
STARTING	electric
CLUTCH	multiplate, oil-bath
GEARBOX	3 speeds, grip-shift
FRAME, WHEELS, SUSPENSION, BRAKES	
FRAME	monocoque
FRONT SUSPENSION	trailing arm with coil spring and damper
REAR SUSPENSION	coil spring and damper
FINAL DRIVE	direct
WHEELS	interchangeable, cantilevered with split rim
FRONT BRAKE	150 mm drum
REAR BRAKE	150 mm drum
TYRES	3.00 x 10 front 3.00 x 10 rear
DIMENSIONS/WEIGHT	
LENGTH	1675 mm
WIDTH	700 mm
SADDLE HEIGHT	790 mm
WHEELBASE	1175 mm
FUEL TANK	5.8 litres
WEIGHT	90 kg
DECLARED PERFORMANCE	
MAXIMUM SPEED	40 kph
ACCELERATION	n.a.
FUEL CONSUMPTION	2l/100 km

50 PK N Speedmatic

V5P1T

1989-1991

Presentation
Milan Show 1989

Price
lire 2,350,000

Production
4,924 examples

Colours
Green, white

Frame numbers
V5P1T 1101-6025

The automatic version of the 50 PK was practically identical to the base model with the obvious exception of the automatic gearbox.

The brake pedal on the platform was replaced by the left-hand handlebar lever given the lack of a clutch. The levers were ergonomically shaped.

The left-hand handlebar grip had two positions, one for neutral, one to engage drive. In styling terms, the new 50 was distinguished by blue and green trim on the side-panels.

The differences with regard to the engine concerned the aluminium (rather than cast-iron) cylinder and reed rather than rotary valve induction.

ENGINE

CYLINDERS/CYCLE	single/2-stroke
DISPLACEMENT	49.8 cc
BORE AND STROKE	38.4 x 43 mm
COMPRESSION RATIO	8.8:1
POWER/REVS	2.5 hp/6250 rpm
TORQUE/REVS	0.35 kgm/3500 rpm
COOLING	forced air
INDUCTION SYSTEM	reed valve
FUEL SYSTEM	Dell'Orto SHB 16/12 carburettor (12 mm)
OIL/FUEL RATIO	2%
IGNITION	electronic
STARTING	kick-start peda, electric
CLUTCH	continuously variable
GEARBOX	automatic

FRAME, WHEELS, SUSPENSION, BRAKES

FRAME	monocoque
FRONT SUSPENSION	trailing arm with coil spring and damper
REAR SUSPENSION	coil spring and damper
FINAL DRIVE	direct
WHEELS	interchangeable, cantilevered with split rim
FRONT BRAKE	150 mm drum
REAR BRAKE	150 mm drum
TYRES	3.00 x 10 front 3.00 x 10 rear

DIMENSIONS/WEIGHT

LENGTH	1675 mm
WIDTH	700 mm
SADDLE HEIGHT	790 mm
WHEELBASE	1175 mm
FUEL TANK	5.8 litres
WEIGHT	90 kg

DECLARED PERFORMANCE

MAXIMUM SPEED	40 kph
ACCELERATION	n.a.
FUEL CONSUMPTION	2l/100 km

vespa 50 N speedmatic

Presentation
Milan Show 1991

Price
L. 2,350,000

Production
n.a.

Colours
white

Frame numbers
n.a.

The upper part of the headset was redesigned and presented softer lines. The central section was black, with the white-faced speedometer in the middle. The glovebox behind the leg-shield was completely redesigned and extended through to the steeringhead, eliminating the shelf. The glovebox was concave in shape to provide greater legroom. This was the last version exclusively equipped with the two-stroke engine.

ENGINE

CYLINDERS/CYCLE	single/2-stroke
DISPLACEMENT	49.8 cc
BORE AND STROKE	38.4 x 43 mm
COMPRESSION RATIO	8.8:1
POWER/REVS	2.5 HP/ 6250 rpm
TORQUE/REVS	0.35 kgm/3500 rpm
COOLING	forced air
INDUCTION SYSTEM	rotary valve
FUEL SYSTEM	Dell'Orto SHB 16/12 carburettor (12 mm)
OIL/FUEL RATIO	2%
IGNITION	electronic
STARTING	kick-start pedal, electric
CLUTCH	continuously variable
GEARBOX	automatic

FRAME, WHEELS, SUSPENSION, BRAKES

FRAME	monocoque
FRONT SUSPENSION	trailing arm with coil spring and damper
REAR SUSPENSION	coil spring and damper
FINAL DRIVE	direct
WHEELS	interchangeable, cantilevered with split rim
FRONT BRAKE	150 mm drum
REAR BRAKE	150 mm drum
TYRES	3.00 x 10 front 3.00 x 10 rear

DIMENSIONS/WEIGHT

LENGTH	1675 mm
WIDTH	700 mm
SADDLE HEIGHT	790 mm
WHEELBASE	1175 mm
FUEL TANK	5.8 litres
WEIGHT	90 kg

DECLARED PERFORMANCE

MAXIMUM SPEED	40 kph
ACCELERATION	n.a.
FUEL CONSUMPTION	2l/100 km

50 PK FL2 Speedmatic   V5P1T

Presentation
Milan Show 1991
Price
L. 3,340,000
Production
n.a.
Colours
white
Frame numbers
n.a.

The new version of the 50 with automatic transmission featured revised styling and was far more attractive than the previous model. The headset was completely redesigned and featured clearly legible and comprehensive instrumentation with a white-faced speedometer. A redesigned glovebox was mounted behind the leg-shield. The concave shape provided greater legroom. The plastic wheel covers were very attractive but rather impractical.

ENGINE

CYLINDERS/CYCLE	single/2-stroke
DISPLACEMENT	49.8 cc
BORE AND STROKE	38.4 x 43 mm
COMPRESSION RATIO	8.8:1
POWER/REVS	2.5 hp/ 6250 rpm
TORQUE/REVS	0.35 kgm/3500 rpm
COOLING	forced air
INDUCTION SYSTEM	rotary valve
FUEL SYSTEM	Dell'Orto SHB 16/12 carburettor (12 mm)
OIL/FUEL RATIO	2%
IGNITION	electronic
STARTING	kick-start pedal – electric
CLUTCH	continuously variable
GEARBOX	automatic

FRAME, WHEELS, SUSPENSION, BRAKES

FRAME	monocoque
FRONT SUSPENSION	trailing link with coilspring and damper
REAR SUSPENSION	coil spring and damper
FINAL DRIVE	direct
WHEELS	interchangeable, cantilevered with split rim
FRONT BRAKE	150 mm drum
REAR BRAKE	150 mm drum
TYRES	3.00 x 10 front 3.00 x 10 rear

DIMENSIONS/WEIGHT

LENGTH	1675 mm
WIDTH	700 mm
SADDLE HEIGHT	790 mm
WHEELBASE	1175 mm
FUEL TANK	5.8 litres
WEIGHT	90 kg

DECLARED PERFORMANCE

MAXIMUM SPEED	40 kph
ACCELERATION	n.a.
FUEL CONSUMPTION	2l/100 km

Presentation
Milan Show 1991

Price
L. 2,840,000

Production
n.a.

Colours
white

Frame numbers
n.a.

The last 125 prior to the epochal shift to the four-stroke ET4, the FL2 version of the PK was distinguished by the sleek styling of the front mudguard and the leg-shield. The headset had a tapering shape and a larger saddle was fitted. The large and comprehensive instrumentation included a fuel gauge and was located in the black centre section of the headset. The choke lever was located on the headset and the wheel covers were perforated. The engine featured a cast-iron cylinder and rotary valve induction. The glovebox extended up to the steering column and had a concave form to provide more legroom. The series was not particularly successful in commercial terms as the new

generation Vespa with a four-stroke engine was on the horizon. It was, however, the most highly evolved version of the 125 two-stroke small frame series.

ENGINE

CYLINDERS/CYCLE	single/2-stroke
DISPLACEMENT	121.2 cc
BORE AND STROKE	55 x 51 mm
COMPRESSION RATIO	9.3:1
POWER/REVS	8.2 hp/ 5500 rpm
TORQUE/REVS	0.95 kgm/4700 rpm
COOLING	forced air
INDUCTION SYSTEM	rotary valve
FUEL SYSTEM	Dell'Orto SHBC 20 carburettor (20 mm)
OIL/FUEL RATIO	2%
IGNITION	electronic
STARTING	electric
CLUTCH	multiplate, oil-bath
GEARBOX	4 speeds, grip-shift

FRAME, WHEELS, SUSPENSION, BRAKES

FRAME	monocoque
FRONT SUSPENSION	trailing arm with coil spring and damper
REAR SUSPENSION	coil spring and damper
FINAL DRIVE	direct
WHEELS	interchangeable, cantilevered with split rim
FRONT BRAKE	150 mm drum
REAR BRAKE	150 mm drum
TYRES	3.00 x 10 front 3.00 x 10 rear

DIMENSIONS/WEIGHT

LENGTH	1710 mm
WIDTH	720 mm
SADDLE HEIGHT	790 mm
WHEELBASE	1175 mm
FUEL TANK	5.8 litres
WEIGHT	90 kg

DECLARED PERFORMANCE

MAXIMUM SPEED	100 kph
ACCELERATION	n.a.
FUEL CONSUMPTION	2.3l/100 km

Presentation
Milan Show 1991
Price
L. 3,140,000
Production
n.a.
Colours
white
Frame numbers
n.a.

The automatic version of the FL2 was practically identical to the base FL2 with the obvious exception of the automatic gearbox. It was distinguished by the absence of the brake pedal, replaced by a left-hand lever. The engine had a light alloy rather than cast-iron cylinder and reed rather than rotary valve induction. The glovebox extended to the steeringhead and had a concave shape to provide extra legroom. The series was not particularly successful as the new generation Vespa with the four-stroke engine was already on the horizon. This was, however, the most highly evolved version of the 125 series with automatic transmission, the small frame and a two-stroke engine. Initially this version was only available on export markets, but was then also introduced in Italy. Compared with the manual gearbox model, the power output was slightly lower (by 1 hp) and performance was therefore slightly weaker. The left-hand grip had a position to keep the transmission in neutral allowing the engine to warm up while stationary. In contrast with the manual version, this model lacked the tool-carrier beneath the saddle due to the different configuration of the engine and the presence of an oil tank.

A minor sign of refinement: in order to reduce noise, the inside of the engine-side hatch was lined with felt.

ENGINE

CYLINDERS/CYCLE	single/2-stroke
DISPLACEMENT	121.2 cc
BORE AND STROKE	55 x 51 mm
COMPRESSION RATIO	9.5:1
POWER/REVS	7.2 hp/ 6250 rpm
TORQUE/REVS	1 kgm/4500 rpm
COOLING	forced air
INDUCTION SYSTEM	reed valve
FUEL SYSTEM	Dell'Orto SHBA 28/20 carburettor (20 mm)
OIL/FUEL RATIO	2%
IGNITION	electronic
STARTING	electric
CLUTCH	centrifugal
GEARBOX	automatic

FRAME, WHEELS, SUSPENSION, BRAKES

FRAME	monocoque
FRONT SUSPENSION	trailing arm with coil spring and damper
REAR SUSPENSION	coil spring and damper
FINAL DRIVE	direct
WHEELS	interchangeable, cantilevered with split rim
FRONT BRAKE	150 mm drum
REAR BRAKE	150 mm drum
TYRES	3.00 x 10 front 3.00 x 10 rear

DIMENSIONS/WEIGHT

LENGTH	1710 mm
WIDTH	720 mm
SADDLE HEIGHT	790 mm
WHEELBASE	1175 mm
FUEL TANK	5.8 litres
WEIGHT	90 kg

DECLARED PERFORMANCE

MAXIMUM SPEED	100 kph
ACCELERATION	n.a.
FUEL CONSUMPTION	2.8l/100 km

Presentation
Milan Show 1987

Price
L. 2,950,000

Production
n.a.

Colours
white, red, green, light blue, blue

Frame numbers
VNR1T 3000001 - 3017315

ENGINE	
CYLINDERS/CYCLE	single/2-stroke
DISPLACEMENT	123.4 cc
BORE AND STROKE	52.2 x 57 mm
COMPRESSION RATIO	9.2:1
POWER/REVS	7.2 hp/ 6250 rpm
TORQUE/REVS	1 kgm/4500 rpm
COOLING	forced air
INDUCTION SYSTEM	rotary valve
FUEL SYSTEM	Dell'Orto carburettor (20 mm)
OIL/FUEL RATIO	2%
IGNITION	electronic
STARTING	kick-start pedal, electric
CLUTCH	multiplate, oil-bath
GEARBOX	4 speeds, grip-shift
FRAME, WHEELS, SUSPENSION, BRAKES	
FRAME	monocoque
FRONT SUSPENSION	trailing arm with coil spring and damper
REAR SUSPENSION	coil spring and damper
FINAL DRIVE	direct
WHEELS	interchangeable, cantilevered with split rim
FRONT BRAKE	170 mm drum
REAR BRAKE	170 mm drum
TYRES	3.00 x 10 front 3.00 x 10 rear
DIMENSIONS/WEIGHT	
LENGTH	1805 mm
WIDTH	700 mm
SADDLE HEIGHT	805 mm
WHEELBASE	1270 mm
FUEL TANK	8 litres
WEIGHT	115 kg
DECLARED PERFORMANCE	
MAXIMUM SPEED	90 kph
ACCELERATION	400 metres from standing start: 25.3 sec.
FUEL CONSUMPTION	100 km/2.4 l

In the late '80s, Piaggio decide to update the styling of the PX with more angular forms. The newborn scooter was initially intended to be known as the Vespa R ("Rinnovata" or "Revised"). It was instead decided to put the new model into production with the name "Cosa" to emphasise the break with the previous image of Vespa. Unfortunately, the Cosa soon proved to be a failure, in part because of its unhappy styling, but above all due to the rejection of the glorious Vespa name. This meant that the interesting modifications introduced with the project tended to be overlooked. The instrumentation was particularly comprehensive (even including a rev-counter), the engine was more powerful and the rear swinging arm was reinforced. With regards to the frame, more leg-room was available and a helmet could be stored in a compartment beneath the saddle.
The Cosa retained the monocoque frame in pressed steel but boasted a number of innovations with respect to the earlier Vespa models. The side-panels were slightly inclined forwards to improve aerodynamics. The indicators were set into the leg-shield while the rear light unit was incorporated below the number plate. The integral braking system (controlled by the foot pedal) spilt braking force between the wheels via a hydraulic circuit and a pressure regulator.

125 Cosa 2

VNR1T   1992-1995

Presentation
Milan Show 1991

Price
L. 4,080,000

Production
n.a.

Colours
white, red, green, light blue, blue

Frame numbers
n.a.

ENGINE

CYLINDERS/CYCLE	single/2-stroke
DISPLACEMENT	123.4 cc
BORE AND STROKE	52.2 x 57 mm
COMPRESSION RATIO	9.2:1
POWER/REVS	8.3 hp/ 6000 rpm
TORQUE/REVS	1.07 kgm/4500 rpm
COOLING	forced air
INDUCTION SYSTEM	rotary valve
FUEL SYSTEM	Dell'Orto carburettor (20 mm)
OIL/FUEL RATIO	2%
IGNITION	electronic
STARTING	kick-start pedal, electric
CLUTCH	multiplate, oil-bath
GEARBOX	4 speeds, grip-shift

FRAME, WHEELS, SUSPENSION, BRAKES

FRAME	monocoque
FRONT SUSPENSION	trailing arm with coil spring and damper
REAR SUSPENSION	coil spring and damper
FINAL DRIVE	direct
WHEELS	interchangeable, cantilevered with split rim
FRONT BRAKE	170 mm drum
REAR BRAKE	170 mm drum
TYRES	3.00 x 10 front 3.00 x 10 rear

DIMENSIONS/WEIGHT

LENGTH	1805 mm
WIDTH	700 mm
SADDLE HEIGHT	805 mm
WHEELBASE	1270 mm
FUEL TANK	8 litres
WEIGHT	115 kg

DECLARED PERFORMANCE

MAXIMUM SPEED	90 kph
ACCELERATION	400 metres from standing start: 25.3 sec.
FUEL CONSUMPTION	2.4 l/100 km

Stylistically, the Cosa 2 was distinguished from the first series above all by the different position of the rear light and number plate holder. The light unit was now set higher with the number plate lower.
A much larger saddle was also fitted. The EBC version featured an integral braking system based on a hydraulic circuit with pressure regulators allowing both brakes to be actuated with the pedal alone.
The EBC system reduced the pressure in the braking circuit when a sensor detected the possibility of locking the front wheel. Numerous modifications were introduced with this series to make the Cosa more comfortable. The saddle was larger and configured with two levels with more substantial upholstery.

The passenger benefited from lateral grab handles. The clutch control was redesigned to reduce lever force. Use of the gearbox was also facilitated with a new single-cable transmission. The instrumentation had yellow graphics.

Presentation
Milan Show 1987

Price
L. 3,147,000

Production
n.a.

Colours
white, red, green, light blue, blue

Frame numbers
VLR1T 3000001 - 3009413

The Cosa 150 featured the same styling as the 125 and consequently was given the same tepid reaction by the public. Mechanically it was interesting, boasting more advanced components than the previous Vespa models. It was also more practical as it offered the possibility of storing a helmet beneath the saddle. However, the very fact that it was burdened with the name "Cosa" contributed to its commercial failure. The Cosa retained the monocoque frame in pressed steel but boasted a number of innovations with respect to the earlier Vespa models. The side-panels were slightly inclined forwards to improve aerodynamics. The indicators were set into the leg-shield while the rear light unit was incorporated below the number plate. The integral braking system (controlled by the foot pedal) split braking force between the wheels via a hydraulic circuit and a pressure regulator.

ENGINE

CYLINDERS/CYCLE	single/2-stroke
DISPLACEMENT	149 cc
BORE AND STROKE	57.8 x 57 mm
COMPRESSION RATIO	9.2:1
POWER/REVS	9 hp/ 6000 rpm
TORQUE/REVS	1.3 kgm/4500 rpm
COOLING	forced air
INDUCTION SYSTEM	rotary valve
FUEL SYSTEM	Dell'Orto carburettor (20 mm)
OIL/FUEL RATIO	2%
IGNITION	electronic
STARTING	kick-start pedal, electric
CLUTCH	multiplate, oil-bath
GEARBOX	4 speeds, grip-shift

FRAME, WHEELS, SUSPENSION, BRAKES

FRAME	monocoque
FRONT SUSPENSION	trailing arm with coil spring and damper
REAR SUSPENSION	coil spring and damper
FINAL DRIVE	direct
WHEELS	interchangeable, cantilevered with split rim
FRONT BRAKE	170 mm drum
REAR BRAKE	170 mm drum
TYRES	3.00 x 10 front 3.00 x 10 rear

DIMENSIONS/WEIGHT

LENGTH	1805 mm
WIDTH	700 mm
SADDLE HEIGHT	805 mm
WHEELBASE	1270 mm
FUEL TANK	8 litres
WEIGHT	115 kg

DECLARED PERFORMANCE

MAXIMUM SPEED	90 kph
ACCELERATION	400 metres from standing start: 24.8 sec.
FUEL CONSUMPTION	100 km/2.5 l

150 Cosa 2

VLR1T

1992-1995

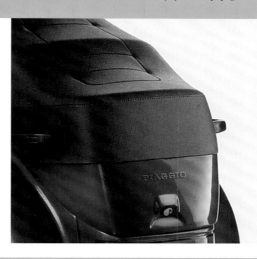

Compared with the Cosa 150, the new version was distinguished by a number of styling changes including the positioning of the rear light immediately below the saddle and above the number plate. A much larger saddle was also fitted and had two staggered seats and two grab handles for the passenger. The clutch and gear change controls were new and more functional. The braking system was enhanced with the sophisticated EBC device that prevented locking of the front wheel thanks to a magnetic sensor.

Presentation	
Milan Show 1991	
Price	
L. 4,280,000	
Production	
n.a.	
Colours	
white, red, green, light blue, blue	
Frame numbers	
n.a.	

ENGINE	
CYLINDERS/CYCLE	single/2-stroke
DISPLACEMENT	149 cc
BORE AND STROKE	57.8 x 57 mm
COMPRESSION RATIO	9.2:1
POWER/REVS	9 hp/ 6000 rpm
TORQUE/REVS	1.3 kgm/4500 rpm
COOLING	forced air
INDUCTION SYSTEM	rotary valve
FUEL SYSTEM	Dell'Orto carburettor (20 mm)
OIL/FUEL RATIO	2%
IGNITION	electronic
STARTING	kick-start pedal, electric
CLUTCH	multiplate, oil-bath
GEARBOX	4 speeds, grip-shift
FRAME, WHEELS, SUSPENSION, BRAKES	
FRAME	monocoque
FRONT SUSPENSION	trailing arm with coil spring and damper
REAR SUSPENSION	coil spring and damper
FINAL DRIVE	direct
WHEELS	interchangeable, cantilevered with split rim
FRONT BRAKE	170 mm drum
REAR BRAKE	170 mm drum
TYRES	3.00 x 10 front 3.00 x 10 rear
DIMENSIONS/WEIGHT	
LENGTH	1805 mm
WIDTH	700 mm
SADDLE HEIGHT	805 mm
WHEELBASE	1270 mm
FUEL TANK	8 litres
WEIGHT	115 kg
DECLARED PERFORMANCE	
MAXIMUM SPEED	92 kph
ACCELERATION	400 metres from standing start: 24.8 sec.
FUEL CONSUMPTION	100 km/2.5 l

Presentation
Milan Show 1987

Price
L. 3,427,000

Production
n.a.

Colours
white, red, green, light blue, blue

Frame numbers
VSR1T 1101 – n.a.

ENGINE	
CYLINDERS/CYCLE	single/2-stroke
DISPLACEMENT	198 cc
BORE AND STROKE	66.5 x 57 mm
COMPRESSION RATIO	8.8:1
POWER/REVS	11 hp/ 6000 rpm
TORQUE/REVS	1.48 kgm/4500 rpm
COOLING	forced air
INDUCTION SYSTEM	rotary valve
FUEL SYSTEM	Dell'Orto carburettor (24 mm)
OIL/FUEL RATIO	2%
IGNITION	electronic
STARTING	kick-start pedal, electric
CLUTCH	multiplate, oil-bath
GEARBOX	4 speeds, grip-shift
FRAME, WHEELS, SUSPENSION, BRAKES	
FRAME	monocoque
FRONT SUSPENSION	trailing arm with coil spring and damper
REAR SUSPENSION	coil spring and damper
FINAL DRIVE	direct
WHEELS	interchangeable, cantilevered with split rim
FRONT BRAKE	170 mm drum
REAR BRAKE	170 mm drum
TYRES	3.00 x 10 front 3.00 x 10 rear
DIMENSIONS/WEIGHT	
LENGTH	1805 mm
WIDTH	700 mm
SADDLE HEIGHT	805 mm
WHEELBASE	1270 mm
FUEL TANK	8 litres
WEIGHT	115 kg
DECLARED PERFORMANCE	
MAXIMUM SPEED	100 kph
ACCELERATION	400 metres from standing start: 22 sec.
FUEL CONSUMPTION	100 km/3 l

The Cosa 200 was mechanically advanced but suffered a tepid welcome. The change of name was difficult to accept and from the point of view of styling it can hardly be said that the Cosa found favour with the public. In technical terms, however, various improvements had been made that turned this scooter into one of the best on the market. Compared with the past, the roadholding was significantly better, the braking featured an integral system and the performance was more than a match for most rivals. The side-pods were inclined forwards to improve aerodynamics. This series represented the height of scooter performance but it was nonetheless unsuccessful: neither its styling nor its name was popular, two defects that compromised its chances from the outset.

Presentation	
Milan Show 1991	
Price	
L. 4,570,000	
Production	
n.a.	
Colours	
white, red, green, light blue, blue	
Frame numbers	
n.a.	

ENGINE

CYLINDERS/CYCLE	single/2-stroke
DISPLACEMENT	198 cc
BORE AND STROKE	66.5 x 57 mm
COMPRESSION RATIO	8.8:1
POWER/REVS	11 hp/ 6000 rpm
TORQUE/REVS	1.48 kgm/4500 rpm
COOLING	forced air
INDUCTION SYSTEM	rotary valve
FUEL SYSTEM	Dell'Orto carburettor (24 mm)
OIL/FUEL RATIO	2%
IGNITION	electronic
STARTING	kick-start pedal, electric
CLUTCH	multiplate, oil-bath
GEARBOX	4 speeds, grip-shift

FRAME, WHEELS, SUSPENSION, BRAKES

FRAME	monocoque
FRONT SUSPENSION	trailing arm with coil spring and damper
REAR SUSPENSION	coil spring and damper
FINAL DRIVE	direct
WHEELS	interchangeable, cantilevered with split rim
FRONT BRAKE	170 mm drum
REAR BRAKE	170 mm drum
TYRES	3.00 x 10 front 3.00 x 10 rear

DIMENSIONS/WEIGHT

LENGTH	1805 mm
WIDTH	700 mm
SADDLE HEIGHT	805 mm
WHEELBASE	1270 mm
FUEL TANK	8 litres
WEIGHT	115 kg

DECLARED PERFORMANCE

MAXIMUM SPEED	100 kph
ACCELERATION	400 metres from standing start: 22 sec.
FUEL CONSUMPTION	100 km/3 l

The most conspicuous styling changes made to the 2nd series concerned the rear end with shifting of the rear light immediately below the saddle and the number plate holder consequently being set lower. The saddle, with two staggered seats, was given more substantial upholstery and was much more comfortable. The passenger was also made more comfortable thanks to two useful grab handles. The clutch and brake controls were more functional and the Cosa 2 was safer especially under braking. The integral braking system was completed with the EBC device that, via a magnetic sensor, prevented the locking of the front wheel. From a technical point of view the Cosa 2 represented the pinnacle of scooter development. It boasted the best performance and a significantly advanced chassis.

Anti-lock bracking systems were a rarity even among the far more expensive, large displacement motorcycles. Unfortunately, the Cosa 2 was unable to shed the burden of two significant defects: its styling and its name.

Presentation
Milan Show 1993

Price
L. 4,140,000

Production
n.a.

Colours
blue, yellow

Frame numbers
n.a.

This version of the PX was characterised by the black finish of the leg-shield edging, the fan cover and the wheel nut covers. The Classic series, produced to celebrate the 50th anniversary of the birth of the Vespa, was characterised by yellow paintwork and a brown saddle. This was the last series of the PX with a front drum brake, identical to the model introduced 15 years earlier. For many Vespisti, this was the last "true" Vespa. During these years the PX continued to satisfy a clientele of enthusiasts who appreciated its still modern styling. Furthermore, there was also the grip-shift transmission, a key feature for many Vespisti. The presentation of the Vespa ET with a four-stroke engine and automatic transmission was approaching and many feared that the PX would be pensioned off. The styling modifications were mere details and not particularly successful.

ENGINE

CYLINDERS/CYCLE	single/2-stroke
DISPLACEMENT	123.4 cc
BORE AND STROKE	52.5 x 57 mm
COMPRESSION RATIO	9.2:1
POWER/REVS	11 hp/ 6000 rpm
TORQUE/REVS	1.48 kgm/4500 rpm
COOLING	forced air
INDUCTION SYSTEM	rotary valve
FUEL SYSTEM	Dell'Orto carburettor (24 mm)
OIL/FUEL RATIO	2%
IGNITION	electronic
STARTING	kick-start pedal, electric
CLUTCH	multiplate, oil-bath
GEARBOX	4 speeds, grip-shift

FRAME, WHEELS, SUSPENSION, BRAKES

FRAME	monocoque
FRONT SUSPENSION	trailing arm with coil spring and damper
REAR SUSPENSION	coil spring and damper
FINAL DRIVE	direct
WHEELS	interchangeable, cantilevered with split rim
FRONT BRAKE	170 mm drum
REAR BRAKE	170 mm drum
TYRES	3.00 x 10 front 3.00 x 10 rear

DIMENSIONS/WEIGHT

LENGTH	1805 mm
WIDTH	700 mm
SADDLE HEIGHT	805 mm
WHEELBASE	1270 mm
FUEL TANK	8 litres
WEIGHT	115 kg

DECLARED PERFORMANCE

MAXIMUM SPEED	90 kph
ACCELERATION	400 metres from standing start: 25.3 sec.
FUEL CONSUMPTION	100 km/2.4 l

Presentation
Milan Show 1993
Price
L. 5,210,000
Production
n.a.
Colours
light green
Frame numbers
n.a.

This PX presented significant innovations, the main one being the front disc brake. The brake fluid reservoir was located on the headset, alongside the brake lever. New were the front suspension with the exposed spring, the wheel hub, the rounded saddle, the leg-shield edge trim in chromed plastic, the chromed mudguard trim and the metallic grey fan cover. The Vespa script was reinstated on the leg-shield and side-panels.

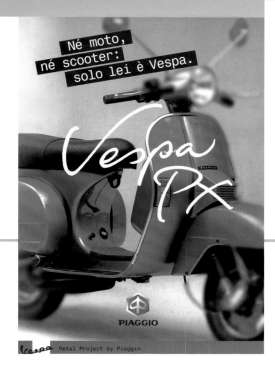

Né moto, né scooter: solo lei è Vespa.

Vespa PX

PIAGGIO

Vespa Metal Project by Piaggio.

ENGINE

CYLINDERS/CYCLE	single/2-stroke
DISPLACEMENT	123.4 cc
BORE AND STROKE	52.2 x 57 mm
COMPRESSION RATIO	9.2:1
POWER/REVS	8.3 hp/ 6000 rpm
TORQUE/REVS	1.07 kgm/4500 rpm
COOLING	forced air
INDUCTION SYSTEM	rotary valve
FUEL SYSTEM	Dell'Orto carburettor (20 mm)
OIL/FUEL RATIO	2%
IGNITION	electronic
STARTING	kick-start pedal, electric
CLUTCH	multiplate, oil-bath
GEARBOX	4 speeds, grip-shift

FRAME, WHEELS, SUSPENSION, BRAKES

FRAME	monocoque
FRONT SUSPENSION	trailing arm with coil spring and damper
REAR SUSPENSION	coil spring and damper
FINAL DRIVE	direct
WHEELS	interchangeable, cantilevered with split rim
FRONT BRAKE	200 mm disc
REAR BRAKE	170 mm drum
TYRES	3.00 x 10 front 3.00 x 10 rear

DIMENSIONS/WEIGHT

LENGTH	1805 mm
WIDTH	700 mm
SADDLE HEIGHT	805 mm
WHEELBASE	1270 mm
FUEL TANK	8 litres
WEIGHT	115 kg

DECLARED PERFORMANCE

MAXIMUM SPEED	90 kph
ACCELERATION	400 metres from standing start: 25.3 sec.
FUEL CONSUMPTION	100 km/2.4 l

Chi si muove sceglie Vespa. Nella sua linea inimitabile è scritta la sua storia, lo stile di un design italiano destinato a piacere in eterno.

Per questo Vespa Px ancora oggi, è considerata da tutti come un'insostituibile compagna di viaggio.

La leggendaria affidabilità del suo motore e la linea inossidabile della sua carrozzeria in metallo completano un mito che ha dato vita ad un movimento perpetuo.

La sua linea inconfondibile racchiude il pregio in un design italiano davvero unico.

La ruota di scorta, trova spazio nella fiancata: una comoda soluzione in caso di emergenza

Il pratico cambio a 4 marce: tradizione e carattere di un certo modo di guidare.

Freno a disco anteriore per migliorare ulteriormente la sicurezza in frenata.

Classici i cofani laterali staccabili per accedere facilmente alle parti meccaniche

Indistruttibile la carrozzeria in metallo: assicura protezione e durata.

Tre cilindrate disponibili subito per rispondere a tutte le esigenze:

Vespa PX 125 cc
Vespa PX 150 cc
Vespa PX 200 cc

Presentation	
Milan Show 1993	
Price	
L. 4,360,000	
Production	
n.a.	
Colours	
blue, yellow	
Frame numbers	
n.a.	

ENGINE

CYLINDERS/CYCLE	single/2-stroke
DISPLACEMENT	149 cc
BORE AND STROKE	57.8 x 57 mm
COMPRESSION RATIO	9.2:1
POWER/REVS	9 hp/6000 rpm
TORQUE/REVS	1.3 kgm/4500 rpm
COOLING	forced air
INDUCTION SYSTEM	rotary valve
FUEL SYSTEM	Dell'Orto carburettor (20 mm)
OIL/FUEL RATIO	2%
IGNITION	electronic
STARTING	kick-start pedal, electric
CLUTCH	multiplate, oil-bath
GEARBOX	4 speeds, grip-shift

FRAME, WHEELS, SUSPENSION, BRAKES

FRAME	monocoque
FRONT SUSPENSION	trailing arm with coil spring and damper
REAR SUSPENSION	coil spring and damper
FINAL DRIVE	direct
WHEELS	interchangeable, cantilevered with split rim
FRONT BRAKE	170 mm drum
REAR BRAKE	170 mm drum
TYRES	3.00 x 10 front 3.00 x 10 rear

DIMENSIONS/WEIGHT

LENGTH	1805 mm
WIDTH	700 mm
SADDLE HEIGHT	805 mm
WHEELBASE	1270 mm
FUEL TANK	8 litres
WEIGHT	115 kg

DECLARED PERFORMANCE

MAXIMUM SPEED	n.a.
ACCELERATION	n.a.
FUEL CONSUMPTION	n.a.

Twenty years on from its presentation, the PX was significantly revised. This was the dawn of a new generation: the front drum brake was replaced with a more efficient disc. This inevitably led to the fitting of a brake fluid reservoir located on the headset, alongside the brake lever. Also new was the exposed spring on the front suspension. In styling terms the new PX was distinguished by the rounded saddle, but there were also a number of details that represented a return to the past such as the leg-shield edging in chromed plastic and the chromed mudguard trim. The cursive Vespa script returned on the leg-shield and the side-panels. The fan cover was finished in metallic grey. The 150 version was still the best of the three displacements with which the PX was offered and the revised version was well received by a large group of enthusiasts. In fact, this series of the PX actually conquered a new clientele. There were many who admired its classic lines that were now combined with a technically more advanced specification to create a scooter that was without doubt safer on the road thanks to its front disc brake. With this second generation the PX became a timeless classic.

Presentation
Milan Show 1997

Price
L. 5,440,000

Production
n.a.

Colours
light green

Frame numbers
n.a.

ENGINE

CYLINDERS/CYCLE	single/2-stroke
DISPLACEMENT	149 cc
BORE AND STROKE	57.8 x 57 mm
COMPRESSION RATIO	9.2:1
POWER/REVS	9 hp/6000 rpm
TORQUE/REVS	1.3 kgm/4500 rpm
COOLING	forced air
INDUCTION SYSTEM	rotary valve
FUEL SYSTEM	Dell'Orto carburettor (20 mm)
OIL/FUEL RATIO	2%
IGNITION	electronic
STARTING	kick-start pedal, electric
CLUTCH	multiplate, oil-bath
GEARBOX	4 speeds, grip-shift

FRAME, WHEELS, SUSPENSION, BRAKES

FRAME	monocoque
FRONT SUSPENSION	trailing arm with coil spring and damper
REAR SUSPENSION	coil spring and damper
FINAL DRIVE	direct
WHEELS	interchangeable, cantilevered with split rim
FRONT BRAKE	200 mm disc
REAR BRAKE	170 mm drum
TYRES	3.00 x 10 front 3.00 x 10 rear

DIMENSIONS/WEIGHT

LENGTH	1805 mm
WIDTH	700 mm
SADDLE HEIGHT	805 mm
WHEELBASE	1270 mm
FUEL TANK	8 litres
WEIGHT	115 kg

DECLARED PERFORMANCE

MAXIMUM SPEED	n.a.
ACCELERATION	n.a.
FUEL CONSUMPTION	n.a.

Twenty years on from its presentation, the PX was thoroughly revised. This represented the birth of a new generation: the front drum brake was replaced by a more efficient disc. This implied the introduction of a brake fluid reservoir located on the headset, alongside the brake lever. The front suspension was also new and featured an exposed spring. The new PX was distinguished above all by the rounded saddle, but there were a number of details that referenced the past such as the edge trim around the leg-shield in chromed plastic and the chromed trim on the mudguard. The cursive Vespa script returned on the leg-shield and the side-panels. The fan cover was finished in metallic grey. The 150 version was always the better balanced of the three displacements offered with the PX and the revised version represented a model popular with a large group of enthusiasts. This series of the PX also attracted a new clientele. Many new Vespisti were in fact attracted by the fact that the styling had remained unchanged but was now combined with updated technology that made the scooter safer to ride, thanks above all to the front disc brake. With this second generation version the PX became a timeless classic.

Presentation	
Milan Show 1993	
Price	
L. 4,580,000	
Production	
n.a.	
Colours	
blue, yellow	
Frame numbers	
n.a.	

The PX continued to be popular and there was always a demand despite the fact that it was never marketed. There were many who were surprised to find it still in the Piaggio catalogue, but for those Vespisti devoted to the manual grip-shift there was no alternative. The 200 also boasted the best performance of the series. In order to keep it up to date, a number of components were characterised by a rather questionable black finish. Many Vespisti were worried that the PX would be dropped following the announcement of the new ET series with the four-stroke engine and automatic transmission; in reality the model's career was far from over. When the new series was launched Piaggio celebrated the 50th anniversary of the Vespa and there was also a new version of the PX to mark the occasion: it was finished in yellow with a brown saddle.

ENGINE

CYLINDERS/CYCLE	single/2-stroke
DISPLACEMENT	198 cc
BORE AND STROKE	66.5 x 57 mm
COMPRESSION RATIO	8.8:1
POWER/REVS	11 hp/6000 rpm
TORQUE/REVS	1.48 kgm/4500 rpm
COOLING	forced air
INDUCTION SYSTEM	rotary valve
FUEL SYSTEM	Dell'Orto carburettor (24 mm)
OIL/FUEL RATIO	2%
IGNITION	electronic
STARTING	kick-start pedal, electric
CLUTCH	multiplate, oil-bath
GEARBOX	4 speeds, grip-shift

FRAME, WHEELS, SUSPENSION, BRAKES

FRAME	monocoque
FRONT SUSPENSION	trailing arm with coil spring and damper
REAR SUSPENSION	coil spring and damper
FINAL DRIVE	direct
WHEELS	interchangeable, cantilevered with split rim
FRONT BRAKE	170 mm drum
REAR BRAKE	170 mm drum
TYRES	3.00 x 10 front 3.00 x 10 rear

DIMENSIONS/WEIGHT

LENGTH	1805 mm
WIDTH	700 mm
SADDLE HEIGHT	805 mm
WHEELBASE	1270 mm
FUEL TANK	8 litres
WEIGHT	115 kg

DECLARED PERFORMANCE

MAXIMUM SPEED	n.a.
ACCELERATION	n.a.
FUEL CONSUMPTION	n.a.

Presentation
Milan Show 1997

Price
L. 5,660,000

Production
n.a.

Colours
light green

Frame numbers
n.a.

A new generation PX was born: 20 years after its birth it evolved into a thoroughly up-dated model. After such a long and glorious career there was only one aspect to be improved: the braking, especially on the 200 version. The front drum brake was replaced with a far more efficient disc while roadholding was also improved with a new front suspension configuration with an exposed spring. The rest of the modifications were details designed to recall aspects of past models: the leg-shield edging in chromed plastic, the chromed mudguard trim and the metallic grey fan shroud.
The cursive Vespa script returned on the leg-shield and the side-panels. With this model the PX was reincarnated. There were only a few die-hard Vespisti who lamented the passing of the drum brake and new riders began to be attracted to the Vespa by its classic styling.

ENGINE
CYLINDERS/CYCLE	single/2-stroke
DISPLACEMENT	198 cc
BORE AND STROKE	66.5 x 57 mm
COMPRESSION RATIO	8.8:1
POWER/REVS	11 hp/6000 rpm
TORQUE/REVS	1.48 kgm/4500 rpm
COOLING	forced air
INDUCTION SYSTEM	rotary valve
FUEL SYSTEM	Dell'Orto carburettor (24 mm)
OIL/FUEL RATIO	2%
IGNITION	electronic
STARTING	kick-start pedal, electric
CLUTCH	multiplate, oil-bath
GEARBOX	4 speeds, grip-shift

FRAME, WHEELS, SUSPENSION, BRAKES
FRAME	monocoque
FRONT SUSPENSION	trailing arm with coil spring and damper
REAR SUSPENSION	coil spring and damper
FINAL DRIVE	direct
WHEELS	interchangeable, cantilevered with split rim
FRONT BRAKE	200 mm disc
REAR BRAKE	170 mm drum
TYRES	3.00 x 10 front 3.00 x 10 rear

DIMENSIONS/WEIGHT
LENGTH	1805 mm
WIDTH	700 mm
SADDLE HEIGHT	805 mm
WHEELBASE	1270 mm
FUEL TANK	8 litres
WEIGHT	115 kg

DECLARED PERFORMANCE
MAXIMUM SPEED	n.a.
ACCELERATION	n.a.
FUEL CONSUMPTION	n.a.

2000s

50 ET2 carburatore
50 ET2 FAST iniezione
50 ET4
50 LX 2T
50 LX 4T
50 LXV
125 ET4
125 LX
125 LXV
125 PX Catalyzed
125 GTL
125 GTV
150 ET4
150 LX
150 PX Time 2000
150 PX Catalyzed
200 GTL
250 GTS
250 GTV
250 GT 60°

Presentation	
Cologne Show 1996	
Price	
Euro 2,150	
Production	
170,000	
Colours	
red, blue, grey, black, solid yellow	
Frame numbers	
from ZAPC 16-00001	

The new 50 ET2 was introduced immediately after the 125 ET4 and was offered with two different engines, one featuring a carburettor and the other a highly innovative unit fitted with fuel injection. The carburettored version is significantly cheaper. The exhaust emissions are not as low as with the more sophisticated version, but the scooter shares the same qualities of lightness, ease of maintenance and good performance. The bodywork is identical to that of the 125 model, with the minimal difference that the lower body has a matte rather than gloss finish.

ENGINE

CYLINDERS/CYCLE	single/2-stroke
DISPLACEMENT	49.3 cc
BORE AND STROKE	40 x 39.3 mm
COMPRESSION RATIO	11:1
POWER/REVS	4.5 hp/6500 rpm
TORQUE/REVS	0.5 kgm/6250 rpm
COOLING	forced air
INDUCTION SYSTEM	disc valve
FUEL SYSTEM	Dell'Orto/Mikuni carburettor (12 mm)
OIL/FUEL RATIO	2%
IGNITION	electronic
STARTING	kick-start lever, electric
CLUTCH	centrifugal
GEARBOX	continuously variable automatic

FRAME, WHEELS, SUSPENSION, BRAKES

FRAME	monocoque
FRONT SUSPENSION	trailing arm with coil spring and damper
REAR SUSPENSION	coil spring and damper
FINAL DRIVE	direct
WHEELS	interchangeable, cantilevered with split rim
FRONT BRAKE	200 mm disc
REAR BRAKE	110 mm drum
TYRES	100/80 x 10 front 120/80 x 10 rear

DIMENSIONS/WEIGHT

LENGTH	1760 mm
WIDTH	670 mm
SADDLE HEIGHT	805 mm
WHEELBASE	1280 mm
FUEL TANK	9 litres
WEIGHT	92 kg

DECLARED PERFORMANCE

MAXIMUM SPEED	45 kph
ACCELERATION	n.a.
FUEL CONSUMPTION	2l/100 km

50 ET2 FAST iniezione

ZAPC 16

Presentation
Cologne Show 1996

Price
Euro 2,300

Production
39,300

Colours
red, blue, grey, black, solid yellow

Frame
from ZAPC 16-00001

Of the two new ET2 models, there is no doubt that the fuel-injected FAST version is by far the more advanced. It in fact boasts an injection system that permits fuel consumption that is generally rather high with two-stroke engines to be drastically reduced. In the new engine, the critical scavenging phase is executed with pure air and no fuel, thus eliminating waste. The fuel-air mixture is injected directly into the cylinder head when the exhaust port is closed, to the benefit of fuel consumption and environmental protection. A two-way volumetric oil pump guarantees lubrication of the engine and the injection pump.

Presentation
Cologne Show 1996

Price
Euro 2,200

Production
42,700

Colours
orange, green, blue, red, grey, white, black, solid green

Frame numbers
from ZAPC 16-00001

In order to respect the ever-stricter anti-smog legislation and to meet the Euro 1 norms, a four-stroke version of the 50 was introduced. The engine is the same as the one fitted to the Zip 50 4T. This was the first 50 cc four-stroke unit to be produced by a European company. Known as the HiPER4, it features a single overhead camshaft, two valves per cylinder and electronic ignition. The Vespa 50 ET4 has particularly low fuel consumption and a range of up to 500 km. Among the 50 cc scooters, the ET 4 stands out as it is the only one with a steel monocoque, exactly like that of the others in the Vespa range. This feature, together with the four-stroke engine, places the ET4 in a category of its own.

ENGINE

CYLINDERS/CYCLE	single/4-stroke
DISPLACEMENT	49.9 cc
BORE AND STROKE	39 x 41.8 mm
COMPRESSION RATIO	8.6:1
POWER/REVS	n.a.
TORQUE/REVS	n.a.
COOLING	forced air
TIMING SYSTEM	Single overhead camshaft
FUEL SYSTEM	Keihin carburettor (18 mm)
IGNITION	electronic
STARTING	kick-start lever, electric
CLUTCH	centrifugal
GEARBOX	continuously variable automatic

FRAME, WHEELS, SUSPENSION, BRAKES

FRAME	monocoque
FRONT SUSPENSION	trailing arm with coil spring and damper
REAR SUSPENSION	coil spring and damper
FINAL DRIVE	direct
WHEELS	interchangeable, cantilevered with split rim
FRONT BRAKE	200 mm disc
REAR BRAKE	110 mm drum
TYRES	100/80 x 10 front 120/70 x 10 rear

DIMENSIONS/WEIGHT

LENGTH	1760 mm
WIDTH	670 mm
SADDLE HEIGHT	795 mm
WHEELBASE	1280 mm
FUEL TANK	9 litres
WEIGHT	96 kg

DECLARED PERFORMANCE

MAXIMUM SPEED	n.a.
ACCELERATION	n.a.
FUEL CONSUMPTION	39 km/l

Giovane, sicura, elegante: va dall'utile al dilettevole nello spazio di un sorriso

Presentation
Milan Show 2005
Price
Euro 2,110
Production
currently in production
Colours
red, black, violet, grey
Frame numbers
from ZAPC 3810-00001

The LX series represents the evolution of the ET. The headlight is now round and the rear-view mirrors are chromed. The lines are slightly more angular, especially the front mudguard and the tail. An 11" front wheel is fitted for the first time. The two-stroke Hi-Per engine is fitted with a two-way catalyst. The 50 cc 2-stroke version of the LX extends the successful career of the ET2 initiated almost ten years earlier. It is very popular among young people who appreciate the extra performance with respect to the four-stroke version. It is nonetheless an environmentally friendly power unit that conforms to the Euro 2 anti-smog standard and is equipped with the advanced SAS secondary air recovery system.

ENGINE

CYLINDERS/CYCLE	single/2-stroke
DISPLACEMENT	49.4 cc
BORE AND STROKE	40 x 39.3 mm
COMPRESSION RATIO	n.a.
POWER/REVS	n.a.
TORQUE/REVS	n.a.
COOLING	forced air
TIMING SYSTEM	disc valve
FUEL SYSTEM	direct injection
IGNITION	electronic
STARTING	electric
CLUTCH	centrifugal
GEARBOX	continuously variable automatic

FRAME, WHEELS, SUSPENSION, BRAKES

FRAME	monocoque
FRONT SUSPENSION	single strut with trailing arm
REAR SUSPENSION	coil spring and damper
FINAL DRIVE	direct
WHEELS	cantilevered
FRONT BRAKE	200 mm disc
REAR BRAKE	110 mm drum
TYRES	100/70 x 11 front 120/70 x 10 rear

DIMENSIONS/WEIGHT

LENGTH	1755 mm
WIDTH	740 mm
SADDLE HEIGHT	775 mm
WHEELBASE	1280 mm
FUEL TANK	8.6 litres
WEIGHT	98 kg

DECLARED PERFORMANCE

MAXIMUM SPEED	n.a.
ACCELERATION	n.a.
FUEL CONSUMPTION	n.a.

<table>
<tr><td>

Presentation
Milan Show 2005

Price
Euro 2,310

Production
in production

Colours
red, black, violet, grey

Frame numbers
n.a.

</td></tr>
</table>

The LX series represents the evolution of the ET. The frame retains its compact dimensions with the addition of a number of styling modifications that recall the past: the headlight is now round and the rear-view mirrors are chromed. A more modern touch is provided by the sharply cut clear plastic indicator covers. The front mudguard is more angular. The saddle has a lock on the left-hand side. Both centre and side stands are provided. An 11" front wheel is fitted for the first time. The rims have a five-spoke design. The tail is also more square-cut with a protruding tail light.

ENGINE

CYLINDERS/CYCLE	single/4-stroke
DISPLACEMENT	49.9 cc
BORE AND STROKE	39 x 41.8 mm
COMPRESSION RATIO	8.6:1
POWER/REVS	n.a.
TORQUE/REVS	n.a.
COOLING	forced air
TIMING SYSTEM	Single overhead camshaft
FUEL SYSTEM	Keihin carburettor (18 mm)
IGNITION	electronic
STARTING	kick-start lever, electric
CLUTCH	centrifugal
GEARBOX	continuously variable automatic

FRAME, WHEELS, SUSPENSION, BRAKES

FRAME	monocoque
FRONT SUSPENSION	trailing arm with coil spring and damper
REAR SUSPENSION	coil spring and damper
FINAL DRIVE	direct
WHEELS	cantilevered with split rim
FRONT BRAKE	200 mm disc
REAR BRAKE	110 mm drum
TYRES	100/80 x 11 front 120/70 x 10 rear

DIMENSIONS/WEIGHT

LENGTH	1760 mm
WIDTH	670 mm
SADDLE HEIGHT	795 mm
WHEELBASE	1280 mm
FUEL TANK	9 litres
WEIGHT	96 kg

DECLARED PERFORMANCE

MAXIMUM SPEED	n.a.
ACCELERATION	n.a.
FUEL CONSUMPTION	39 km/l

Presentation
Milan Show 2005
Price
Euro 2,540
Production
currently in production
Colours
green, blue, white
Frame numbers
n.a.

This version is based on the smallest of the LX series and deliberately references the styling of the Vespas from the 1960s. Of particular note are the tubular handlebars as used in that period. The instrumentation also has a classic appearance with the analogue element is inserted within a chromed bezel. The final touch is provided by the instrumentation graphics that reference the style used in the '60s. Another feature is the separate saddles for driver and passenger. The look is dated but the comfort level meets the standards demanded today. The appeal of the old, the taste of the modern.

ENGINE

CYLINDERS/CYCLE	single/2-stroke
DISPLACEMENT	49.4 cc
BORE AND STROKE	40 x 39.3 mm
COMPRESSION RATIO	n.a.
POWER/REVS	n.a.
TORQUE/REVS	n.a.
COOLING	forced air
TIMING SYSTEM	disc valve
FUEL SYSTEM	direct injection
IGNITION	electronic
STARTING	electric
CLUTCH	centrifugal
GEARBOX	continuously variable automatic

FRAME, WHEELS, SUSPENSION, BRAKES

FRAME	monocoque
FRONT SUSPENSION	single strut with trailing arm
REAR SUSPENSION	coil spring and damper
FINAL DRIVE	direct
WHEELS	cantilevered
FRONT BRAKE	200 mm disc
REAR BRAKE	110 mm drum
TYRES	100/70 x 11 front 120/70 x 10 rear

DIMENSIONS/WEIGHT

LENGTH	1755 mm
WIDTH	740 mm
SADDLE HEIGHT	775 mm
WHEELBASE	1280 mm
FUEL TANK	8.6 litres
WEIGHT	98 kg

DECLARED PERFORMANCE

MAXIMUM SPEED	n.a.
ACCELERATION	n.a.
FUEL CONSUMPTION	n.a.

Presentation	
Milan Show 2005	
Price	
Euro 3,050	
Production	
83,000	
Colours	
orange, green, blue, red, grey, white, black, pale green	
Frame numbers	
from ZAPM 1900-00001	

In the mid-'90s, Piaggio was faced with the extremely difficult task of celebrating the 50th anniversary of the birth of the Vespa with a new model capable of venturing into the new millennium without disowning the past. Piaggio rose to this challenge with consummate skill in presenting the ET4 in 1996. This model carried forward the Primavera and PK theme with the small frame shared with the 50 cc models. However, what was most striking was the engine: for the first time a Vespa was powered by a four-stroke unit. While this was not an absolute first for the company (the technology had previously been used on the Sfera) it was an important step in that the decision derived from the ever-stricter legislation regarding the reduction of fuel consumption and toxic emissions.

The styling of the ET4 is successful, decidedly modern with its upward sloping tail yet softly sculpted with clear references to the Vespas of the past. The frame is a steel monocoque, an act of faith with respect to the Vespa design that distinguishes the ET4 from its rivals which all use tubular frames with plastic panels. The design boasts great elegance and attention to detail: the badging is in a cursive script as on the classic Vespas, there are no exposed screws with the exception of those on the front suspension cover. Other innovations include: the helmet store below the saddle, the extractable hook in the front section of the saddle, the instrumentation complete with a clock and fuel gauge, the light-alloy luggage rack, the front disc brake and the key with electronic anti-theft protection.

ENGINE

CYLINDERS/CYCLE	single/4-stroke
DISPLACEMENT	124.2 cc
BORE AND STROKE	57 x 48.6 mm
COMPRESSION RATIO	10.6:1
POWER/REVS	12 hp/7750 rpm
TORQUE/REVS	1 kgm/6500 rpm
COOLING	forced air
TIMING SYSTEM	Single overhead camshaft
FUEL SYSTEM	Mikuni carburettor (24 mm)
IGNITION	electronic
STARTING	kick-start lever, electric
CLUTCH	centrifugal
GEARBOX	continuously variable automatic

FRAME, WHEELS, SUSPENSION, BRAKES

FRAME	monocoque
FRONT SUSPENSION	trailing arm with coil spring and damper
REAR SUSPENSION	coil spring and damper
FINAL DRIVE	direct
WHEELS	interchangeable, cantilevered
FRONT BRAKE	200 mm disc
REAR BRAKE	110 mm drum
TYRES	100/80 x 10 front 120/80 x 10 rear

DIMENSIONS/WEIGHT

LENGTH	1760 mm
WIDTH	670 mm
SADDLE HEIGHT	805 mm
WHEELBASE	1280 mm
FUEL TANK	9 litres
WEIGHT	102 kg

DECLARED PERFORMANCE

MAXIMUM SPEED	95 kph
ACCELERATION	n.a.
FUEL CONSUMPTION	n.a.

Presentation
Milan Show 1999
Price
Euro 3,080
Production
80,300
Colours
n.a.
Frame numbers
from ZAPM 1900-

The 2nd series of the ET4 is distinguished by its new LEADER engine that boasts low fuel consumption and emissions. In styling terms, the new ET4 can be recognised by its round black crankcase cover and its white indicators. The ET4 has been constantly updated and has enjoyed great commercial success. The public has demonstrated its appreciation of this small frame series and both the styling and the four-stroke engine have been popular. This success recalls that of the Primavera in the 1970s and is very different to lack of enthusiasm for the PK in the 1980s.

125 LX

Presentation
Milan Show 2005

Price
Euro 2,910

Production
in production

Colours
red, black, violet, grey

Frame numbers
from ZAPM 441-00001

The LX replaces the ET4 series. Aesthetically it resembles the Granturismo: the headlight is round and the rear-view mirrors are chromed. The lines are more angular. The indicators are larger and with transparent plastic covers. The instrumentation is comprehensive with a fuel level gauge and a digital clock. The saddle has a grab handle for the passenger. The diameter of the front wheel has been increased from 10" to 11" to provide greater stability while the rims have a new five-spoke design. The engine is from the LEADER (Low Emission Advanced Engine Range) series, an advanced design that uses a catalyst and a secondary air recovery system to conform to the Euro2 anti-smog standard.

ENGINE

CYLINDERS/CYCLE	single/4-stroke
DISPLACEMENT	124 cc
BORE AND STROKE	57 x 48.6 mm
COMPRESSION RATIO	n.a.
POWER/REVS	10.3 hp/8000 rpm
TORQUE/REVS	9.6 Nm/6000 rpm
COOLING	forced air
FUEL SYSTEM	direct injection
IGNITION	electronic
STARTING	electric
CLUTCH	centrifugal
GEARBOX	continuously variable automatic

FRAME, WHEELS, SUSPENSION, BRAKES

FRAME	monocoque
FRONT SUSPENSION	single strut with trailing arm
REAR SUSPENSION	coil spring and damper
FINAL DRIVE	direct
WHEELS	cantilevered
FRONT BRAKE	200 mm disc
REAR BRAKE	110 mm drum
TYRES	100/70 x 11 front 120/70 x 10 rear

DIMENSIONS/WEIGHT

LENGTH	1800 mm
WIDTH	740 mm
SADDLE HEIGHT	785 mm
WHEELBASE	1290 mm
FUEL TANK	8.6 litres
WEIGHT	110 kg

DECLARED PERFORMANCE

MAXIMUM SPEED	n.a.
ACCELERATION	n.a.
FUEL CONSUMPTION	n.a.

Presentation
Milan Show 2005

Price
Euro 3,210

Production
currently in production

Colours
green, blue, white

Frame numbers
n.a.

This version is based on the LX 125 and is distinguished by a number of styling features that constitute a worthy tribute to the models from the '60s. The most eye-catching of these are tubular handlebars identical to those used in the period. A classic touch is also provided by the analogue instrumentation enclosed within a chrome frame. The instrumentation graphics also reflect those in vogue in the past. The separate saddles for the driver and passenger also contribute to the theme. The styling is that of the past, the comfort that of today. A combination sure to appeal to many enthusiasts.

ENGINE

CYLINDERS/CYCLE	mono/4-stroke
DISPLACEMENT	124 cc
BORE AND STROKE	57 x 48.6 mm
COMPRESSION RATIO	n.a.
POWER/REVS	10.3 hp/8000 rpm
TORQUE/REVS	9.6 Nm/6000 rpm
COOLING	forced air
FUEL SYSTEM	direct injection
IGNITION	electronic
STARTING	electric
CLUTCH	centrifugal
GEARBOX	continuously variable automatic

FRAME, WHEELS, SUSPENSION, BRAKES

FRAME	monocoque
FRONT SUSPENSION	single strut with trailing link
REAR SUSPENSION	coil spring and damper
FINAL DRIVE	direct
WHEELS	cantilevered
FRONT BRAKE	200 mm disc
REAR BRAKE	110 mm drum
TYRES	100/70 x 11 front 120/70 x 10 rear

DIMENSIONS/WEIGHT

LENGTH	1800 mm
WIDTH	740 mm
SADDLE HEIGHT	785 mm
WHEELBASE	1290 mm
FUEL TANK	8.6 litres
WEIGHT	110 kg

DECLARED PERFORMANCE

MAXIMUM SPEED	97 kph
ACCELERATION	4.5 sec/30 m
FUEL CONSUMPTION	30 km/l

Presentation
Milan Show 1999

Price
Euro 2,850

Production
n.a.

Colours
grey

Frame numbers
from ZAPM 09040-00001

The Catalyzed version was introduced to meet the anti-smog normatives. It was equipped with a two-way catalytic converter to meet the Euro 1 anti-smog standards. The Catalyzed series introduced a number of styling modifications. The rear section of the saddle had a new shape. The plastic indicator covers were now white while the engine fan cover was black.
Even though it received little marketing support in this period, the PX series continued to enjoy great success with a clientele unwilling to abandon this remarkable model.
20 years on from its launch, the PX 125 continues on its merry way in continuously updated form. Even the ever-stricter pollution norms are unable to stop it.

The 200 version was instead dropped, a victim of those same anti-smog norms.

ENGINE	
CYLINDERS/CYCLE	mono/4-stroke
DISPLACEMENT	124 cc
BORE AND STROKE	52,2 x 57 mm
COMPRESSION RATIO	9.2:1
POWER/REVS	8.3 hp/6000 rpm
TORQUE/REVS	1.07 kgm/4500 rpm
COOLING	forced air
INDUCTION SYSTEM	rotary valve
FUEL SYSTEM	Dell'Orto carburettor (20 mm)
IGNITION	electronic
STARTING	kick-start lever - electric
CLUTCH	multiplate, oil-bath
GEARBOX	4 speeds, grip-shift
FRAME, WHEELS, SUSPENSION, BRAKES	
FRAME	monocoque
FRONT SUSPENSION	trailing link with coil spring and damper
REAR SUSPENSION	coil spring and damper
FINAL DRIVE	direct
WHEELS	interchangeable, cantilevered with split rim
FRONT BRAKE	200 mm disc
REAR BRAKE	170 mm drum
TYRES	3.00 x 10" front 3.00 x 10" rear
DIMENSIONS/WEIGHT	
LENGTH	1805 mm
WIDTH	700 mm
SADDLE HEIGHT	805 mm
WHEELBASE	1270 mm
FUEL TANK	8 litres
WEIGHT	115 kg
DECLARED PERFORMANCE	
MAXIMUM SPEED	90 kph
ACCELERATION	25.3 sec/(400 metres from a standing start)
FUEL CONSUMPTION	2.4l/100 km

Presentation
Milan Show 2001

Price
Euro 2,980

Production
n.a.

Colours
n.a.

Frame numbers
n.a.

This series has many new features. The headset has new instrumentation incorporating the speedometer, fuel gauge and various tell-tales. The indicators have transparent plastic covers and the headlight has a halogen bulb. The two-tone rectangular badge returned to the leg-shield. The front mudguard trim, the handlebar grip ends and the indicator and rear light bezels are chromed. The PX with its continual modifications is constantly updated and is approaching perfection. The grip-shift is particularly popular.

Presentation
Milan Show 2003

Price
Euro 4,076

Production
in production

Colours
green, grey, blue, alabaster, black

Frame numbers
from ZAPM 311-00001

With the new Granturismo, Vespa relaunched the large frame series to be produced alongside the small frame LX series. The frame has been completely revised with a number of references to the past: the leg-shield features the historic blue and white badge and the platform has classic longitudinal rubber strips. There are multiple details that make the Granturismo particularly up-to-date: the passenger is provided with foldaway rear footrests and there is a large compartment beneath the saddle that can take two open-face helmets.

The flush rear lighting unit and the LED lights are perhaps excessively modern for a model deliberately referencing the past. In mechanical terms, the four-stroke liquid cooled engine stands out. For the first time it is fitted with a four-valve system. It was not easy to conceal the radiator, but the problem has been resolved brilliantly with the air intakes located either side of the glovebox behind the leg-shield. The 12" wheels, dual rear dampers (another first) and front and rear disc brakes show their worth on the road.

ENGINE

CYLINDERS/CYCLE	single/4-stroke
DISPLACEMENT	124 cc
BORE AND STROKE	57 x 48.6 mm
COMPRESSION RATIO	11.5:1
POWER/REVS	15 hp/10,000 rpm
TORQUE/REVS	1.17 kgm/8500 rpm
COOLING	liquid
TIMING SYSTEM	single overhead camshaft
FUEL SYSTEM	Walbro carburettor (29 mm)
IGNITION	electronic
STARTING	electric
CLUTCH	centrifugal
GEARBOX	continuously variable automatic

FRAME, WHEELS, SUSPENSION, BRAKES

FRAME	monocoque
FRONT SUSPENSION	single strut with trailing arm
REAR SUSPENSION	dual dampers
FINAL DRIVE	direct
WHEELS	cantilevered
FRONT BRAKE	220 mm disc
REAR BRAKE	220 mm drum
TYRES	120/70 x 12 front 130/70 x 12 rear

DIMENSIONS/WEIGHT

LENGTH	1940 mm
WIDTH	755 mm
SADDLE HEIGHT	790 mm
WHEELBASE	1395 mm
FUEL TANK	10 litres
WEIGHT	138 kg

DECLARED PERFORMANCE

MAXIMUM SPEED	n.a.
ACCELERATION	n.a.
FUEL CONSUMPTION	n.a.

Presentation
Milan Show 2005
Price
Euro 4,150
Production
currently in production
Colours
grey
Frame numbers
n.a.

The Vintage version is derived from the GT 125 and represents a tribute to the models of the '50s. The principal feature is the headlamp mounted on the mudguard, as was the case with the first Vespas to leave Pontedera. The tubular handlebars also reference the typical style of the period. The circular analogue instrumentation has retro graphics combined with a modern display keeping a check on all vital functions. Split saddles are fitted, as used in the '50s: one for the driver and one for the passenger. A perfect and appealing combination of classic and modern styling.

ENGINE

CYLINDERS/CYCLE	single/4-stroke
DISPLACEMENT	124 cc
BORE AND STROKE	57 x 48.6 mm
COMPRESSION RATIO	11.5:1
POWER/REVS	15 hp/10000 rpm
TORQUE/REVS	1.17 kgm/8500 rpm
COOLING	liquid
TIMING SYSTEM	single overhead camshaft
FUEL SYSTEM	Walbro overhead carburettor (29 mm)
IGNITION	electronic
STARTING	electric
CLUTCH	centrifugal
GEARBOX	continuously variable automatic

FRAME, WHEELS, SUSPENSION, BRAKES

FRAME	monocoque
FRONT SUSPENSION	single strut with trailing link
REAR SUSPENSION	twin dampers
FINAL DRIVE	direct
WHEELS	cantilevered
FRONT BRAKE	220 mm disc
REAR BRAKE	120 mm disc
TYRES	120/70 x 12 front 130/70 x 12 rear

DIMENSIONS/WEIGHT

LENGTH	1940 mm
WIDTH	755 mm
SADDLE HEIGHT	790 mm
WHEELBASE	1395 mm
FUEL TANK	10 litres
WEIGHT	138 kg

DECLARED PERFORMANCE

MAXIMUM SPEED	102 kph
ACCELERATION	4.6 sec/30 m
FUEL CONSUMPTION	37 km/l

Presentation
Milan Show 1999

Price
Euro 3,150

Production
32,000

Colours
silver, red, white, blue, green, black, purple

Frame numbers
from ZAPM 1900-00001

Presented three years after its sister models sharing the same frame, the 150 revived what is a classic Vespa displacement that permits the scooter to be ridden on the autostrada. The long wait for a small increase in cylinder capacity was justified by the fact that the 150 engine was an all-new design and the first of the LEADER (Low Emission Advanced Engine Range) family. This series of engines represents a significant advance with respect to the reduction in toxic emissions and required particularly intensive development. In styling terms, the ET4 150 was distinguished from its 125 cc sister by two trim elements on the side-panels and transparent rather than orange front indicators. Another small difference: the oil level could be checked with a practical dipstick rather than a sightglass.

ENGINE

CYLINDERS/CYCLE	single/4-stroke
DISPLACEMENT	149.5 cc
BORE AND STROKE	62.6 x 48.6 mm
COMPRESSION RATIO	10.6:1
POWER/REVS	12.5 hp/7500 rpm
TORQUE/REVS	1.3 kgm/6000 rpm
COOLING	forced air
TIMING SYSTEM	single overhead camshaft
FUEL SYSTEM	Walbro VWF6 carburettor (24 mm)
IGNITION	electronic
STARTING	kick-start lever, electric
CLUTCH	centrifugal
GEARBOX	continuously variable automatic

FRAME, WHEELS, SUSPENSION, BRAKES

FRAME	monocoque
FRONT SUSPENSION	trailing arm with coil spring and damper
REAR SUSPENSION	coil spring and dampers
FINAL DRIVE	direct
WHEELS	interchangeable, cantilevered
FRONT BRAKE	200 mm disc
REAR BRAKE	110 mm drum
TYRES	100/80 x 10 front 120/80 x 10 rear

DIMENSIONS/WEIGHT

LENGTH	1760 mm
WIDTH	670 mm
SADDLE HEIGHT	805 mm
WHEELBASE	1280 mm
FUEL TANK	9 litres
WEIGHT	105 kg

DECLARED PERFORMANCE

MAXIMUM SPEED	97 kph
ACCELERATION	n.a.
FUEL CONSUMPTION	n.a.

Presentation
Milan Show 1999

Price
Euro 3,180

Production
30,600

Colours
silver, red, white, blue, green, black, purple

Frame numbers
from ZAPM 1900-

The 2nd series of the 150 ET4 differed in that the displacement was increased from 149 to 151 cc to allow it to be ridden on the autostrada.

Ever more intense urban traffic has encouraged many motorists to move to two wheels and the protection offered by the scooter frequently makes it the preferred option. For those who have to tackle even short stretches of motorway or ring-road being denied access by a small shortfall in cylinder capacity represents a significant blow and to satisfy this group of uses the displacement of the ET4 was increased slightly. The 150 found favour with the public who saw it as an excellent compromise between size and performance.

The ET4 evolved into the stylistically more up-to-date LX series. The bodywork is identical, but numerous details bring the LX closer to the Granturismo: the headlight is round and the indicators are of a different shape and larger, more angular and fitted with transparent plastic covers. The front mudguard is more modern and angular. The instrumentation is particularly comprehensive with a rev-counter and speedometer, a fuel level gauge and a digital clock. The saddle has a grab handle for the passenger and a lock on the left-hand side. The diameter of the front wheel has been increased from 10" to 11" to provide greater stability while the rims have a new five-spoke design. The engine is from the LEADER series.

Presentation
Milan Show 2005
Price
Euro 3,160
Production
in production
Colours
red, black, violet, grey
Frame numbers
from ZAPM 442-0001

ENGINE

CYLINDERS/CYCLE	single/4-stroke
DISPLACEMENT	151 cc
BORE AND STROKE	62.8 x 48.6 mm
COMPRESSION RATIO	n.a.
POWER/REVS	11 hp/7750 rpm
TORQUE/REVS	11.6 kgm/6000 rpm
COOLING	forced air
FUEL SYSTEM	direct injection
IGNITION	electronic
STARTING	electric
CLUTCH	centrifugal
GEARBOX	continuously variable automatic

FRAME, WHEELS, SUSPENSION, BRAKES

FRAME	monocoque
FRONT SUSPENSION	single strut with trailing arm
REAR SUSPENSION	coil spring and dampers
FINAL DRIVE	direct
WHEELS	cantilevered
FRONT BRAKE	200 mm disc
REAR BRAKE	110 mm drum
TYRES	110/70 x 11 front 120/70 x 10 rear

DIMENSIONS/WEIGHT

LENGTH	1800 mm
WIDTH	740 mm
SADDLE HEIGHT	785 mm
WHEELBASE	1290 mm
FUEL TANK	8.6 litres
WEIGHT	110 kg

DECLARED PERFORMANCE

MAXIMUM SPEED	n.a.
ACCELERATION	n.a.
FUEL CONSUMPTION	n.a.

Presentation
Milan Show 1999

Price
Euro 3,050

Production
2.000

Colours
n.a.

Frame numbers
n.a.

The Time 2000 model was introduced as a limited edition to celebrate the beginning of the third millennium. It was distinguished by a grey-blue colour scheme with a body-coloured saddle, a chromed rear luggage rack and a leather bag with buckles. There was a silver plaque on the top of the glovebox that read Millennium followed a progressive number. The Time 2000 was only in production for a couple of years and even though differed only slightly with respect to the standard version, it nonetheless had a particular role to play. It was significant that Piaggio decided to commemorate the arrival of the year 2000 exclusively with a model from the PX series that continued to be produced almost a quarter of a century on from its launch. The Time 2000 was presented at Rimini, in the June of 2000, within the ambit of NightWave, the entertainment and discotheque trade fair. Production was limited to just 2000 examples, by no means a random number...

ENGINE

CYLINDERS/CYCLE	mono/2-stroke
DISPLACEMENT	149 cc
BORE AND STROKE	57.8 x 57 mm
COMPRESSION RATIO	9.2:1
POWER/REVS	9 hp/6000 rpm
TORQUE/REVS	1.3 kgm/4500 rpm
COOLING	forced air
TIMING SYSTEM	rotary valve
FUEL SYSTEM	Dell'Orto carburettor (20 mm)
OIL/FUEL RATIO	2 %
IGNITION	electronic
STARTING	kick-start lever - electric
CLUTCH	multiplate, oil-bath
GEARBOX	4 speeds, grip-shift

FRAME, WHEELS, SUSPENSION, BRAKES

FRAME	monocoque
FRONT SUSPENSION	trailing link with coil spring and damper
REAR SUSPENSION	coil spring and damper
FINAL DRIVE	direct
WHEELS	interchangeable, cantilevered with split rim
FRONT BRAKE	200 mm disc
REAR BRAKE	170 mm drum
TYRES	3.00 x 10" front 3.00 x 10" rear

DIMENSIONS/WEIGHT

LENGTH	1805 mm
WIDTH	700 mm
SADDLE HEIGHT	805 mm
WHEELBASE	1270 mm
FUEL TANK	8 litres
WEIGHT	115 kg

DECLARED PERFORMANCE

MAXIMUM SPEED	n.a.
ACCELERATION	n.a.
FUEL CONSUMPTION	n.a.

Presentation
Milan Show 1999

Price
Euro 3,150

Production currently
n.a.

Colours
grey

Frame numbers
from ZAPM 09045-00001

The PX continues to be renewed while remaining faithful to its original configuration. Following the introduction of the disc brake it was the turn of the two-way catalytic converter; this allowed the PX to conform to the Euro 1 standard while retaining its historic two-stroke engine. The PX has continued to enjoy commercial success, satisfying the demand from the fans of manual transmission. From this point the 150 is the PX with the largest displacement. The 200 model failed to meet the anti-smog norms.

ENGINE

CYLINDERS/CYCLE	mono/2-stroke
DISPLACEMENT	149 cc
BORE AND STROKE	57.8 x 57 mm
COMPRESSION RATIO	9.2:1
POWER/REVS	9 hp/6000 rpm
TORQUE/REVS	1.3 kgm/4500 rpm
COOLING	forced air
TIMING SYSTEM	rotary valve
FUEL SYSTEM	Dell'Orto carburettor (20 mm)
OIL/FUEL RATIO	2 %
IGNITION	electronic
STARTING	kick-start lever - electric
CLUTCH	multiplate, oil-bath
GEARBOX	4 speeds, grip-shift

FRAME, WHEELS, SUSPENSION, BRAKES

FRAME	monocoque
FRONT SUSPENSION	trailing link with coil spring and damper
REAR SUSPENSION	coil spring and damper
FINAL DRIVE	direct
WHEELS	interchangeable, cantilevered with split rim
FRONT BRAKE	200 mm disc
REAR BRAKE	170 mm drum
TYRES	3.00 x 10" front 3.00 x 10" rear

DIMENSIONS/WEIGHT

LENGTH	1805 mm
WIDTH	700 mm
SADDLE HEIGHT	805 mm
WHEELBASE	1270 mm
FUEL TANK	8 litres
WEIGHT	115 kg

DECLARED PERFORMANCE

MAXIMUM SPEED	92 kph
ACCELERATION	23,7 sec.
FUEL CONSUMPTION	24,5 km/l

Presentation
Milan Show 2001

Price
Euro 3,070

Production
in production

Colours
n.a.

Frame numbers
n.a.

This series is distinguished by numerous details. The headset features new instrumentation incorporating the speedometer, fuel gauge and various tell-tales. The indicators have transparent plastic covers and the headlight has a halogen bulb.
The two-tone rectangular badge returned to the leg-shield. The front mudguard trim, the handlebar grip ends and the indicator and rear light bezels are chromed.

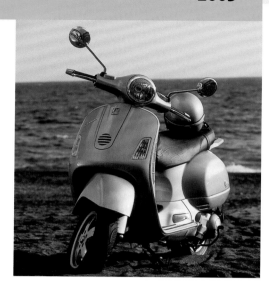

The 200 version of the Granturismo was identical to the 125 model but provided significantly better performance. The power output rose from 15 to 20 hp. On its presentation it was the largest and most powerful Vespa ever produced. The engine features a single overhead camshaft and four valves and powers the scooter to a maximum speed of 120 kph. The Granturismo series is the first in the history of the Vespa with disc brakes front and rear. The 200 is therefore well suited for use outside urban centres.

Presentation
Milan Show 2003

Price
Euro 4,076

Production
in production

Colours
green, grey, blue, alabaster, black

Frame numbers
from ZAPM 312-00001

ENGINE

CYLINDERS/CYCLE	single/4-stroke
DISPLACEMENT	198 cc
BORE AND STROKE	72 x 48.6 mm
COMPRESSION RATIO	11.5:1
POWER/REVS	21 hp/8500 rpm
TORQUE/REVS	1.78 kgm/6500 rpm
COOLING	liquid
TIMING SYSTEM	Single overhead camshaft
FUEL SYSTEM	Walbro carburettor (29 mm)
IGNITION	electronic
STARTING	electric
CLUTCH	centrifugal
GEARBOX	continuously variable automatic

FRAME, WHEELS, SUSPENSION, BRAKES

FRAME	monocoque
FRONT SUSPENSION	single strut with trailing arm
REAR SUSPENSION	twin dampers
FINAL DRIVE	direct
WHEELS	cantilevered
FRONT BRAKE	220 mm disc
REAR BRAKE	220 mm disc
TYRES	120/70 x 12 front 130/70 x 12 rear

DIMENSIONS/WEIGHT

LENGTH	1940 mm
WIDTH	755 mm
SADDLE HEIGHT	790 mm
WHEELBASE	1395 mm
FUEL TANK	10 litres
WEIGHT	138 kg

DECLARED PERFORMANCE

MAXIMUM SPEED	119 kph
ACCELERATION	4.1 sec/30 m
FUEL CONSUMPTION	33 km/l

Presentation
Milan Show 2005

Price
Euro 4,345

Production currently
in production

Colours
red, grey, black

Frame numbers
from ZAPM 451-00001

This version of the Granturismo is particularly innovative. The engine is all-new and is part of the Quasar series featuring four valves and liquid cooling. Never before has a Vespa had such a large displacement and the power output breaks all records at no less than 22 hp. The fuel system boasts electronic injection helping to allow the GTS to be homologated in conformity with the Euro 3 standard ahead of the deadline imposed. The bodywork is that of the Granturismo series and is part of the large frame family. A number of styling modifications makes the 250 unique and represents a return to the past. The leg-shield is characterised by the centrally placed chromed horn grille, while the mudguard features chromed trim. The instrumentation is particularly comprehensive and boasts an analogue speedometer on a dark ground and a digital display with a strip rev-counter. The new tail improves the only aspect of the Granturismo 125 and 200 that had come in for criticism: the flush tail light. Here it instead stands proud and more clearly references the models of the past. From this point of view the design of the rear luggage rack is particularly successful. There is an optional ABS anti-lock braking system and 12" wheels are fitted. 50 years exactly from the launch of the Vespa GS (Gran Sport), the Vespa sporting legend has been revived at Pontedera with this high performance model capable of a maximum speed of over 120 kph.

ENGINE	
CYLINDERS/CYCLE	single/4-stroke
DISPLACEMENT	244 cc
BORE AND STROKE	72 x 60 mm
COMPRESSION RATIO	11.7:1
POWER/REVS	22 hp/8250 rpm
TORQUE/REVS	1.96 kgm/6500 rpm
COOLING	liquid
TIMING SYSTEM	Single overhead camshaft
FUEL SYSTEM	electronic injection
IGNITION	electronic
STARTING	electric
CLUTCH	centrifugal
GEARBOX	continuously variable automatic

FRAME, WHEELS, SUSPENSION, BRAKES	
FRAME	monocoque
FRONT SUSPENSION	single strut with trailing arm
REAR SUSPENSION	twin dampers
FINAL DRIVE	direct
WHEELS	cantilevered
FRONT BRAKE	220 mm disc
REAR BRAKE	220 mm disc
TYRES	120/70 x 12 front 130/70 x 12 rear

DIMENSIONS/WEIGHT	
LENGTH	1940 mm
WIDTH	755 mm
SADDLE HEIGHT	790 mm
WHEELBASE	1395 mm
FUEL TANK	9.5 litres
WEIGHT	148 kg

DECLARED PERFORMANCE	
MAXIMUM SPEED	n.a.
ACCELERATION	n.a.
FUEL CONSUMPTION	n.a.

Presentation
Milan Show 2005
Price
Euro 4,470
Production
currently in production
Colours
green, blue, white
Frame numbers
n.a.

This is the model in the vintage series with the largest displacement and is based on the GT 250. The most eye-catching feature is the positioning of the headlight on the front mudguard, as used on the Vespas from the early '50s. The tubular handlebars are also a retro feature typical of the period. The instrumentation is very up-to-date but enclosed in a classic circular fitting and featuring retro graphics. The saddle is divided into two sections, one for the driver and one for the passenger, as was the custom in the '50s. The level of comfort is, instead, that of today. A perfectly executed nostalgia trip.

ENGINE

CYLINDERS/CYCLE	single/4-stroke
DISPLACEMENT	244 cc
BORE AND STROKE	72 x 60 mm
COMPRESSION RATIO	11.7:1
POWER/REVS	22 hp/8250 rpm
TORQUE/REVS	1.96 kgm/6500 rpm
COOLING	liquid
TIMING SYSTEM	Single overhead camshaft
FUEL SYSTEM	electronic injection
OIL/FUEL RATIO	n.a.
IGNITION	electronic
STARTING	electric
CLUTCH	centrifugal
GEARBOX	continuously variable automatic

FRAME, WHEELS, SUSPENSION, BRAKES

FRAME	monocoque
FRONT SUSPENSION	single strut with trailing arm
REAR SUSPENSION	twin dampers
FINAL DRIVE	direct
WHEELS	cantilevered
FRONT BRAKE	220 mm disc
REAR BRAKE	220 mm disc
TYRES	120/70 x 12 front 130/70 x 12 rear

DIMENSIONS/WEIGHT

LENGTH	1940 mm
WIDTH	755 mm
SADDLE HEIGHT	790 mm
WHEELBASE	1395 mm
FUEL TANK	9.5 litres
WEIGHT	148 kg

DECLARED PERFORMANCE

MAXIMUM SPEED	122 kph
ACCELERATION	4.0 sec/30 m
FUEL CONSUMPTION	30 km/l

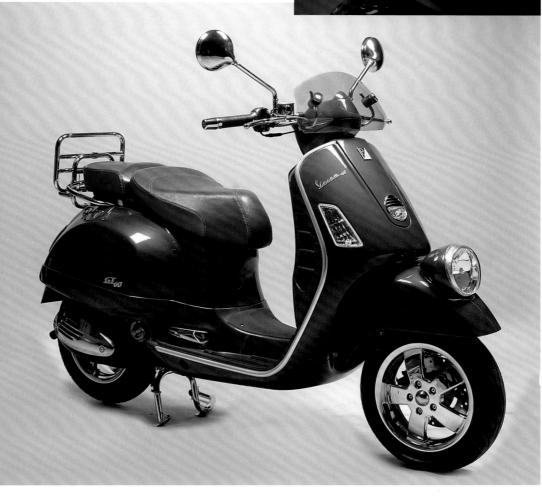

Presentation
Milan Show 2005
Price
Euro 4,590
Production currently
currently in production
Colours
grey
Frame numbers
n.a.

The Limited Edition, produced in 999 units only, is the top of the range in the Vintage series: it has the largest displacement and is the most sophisticated model. The styling is a glowing tribute to the Vespa models produced fifty years ago and characterised by the positioning of the headlight on the front mudguard. The tubular handlebars also reference the styling of the period. The circular instrumentation also features classic graphics. As in the '50s the saddle is divided into two sections, one for the driver and one for the passenger.
The Limited Edition features exclusive colour schemes and only a restricted number of examples will be built.

ENGINE

CYLINDERS/CYCLE	mono/4-stroke
DISPLACEMENT	244 cc
BORE AND STROKE	72 x 60 mm
COMPRESSION RATIO	11.7:1
POWER/REVS	22 hp/8250 rpm
TORQUE/REVS	1.96 kgm/6500 rpm
COOLING	liquid
TIMING SYSTEM	Single overhead camshaft
FUEL SYSTEM	electronic injection
OIL/FUEL RATIO	n.a.
IGNITION	electronic
STARTING	electric
CLUTCH	centrifugal
GEARBOX	continuously variable automatic

FRAME, WHEELS, SUSPENSION, BRAKES

FRAME	monocoque
FRONT SUSPENSION	single strut with trailing link
REAR SUSPENSION	twin dampers
FINAL DRIVE	direct
WHEELS	cantilevered
FRONT BRAKE	220 mm disc
REAR BRAKE	220 mm disc
TYRES	120/70 x 12 front 130/70 x 12 rear

DIMENSIONS/WEIGHT

LENGTH	1940 mm
WIDTH	755 mm
SADDLE HEIGHT	790 mm
WHEELBASE	1395 mm
FUEL TANK	9.5 litres
WEIGHT	148 kg

DECLARED PERFORMANCE

MAXIMUM SPEED	122 kph
ACCELERATION	4.0 sec/30 m
FUEL CONSUMPTION	30 km/l

Printed by
Grafiche Flaminia, Italy,
May 2006